Enhancing Trader Performance

Founded in 1807, John Wiley & Sons is the oldest independent publishing company in the United States. With offices in North America, Europe, Australia and Asia, Wiley is globally committed to developing and marketing print and electronic products and services for our customers' professional and personal knowledge and understanding.

The Wiley Trading series features books by traders who have survived the market's ever-changing temperament and have prospered—some by reinventing systems, others by getting back to basics. Whether a novice trader, professional or somewhere in-between, these books will provide the advice and strategies needed to prosper today and well into the future.

For a list of available titles, please visit our Web site at www.WileyFinance.com

Enhancing Trader Performance

*Proven Strategies from
the Cutting Edge of
Trading Psychology*

BRETT N. STEENBARGER

BICENTENNIAL
1807
WILEY
2007
BICENTENNIAL

John Wiley & Sons, Inc.

Published by John Wiley & Sons, Inc., Hoboken, New Jersey.
Published simultaneously in Canada.

For general information on our other products and services or for technical support, please contact our Customer Care Department within the United States at (800) 762–2974, outside the United States at (317) 572–3993 or fax (317) 572–4002.

Wiley also publishes its books in a variety of electronic formats. Some content that appears in print may not be available in electronic books. For more information about Wiley products, visit our web site at www.wiley.com.

Steenbarger, Brett N.
  Enhancing trader performance : proven strategies from the cutting edge of trading psychology / Brett N. Steenbarger.
    p. cm.—(Wiley trading series)
  Includes bibliographical references.
  ISBN-13: 978–0-470–03866–6 (cloth)
  ISBN-10: 0–470–03866–7 (cloth)
  1. Stocks—Psychological aspects.   2. Speculation—Psychological aspects.
  3. Investments—Psychological aspects.   4. Stockbrokers—Psychological aspects.
  I. Title.   II. Series.
  HG6041.S758 2007
  332.6401'9—dc22   2006013294

Printed in the United States of America

10   9   8   7   6   5   4   3

For Margie, my partner in unchanging youth

To hold an unchanging youth is to reach at the end, the vision with which one started.

—Ayn Rand

Contents

Introduction

*The greater the difficulty the more glory in sur-
mounting it. Skillful pilots gain their reputation
from storms and tempests.*

—Epictetus

This is a book forged from storms and tempests. Roughly one year after the publication of *The Psychology of Trading*, I left the protected world of academic medicine to tackle the rough-and-tumble world of proprietary trading in Chicago. Gone were orderly therapy sessions in my Syracuse office. Now my day started at 4:05 A.M. and proceeded into evenings: a steady blur of tracking overseas markets, updating research, commuting into the city, moving from office to office to help traders as they traded, and then returning home to prepare for the next trading session. If *The Psychology of Trading* was my view from the ivory tower—my integration of academic psychology and practical trading—*Enhancing Trader Performance* is my perspective from the trenches. And quite a view it has been . . .

THE WINDING PATH FROM TRADING PSYCHOLOGY TO TRADER PERFORMANCE

So much has happened since late 2002, when I sat in the food court of Wegman's grocery finishing my book, plunking away at my laptop, sipping my coffee. My e-mail inbox is fuller than it was back then—it stands at 432 as I write—and I've encountered traders from just about every conceivable setting and market. My personal web site and research blog register thousands of hits weekly, including a surprising number from Europe, Asia, and the Pacific Rim. Each day, I hear of the hopes, dreams, frustrations, and hurdles of traders around the world. Such is the privilege—and the challenge—of work in the trenches.

Nothing, however, could have fully prepared me for the frontline exposure I faced at Kingstree Trading, LLC, in Chicago. No longer was I merely talking with traders about trading. Now I was *in* the trading, live, real-time. It is one thing to talk about what to do when a trader is caught in adverse market movement with a thousand-lot on. It is quite another to work with someone while that thousand-lot is veering into the red at $12,500 a tick. Day after day on those front lines, you learn a lot about trading and traders. You also learn quite a bit about yourself.

This book reflects that learning.

Every worthy book is like a symphony: It is held together by a theme that it explores and develops. One of my great joys as a writer is that *The Psychology of Trading* continues to sell as well today as it did when it first hit the bookshelves. I believe this is because its central theme—that the emotional problems faced by traders are extensions of the same problems we all face in dealing with life's risks and uncertainties—was both unique and empowering, transcending the simplistic advice too often associated with trading psychology.

I did not want to write another book until I had one that embodied an equally promising theme. For those of us devoted to writing, a book is something precious. It is an opportunity to communicate with the many people—present and future—that we will never be able to meet. There is very little of permanence that we leave behind when we depart this earth. Books, even more than wealth or kin, have the potential to outlive us, to make their mark on those yet unborn. When you're an author, you don't want to squander that opportunity: You want to do it right.

And yet, writing a book is like living a life. You start with a set of plans neatly outlined in your head, only to look back later and wonder how you could have possibly gotten to this point. Edges of leaves, contours of clouds, hills, and plains—there are very few straight lines in nature. Nature is jagged and rough, bent and twisted. She may not be neat, but she's real. Real like a life lived. Real like words flowing from an author's hand. The best we can hope for, in books as in life, is that we've been faithful to our themes, that we've followed their twists and turns with integrity.

There have, indeed, been many twists and turns on the path to this book, but the theme has remained constant: *Trading is a performance discipline and trading performance can be cultivated through the same kinds of training activities that generate expertise in such diverse domains as athletics, chess, and the performing arts.* That theme has led me to scour research on performance; scrutinize the training programs of athletes, elite military troops, and medical professionals; and, especially, study the traders I've worked with—all in a quest to identify the ingredients of sustained trading success.

If I try to summarize the fruits of this quest in a single sentence, my conclusion would be: *Trading performance is less a function of what traders learn than of how they learn it.* Expertise is the outcome of a process. This process has clearly identifiable features and important applications to the development of traders. We see this process at work among Olympic athletes, and we witness it in world-class manufacturing plants and educational programs. The "what" of learning is always changing: Physicians must keep up with the latest research; traders face different market conditions every few years. The "how" of expertise development, however, is a constant. The same processes that generated exemplary performance in ancient Greece are present today in every field in which outcomes matter.

Winding my way through performance research and the daily work with traders, perhaps my greatest shock has been the recognition that *a significant proportion of emotional problems affecting traders result from departures from the principles of sound training.* When traders do not find the markets and trading styles that match their talents and personalities, when they do not employ systematic training to translate talents into skills, and when they violate prudent risk management in eager hopes of rapid profits, they create needless frustrations and even traumas.

Having never experienced a structured training process and built the competence and confidence conferred by such learning, these traders are ill equipped to adapt to changing market conditions. This, no doubt, has been my most eye-opening experience in trading's rough-and-tumble world: *that trading success in the present so rarely ensures future success.* Market conditions—and the edges that we find in markets—change so radically that ongoing success is guaranteed to no one. The winners in this trading world are not only those who train, but those who *sustain* enhanced learning processes. That is why this book is not only for those traders looking to make themselves successful, but also for those seeking to remake themselves.

I hope that these pages, drawing upon the insights of researchers and practitioners far more steeped in the cultivation of expertise than I, will help traders think—and rethink—what it takes to achieve elite performance in this most rewarding and challenging of arenas. There is much in the trading world that promises you success as a function of *what* you learn: chart patterns, indicator readings, software displays, and self-help skills. There are few guideposts to the *how* of expertise. My deepest wish is that *Enhancing Trader Performance* becomes such a guidepost for you—not only in trading, but in every area of your life in which performance counts.

A LOOK TO THE FUTURE

The future for traders is rapidly changing. The booms in automated trading, arbitrage, and globalization are creating new areas of opportunity even as they wring others dry. It is no longer enough to know when and how to trade: *What* to trade—where to find one's greatest opportunity—is equally important. After all, even the best fishermen will come home empty-handed if they dip their lines into unstocked ponds.

As I write this, many traders are coming home empty-handed. The old ways of trading—sticking with the well-populated stock indexes and trading patterns of momentum and trend—are no longer working. I recently wrote an article for the Trading Markets web site in which I tracked the proportion of two-day trending periods in the S&P 500 Index over the past 40 years. The resulting graph sloped steadily downward. Many individual stocks, however—particularly those not typically included in the baskets of stocks employed in program trading and arbitrage—showed an upward slope, as did selected alternative trading vehicles. Future performance is likely to require increasing degrees of creativity in matching trading styles and markets. My personal research and trading have shifted in that direction, and I invite you to join me in the quest for alpha by staying in touch through the web sites.

I hope that this book will not only assist individual traders, but also help to speed developments within the trading industry. Until now, much of trading education has consisted of the provision of content: seminars, articles, and information. Increasingly, I believe we'll see a shift toward ongoing training and the professionalization of trading as a discipline. We are already seeing the start of such a development in the software field. Just a few years ago, we had separate applications for market analytics, charting, screening, and order execution. Now we are seeing vendors roll all of these features into single, integrated applications that streamline the process from trade idea development through trade management. I recently sipped coffee at a Chicago Starbucks with Joe Kohnen of CQG, Inc., and reviewed the path his company had taken: depth of market, charting, analytics, and order execution now exist on a single page, with order entry as simple as releasing the mouse on the bar of a chart. Rapidly, these performance efficiencies are becoming the norm for all electronic traders.

The greatest of these developments, I believe, will be the integration of education and training through realistic simulation, detailed performance metrics to track performance, and archives of past market data to replay—and retrade—markets for concentrated practice. We will see education and training integrated into order execution platforms on a real-time basis, so that every credible platform is also a sophisticated tool of trader development.

The history of the trading industry is one of democratization. What was once available to institutions eventually reaches the trading public. This includes access to information and research, the leveled playing field and reduced trading expenses afforded by the electronic medium, and the ability to monitor multiple market events in real time and execute complex trading strategies. I have no doubt that this trend will continue. At present, only a few professional firms have the resources to hire in-house trading psychologists and mentors. Before long, however, those all-in-one trading platforms will feature real-time education and mentorship via videoconference, bringing elite training to the trading public. If this book is but a small catalyst toward such a future, I will be gratified and honored indeed.

Most important, however, is to look to *your* future. If it is your ambition to develop trading expertise, do you have a process in place to guide your development? Do you know what you will need to build the skills required for sustained success? You are like an Olympic hopeful; what stands between you and an opportunity for the gold is training: transforming talents into skills and skills into performance. If you read between the lines, you'll see that this is a book about the development of traders, but also about the development of performance itself—in any field. You may or may not choose the path of the trader, but I do hope that you find *your* path: the field of endeavor that best develops you as a performer. In mastering performance, we master ourselves and, in so doing, become more than who we are. What greater calling can there be?

Brett N. Steenbarger, Ph.D.
Naperville, Illinois
March 2006

Acknowledgments

One element has remained unchanged since the writing of *The Psychology of Trading*: the depth of my gratitude to the many people who have provided me with inspiration, insight, and support through all the storms and tempests. First among these are my parents, Jack and Connie Steenbarger, who instilled and modeled the values of entrepreneurship and caring from an early age. Words cannot express my debt to them or my admiration for their many strengths.

I owe much to my own family—Margie, Devon, and Macrae—who encouraged me through the long hours of the working and writing, as well as to our big kids—Debra, Peter, Steve, Lea, Laura, and Ed—who have been constant supports. My appreciation also embraces the larger family: Marc, Lisa, Arnold, Rose, Bert, Ralph, Adrienne, and their supportive families as well.

I have learned much about trading—and even more about working with traders—from Chuck McElveen, who opened the door and brought me to Kingstree. He has been a role model from the start in his caring for traders and commitment to them. This book would never have been possible had it not been for Chuck's vision in creating Kingstree, which was designed from the start as an incubator of the success that results when talent meets opportunity. Marc Greenspoon deserves special mention, not only because he was the initial impetus for my coming to Kingstree, but also for all he has taught me about successful trading and its relationship to continual self-improvement. Readers will also recognize the size of my debt to Scott Pulcini, whose competitive spirit and sheer skill at reading markets have been the source of so much inspiration. Throughout my tenure at Kingstree, Pablo Melgarejo has been a model of market insight and trading perspective. Readers will find his hard-earned wisdom invaluable. In all, I cannot thank the staff and traders and Kingstree enough for their friendship and collegiality.

A very special treat since relocating to Chicagoland has been my continued connection to Upstate Medical University in Syracuse and its Department of Psychiatry and Behavioral Sciences. For that I am grateful to Department Chair Mantosh Dewan, M.D., and Psychology Division Head Roger Greenberg, Ph.D. They are dearly valued friends and colleagues.

Some of my greatest professional debts are to the many fine traders who have provided me with mentorship and guidance, as well as friendship. Victor Niederhoffer has been both teacher and role model, the embodiment of the scientific ideal in trading. I thank him and Laurel Kenner for their continued nurturance of the Spec List, an intellectual haven for inquiring traders. I've learned much from Jon Markman; Jim Dalton; Linda Raschke; Trevor Harnett at Market Delta; David Norman from TraderDNA; Larry Connors, Eddie Kwong, and Ashton Dorkins of Trading Markets; Todd Harrison and Matt Ford of Minyanville; Yale and Jeff Hirsch; John Forman; Terry Liberman of WINdoTRADEr; Henry Carstens; David Aferiat of Trade Ideas; Charles Kirk of The Kirk Report; Gail Osten; Breon Klopp of PIT Instruction and Training; and Gene O'Sullivan and Joseph Koehnen at CQG. Curt Zuckert, DeBorah Lenchard, Robin Gemeinhardt, Tony Zaccaria, Linda Goldsmith, and the staff of the Education Department at the Chicago Mercantile Exchange have been industry leaders in the field of training traders, and I have been their eager student.

But if we save dessert for last, a special note of appreciation goes out to my friend and editor, Pamela Van Giessen, whose work at Wiley has exemplified astuteness, integrity, and a love of authors and writing. She has been the midwife to many fine trading works. Thanks, too, to Jennifer MacDonald and the staff at Wiley for their capable help in bringing this book project to fruition.

Finally, I want to express heartfelt appreciation to the many traders I have worked with personally and who have stayed in touch over the years through the book, articles, and web sites. I have learned more from you than I can ever possibly convey in words.

Author's Note

As with my previous book, *The Psychology of Trading*, I present a number of case examples throughout this book. Most of these are composites of actual traders and trading situations I've worked with, but I have altered and blended identifying details to ensure confidentiality. These composite cases are identified by a fictional first name only. At other points in the book, I discuss actual expert traders I have worked with and identify them—with their permission, of course—by first and last name. To ensure accuracy, all of the traders named in the book reviewed what I wrote about them, made their desired changes, and approved the final text. To their credit, none of the traders sought to embellish their depiction in the text. What you see is what they've got.

Finally, a disclaimer: I mention commercial products and services that I have found to be useful as performance aids and include a list of those resources in the appendix. None of these mentions were solicited by the firms or individuals listed, nor do I hold any commercial interest in or receive any compensation from those mentioned.

B.N.S.

CHAPTER 1

Where Expertise Begins

The Performance Niche

I'm a big believer in starting with high standards and raising them. We make progress only when we push ourselves to the highest level.

—Dan Gable

He was cut from his team in his sophomore year of high school. Any hopes of obtaining a college scholarship were quickly receding. Most aspiring athletes would take their lumps, join a local league or intramural squad, and move on with their lives. Michael Jordan, however, was not like most young athletes. He responded to the cut by practicing day after day. When he felt too tired to continue, he forced himself to recall his cut from the team and drove himself harder. Two years later, he was a McDonald's All-American and the MVP of the McDonald's game. The year after that, he hit the game-winning shot for the University of North Carolina in the NCAA finals. By the time his NBA career ended, Jordan had made an astonishing 25 game-winning shots, perhaps none as memorable as the jumper he nailed against Utah on June 14, 1998. With 5.2 seconds left and no one in the house doubting who would take the last shot, he sealed his sixth championship for the Chicago Bulls.

Michael Jordan was an elite performer, one of many we will encounter in this book. Yet Michael Jordan was not always Michael Jordan. His rise from high school reject to college star was dramatic, but not stellar. He never averaged more than 20 points per game during his college career and was selected third in 1984's NBA draft. All signs pointed to stardom, but not superstardom. Nonetheless, Michael Jordan—along with a small handful of other athletes—stands today as a towering symbol of expert performance. What makes expert performers tick? How are they different from average performers? Is expertise the result of natural, inborn talent, or can it be cultivated? And, most important of all, what can we learn about trading expertise by studying expert performance in other fields? In this book, we will find common factors that contribute to the success of chess experts, Olympic athletes, world-class performing artists, and successful traders. One of those factors is finding a performance niche: a specific activity that is most likely to capitalize on your talents and interests. Michael Jordan had a niche in basketball; he did not find one in baseball. Dan Gable started his athletic career as an undistinguished swimmer, later to discover his own world-class talent as a wrestler—and then as a wrestling coach. Discovering your trading niche may well make the difference between a hall-of-fame trading career and a disappointing one that never quite makes prime time. Sadly, most traders stumble into their markets and trading styles, never to discover where their opportunities might truly lie.

A TALE OF TWO TRADERS

Al and Mick were two short-term traders at a professional trading firm. Both traded the electronic Standard & Poor's (S&P) 500 (ES) E-mini futures contract, and both gave me carte blanche to stand by their screens during market hours so that I could help them with their trading.

I began the day watching Al. The market was trading in a narrow range early in the morning after an attempted rally fizzled. The average price from the day before was about three points below the market's current level, and I had a strong sense (based on my historical studies) that we would take out that average price. Al, Mick, and a handful of other traders had met with me before the trade, and we discussed using the likelihood of the market hitting that level as a potential trade idea. Nevertheless, Al was leaning to the long side. I was skeptical, but decided not to press the point.

As the market ground lower and Al's position went into the red, he shook his head in recognition of his error. Very soon afterward, however, he stopped himself out of the position and flipped to the short side. He was able to pick up a few ticks before the market reversed on him once again. The choppy action continued through the morning, with a mild downward drift. Al was patient, but not making much money for the day. He took a break at lunchtime and expressed to me his hope that the afternoon trade would pick up. Throughout the morning he maintained his composure and held his own in a difficult trade. He expressed optimism that taking a lunch break and clearing his head would help him focus through the afternoon and take advantage of opportunity. Never once did he lose his composure or his positive attitude.

When I moved over to Mick, however, it was a very different story. Mick also tried to play the market's upside and found his position underwater. Enraged, he held onto the position past his stop point, only to see his losses expand. My cautionary comment to Mick was "If your morning losses are small enough, you'll have a fighting shot to make them up in the afternoon." He eventually did exit the position, but refused to take a break at midday. He reviewed every piece of market data from the morning, replaying his bad decisions. All the while he shifted in his chair, pounded the table, raised his voice, and otherwise expressed his frustration. He became particularly agitated when he reviewed the morning trade on his videorecorder. "I can't believe I was so stupid," he fumed. He then proceeded to tell me five things he should have seen in the market to tell him we were going lower. Come hell or high water, he practically shouted, he was going to focus on those five things in the afternoon.

Al and Mick: two very different traders. One of them made a high five-figure sum during the afternoon; the other one struggled to break even all day.

One was an expert trader, the other was struggling.

Al kept himself emotionally balanced, taking liberal time away from the screen after setbacks. He honored his stops religiously and didn't become irate at losses. He consistently expressed optimism over his development and a love of trading.

Mick was anything but balanced, taking losses almost as personal affronts. He periodically violated his risk management guidelines and could not break from the markets until he had rehashed all his mistakes and fumed over each. At such times, he spoke of the market and himself with equal derision.

Most of the trading psychology books you'd read would give the trading edge to Al, the more disciplined, less emotional performer. But Al, the novice, never did succeed at trading. Mick was—and remains—a multi-million-dollar performer. The experience of working with many Micks and Als—and seeing common wisdom about trading success shot down time and again—convinced me to write this book.

THE CORNERSTONE OF EXPERTISE

No doubt, there's a bit of the young Michael Jordan in Mick. He doesn't accept defeat lightly, and he uses losses to drive himself forward. That is characteristic of elite performers, we shall learn, but there's something even more basic that distinguished Mick from Al. In fact, it's so basic that K. Anders Ericsson, perhaps the most prolific researcher in the field of performance, considers it the cornerstone of expertise.

Think of the difference between Al and Mick as something that occurs every day, for approximately 250 trading days a year. Both Al and Mick trade frequently enough that they have winning and losing trades each day. Al puts his losses behind him and clears his head, to focus on the upcoming trade. Mick fusses and fumes, but uses the losses to review his trading, figure out the market (and his mistakes), and get his money back.

Over the course of a year, Mick's reviews ensure that he has easily experienced twice as much market action as Al. Moreover, Mick has systematically reviewed his performance and made constant adjustments. Al, though more relaxed, has little basis for detecting and correcting his errors. Mick, for all his emotionality, has become a learning machine, using losses to improve his trading. Ericsson refers to this as *deliberative practice*, and it is a hallmark of expert performers. Through guided practice, experts open themselves to feedback and, as a result, become better decision makers.

We often hear the phrase "practice makes perfect," but performance experts in sports emphasize that it is *perfect practice that makes perfect.* How practice time is structured makes the difference between a performer with 10 years of experience and one who has a single year of experience repeated 10 times over.

All performers face a chicken-and-egg dilemma: They need confidence and motivation to win, but they need to win to develop such a winning mind-set. *This is why rehearsals are so important: They permit repeated experiences of mastery that provide the emotional fuel for formal competition and performance.* Mick would not allow himself to take a break until he had reviewed every one of his mistakes and figured out what he had done wrong. Al was much more concerned with keeping a level head. By the time the afternoon began, Al was feeling calm and Mick was feeling confident. Mick had figured things out and knew it. What's more, he knew that if he just spent enough time in review, he could figure out any market. His emotionality, which so many would consider a trading liability, was the intensity of a competitor. Vince Lombardi once commented that good losers usually lose. So it was with Mick and Al.

> Competence precedes confidence: Winning mind-sets result from mastery, not the reverse.

Dan Gable was not a good loser. He also knew that practice is the cornerstone of expertise. After a lengthy and exhausting practice, he would order his wrestlers to perform "buddy carries"—hauling other wrestlers up the gymnasium steps. Author Nolan Zavoral tells of Coach Gable's epic sessions with wrestlers, coaxing them to ride the exercise bike with layers of sweat clothes beneath plastic gear, the sweat pouring from them in buckets once the gear was removed. Every fiber of the wrestlers' being wanted to get off the bike and get a drink of water, yet they persisted. By the time they reached the tournament, they had faced every physical challenge imaginable. They could dig deep during the exhaustion of a close match in the third period because they had mastered similar physical adversity day after day in practice.

Practice is the cornerstone of expertise because it multiplies experience. It provides us with far more experience than we could ever gain during formal performance or competition. Gable's wrestlers executed and escaped many more moves than their competitors, thanks to the rigors of practice. Mick reviewed market after market when he was down money; Al did not. Guess who was prepared and confident the next time a similar frustrating market condition presented itself.

One of the expert traders we'll be meeting in this book is Scott Pulcini, a trader of S&P E-minis at a proprietary firm in Chicago—Kingstree Trading, LLC. I met Scott when I joined Kingstree as director of trader development, and I've been honored to be part of his professional development ever since. What initially impressed me about Scott was not the fact that he had made $10 million the year prior to my arrival. It was that he sat in front of the screen until the very close of the market every single day following every order that came and went from the order book. Note that I am not saying he followed every price tick; that went without saying. He tracked every order that traded and every one that did not. Every day. And, as markets changed, he followed that with a review of the day's trading on videotape.

How many years' worth of market data has Scott seen in his relatively few years of trading? How many years' worth of experience is lost by traders during their periods of emotional outbursts, breaks from the screen, and days off?

When I first came to Kingstree, I was impressed with its game room and well-stocked kitchen. I also was struck by who haunted those facilities and who, like Scott, didn't.

Slowly, it dawned on me: I never saw the really good traders hanging out. They were always in front of their screens. They were Mick, not Al.

LEARNING LOOPS: THE ENGINE OF PERFORMANCE

The first thing we notice about deliberative practice is that it invariably takes place apart from formal competition or performance. Think of the practices of a basketball team or a theater company. The goal of practice is to rehearse skills that will be utilized when the game buzzer sounds or when the curtain rises. Performers receive feedback about their actions during practice, so that they can make appropriate adjustments prior to actual performance events.

In relatively solitary performance activities, such as chess, performers obtain feedback on their own. They record their chess moves and then replay games, observing how different lines of play might have ended. They also spend countless hours studying the games of chess grandmasters. During such study they don't just read the moves, but actually replay games themselves so that they can anticipate the moves of experts. When the student's moves differ from those of the expert, the student can follow the expert's reasoning and see why the move is superior.

Most team performance activities rely on coaches or mentors to structure the development process. Basketball coaches watch the practice sessions of their teams and frequently interrupt the action to work on a player's movement or to coordinate teamwork. Similarly, a director will listen to actors deliver their lines and intervene when the intonation or action does not capture the playwright's meaning. Immediacy and accuracy of feedback is essential to the learning process.

The essence of deliberative practice is what I call the *learning loop*. A learning loop is an attempted performance, followed by specific feedback about the success/failure of the performance, followed by renewed efforts that incorporate the feedback (see Exhibit 1.1). Mick created a learning loop when he used his losing trades to review his trading, identify where he went wrong, and then make adjustments upon his return to the screen. Chess champions enter a learning loop each time they make errors during a practice game and force themselves to replay the game with other lines of attack. During team practices, basketball, football, wrestling, and swimming coaches initiate learning loops for their athletes. In no small measure, basic training in the military is a series of learning loops fueled by feedback from drill instructors.

Wendy Whelan is a prima ballerina for the New York City Ballet, considered by many to be the best in the United States. As described by Chip Brown in an intriguing article for the *New York Times Magazine*, Whelan describes the process that brought her from being a dance student with scoliosis to being among the world's elite: "I used to watch tapes if I wasn't sure of the image I was giving off, or if I needed to learn steps. When I dance, I can't see what I'm doing, I can only feel it. . . ." This is similar to active trading: When we're immersed in markets, we can't see what we're doing. We feel market action, but we can't see ourselves. The prima ballerinas of the world take conscious steps to stand outside themselves and watch their performances, correct mistakes, and jump-start a learning

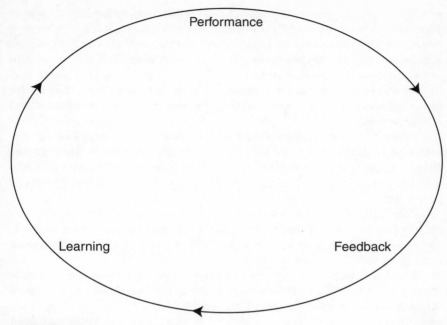

EXHIBIT 1.1 The Learning Loop

process. Think of Nolan Ryan watching tapes of batters, figuring out who will hit the high fastball and who will sit on a curve. Consider serious weight lifters and ask yourself why they always train in rooms with mirrored walls.

All of this seems straightforward. We observe learning loops in classrooms, recital halls, and gymnasiums. Wherever we encounter expertise, we find evidence of learning through deliberative practice.

Then why is such practice so rarely found among traders?

WHAT KEEPS TRADERS OUT OF LEARNING LOOPS?

Let's return to Dan Gable, one of the great competitors in the history of sport. To say that he's an expert performer is a considerable understatement. As a high school wrestler, he won his state championship three times and was undefeated in 64 consecutive matches. He proceeded to win 117 consecutive matches at Iowa State University and twice won the national championship. He was an Olympic gold medalist, outscoring his opponents 130–1 in his final 21 qualification and Olympic matches. As a wrestling coach for the University of Iowa, his teams went 355–21–5, yielding 45 national champions. In his book *A Season on the Mat*, Nolan Zavoral provides a simple assessment of Gable: "Nobody trained harder." Gable was known to practice so hard that he would literally have to crawl to exit the wrestling room. Often, while crawling, he would find a second wind and continue training.

The effort expended by elite performers may not always be as dramatic as that shown by Gable, but it is always significant. In 1869, Sir Francis Galton identified the essence of remarkable ability and achievement as a "laboring instinct," an inner urge to reach ever higher levels of performance.

Next to the leave-everything-on-the-mat work ethic of a Dan Gable, the effort of maintaining a trading journal hardly requires a laboring instinct. Yet the majority of traders won't sustain even this level of performance commitment. Why is that?

Ironically, part of the problem is that new traders themselves view trading as a kind of antiperformance activity. Because they see young people seemingly no different from themselves succeed in the markets, they assume they can do it, too. One trader I worked with was losing day after day and began to fear that his firm would fire him. "I don't want that to happen," he explained. "I want to be a trader. I don't want to have to work for someone else 9 to 5."

There it was.

This was not a trader who was drawn to markets the way Gable fiercely embraced wrestling or Jordan pursued basketball. He wanted to trade because he didn't like the alternatives. The alternatives meant eight hours a day of effort and the loss of the freedom to do what he wanted to do. *But elite performers* are *doing what they want to do when they labor far more than eight hours a day on their craft.* Wendy Whelan, the prima ballerina, loves vigorous rehearsals. "I'm like a Weimeraner," she told author Chip Brown. "I need to run in the park every day. It helps calm me down." Nothing my trader could have said could have so accurately predicted his eventual demise. Without an intrinsic love for the performance activity itself, no one can sustain Galton's laboring instinct to "fret and strive" and overcome barriers to success.

The reality is that expert performance requires an effortful commitment to learning. The perfect practice that makes perfect is sustained by a laboring instinct and a drive to reach perfection. But what sustains that laboring instinct? Why do some traders progress from learning loop to learning loop while others simply run in circles—or stop running altogether?

FROM ENJOYMENT TO EXPERTISE: ELITE PERFORMANCE AS A DEVELOPMENTAL PROCESS

Not all underperforming traders are looking for easy ways to riches. The majority, in fact, fail to sustain learning loops for a very different reason—one that is rarely if ever recognized.

We often talk about expertise as if it's a quality that one possesses. One person is an expert; another is not. Such talk makes it sound as though expertise is an all-or-none *thing*. Research tells us, however, that expertise is a *process*—one that unfolds over a considerable period of time. Moreover, it progresses in stages, with important differences from one stage to the next. The steps needed to advance from an early phase of expertise are very different from those required later in the process.

Benjamin Bloom, Ph.D., of the University of Chicago, coordinated the Development of Talent Research Project in the 1980s, tracking the development of 120 individuals acknowledged by professional peers as world-class talents. These included concert pianists, sculptors, mathematicians, Olympic swimmers, tennis players, and research neurologists. This extraordinary project featured interviews with the elite performers, their parents, and their teachers to better understand the development of their expertise. What the investigators found is that superior performance develops in three stages (Exhibit 1.2):

- *An early phase.* During these years of *initiation* into a performance field, the new performer is engaged in play and exploration. The performance activity is pursued largely for its enjoyment value and is sustained

EXHIBIT 1.2 Phases of Expertise Development (adapted from Bloom, 1985)

	Early Phase	Middle Phase	Late Phase
Primary motivation	Having fun	Developing competence	Building expertise
Primary activity	Play	Skills practice	Honing of technique
Role of the mentor	Supportive	Teaching core skills	Structuring intensive practice
Time commitment	Low	Moderate	High
Primary purpose	Initiation	Development	Mastery

by the ready availability of resources in the immediate environment. Much of the initiation into the performance activity occurs in a social context, with the encouragement of family members, instructors, and peers, who provide positive attention and support. Very often, early success provides a feeling of specialness that sustains the performer's motivation and interest. Teachers during this period are chosen less for their distinctive achievements than for their ability to structure learning in a supportive manner. Performance, at this stage, is pure fun: indulging in something that the performer likes and does well.

- *A middle phase.* At this point of *development*, the performer concentrates on one or more specific fields of performance for serious pursuit. For example, a young athlete who excelled in several sports in high school might focus on just one in college. The performer acquires a great deal of basic knowledge and skills during this period, as the fun side of performance is now joined with directed, effortful activity to learn techniques specific to the performance field. Teachers and coaches are very important in this phase, providing performance feedback and structuring the perfect practice that makes perfect. The development of competence—and the pride it brings—is an important motivation during the middle period as the talented performer begins to excel relative to peers. Family support is also crucial, requiring that significant others adapt to the rising demands of the training regimen.
- *A late phase.* For a limited number of individuals, *mastery* of the performance activity becomes a primary life focus. The goal is no longer competence, but the development of one's talents and skills to the fullest. There is a commitment to self-development, often in the context of working with a recognized mentor who specializes in work with elite performers. The performance field by this time has become a significant part of the talented person's identity: Intensive practice occupies a sizable part of each day. The aim of such practice is the internalization of complex skills, so that high levels of performance become routine. Although such focused and time-intensive effort requires substantial support from family and significant others, by this time the pursuit of excellence is an intrinsic motivation for the performer.

Indeed, Bloom's stages describe many of our lifetime endeavors. Consider, for example, how the stages capture the unfolding of romantic relationships. We start with a stage of dating, having fun, and becoming acquainted with another person. This process is fueled by novelty, excitement, and a feeling of specialness. If all proceeds positively, there follows an intermediate stage of more serious and exclusive dating, in which the couple cultivates an acknowledged relationship. Still later, this relationship becomes a primary life focus with a marriage commitment and the decision to raise a family. As with the development of expertise, what starts as fun becomes, over time, a serious and all-embracing commitment.

Whether in a career, relationship, or high-performance domain, Bloom's work suggests that *working our way through the earlier steps in the developmental process is necessary for moving on to the later phases*. Without a middle period of competence development, there is no readiness for the rigors of mastery. Absent the joys of an initial, exploratory phase, there will be no sustained commitment to skill development.

Most important of all, Bloom's work underscores that *the achievement of elite performance cannot begin with the hard-core pursuit of mastery*. It begins with the simple process of exploration: encountering a field, having fun with it, and seeing if it truly speaks to you.

This insight may seem commonsensical, but it is rarely acknowledged in the trading world.

When we think about developing trader expertise, we naturally focus on the final, mastery stage. We try to teach new traders the nuances of entries, exits, reading order flow, limiting losses, and mastering emotions. This seems quite reasonable at first blush, but is laughably backward from Bloom's perspective. Why would we start traders on the *final* steps of a developmental process?

Think of it this way: Would we recommend that a young couple on a first date accelerate the mastery of their relationship by announcing an engagement?

In fact, there would be no better way to sabotage a fledgling relationship than to artificially accelerate its progression toward marriage. A couple faced with such pressure would rightfully protest that they need more time to learn about each other; they're not ready for such a commitment.

But might that be true for traders as well? Might the premature focus on expertise development—including the intensive practice of a Dan Gable or a Wendy Whelan—sabotage traders' relationships with their craft? Could this be a reason why many traders, especially early in their careers, resist the rigors of keeping journals and imposing discipline? Early in dating, the "discipline" of an exclusive, monogamous commitment might be onerous; later, it is avidly sought. Perhaps traders regard discipline similarly over the course of their development.

Bloom's research supports such an analysis. He found that two factors were crucial to the earliest, initiation phase of performance development: (1) having fun and (2) obtaining support from the social environment. Without the initial fun factor, young persons never develop the interest to sustain them through the subsequent rigors of perfect practice. Part of the early enjoyment of the activity, no doubt, is the praise and attention received from family members, friends, and teachers. Another part is talent: It is difficult to imagine enjoying an activity for which one has little or no aptitude. The combination of early success and early encouragement provides the motivational impetus to continue the activity, which in turn fuels the drive for future development.

Even in the later phases of development, the fun factor remains an important motivational element. In a fascinating program of research, Dr. Janet Starkes and colleagues from McMaster University found that expert performers in sports rated the practice activities most relevant to their development as also the most enjoyable. This finding has been replicated among wrestlers and skaters, as well as soccer and field hockey players and students of the martial arts. In fact, expert athletes demonstrate strong positive correlations among activities that are most effortful, most relevant for development, and most enjoyable. Like Wendy Whelan, they love the runs in the park.

For most of us, the daily physical and mental demands of cultivating expertise at figure skating or the martial arts would be overwhelming. Elite performers in those disciplines, however, routinely report loving the training process. Bloom's insight is that *they didn't start out that way. This is because with performance, as with relationships, the developmental process is one in which extrinsic and hedonistic motivations are gradually transformed into intrinsic, effortful ones.* Building skills while having fun is transformed into an enjoyment of skill building for its own sake.

> Performance, like relationships, begins with a positive chemistry between performer and performance field.

The implications are profound: To develop expertise as a trader, the imposition of discipline and deliberative practice is *not* the first step to be taken. The first step—and the one so often forgotten by new traders—*is to simply have fun.* If Bloom and colleagues are correct, we need to date our performance field before we can marry it.

TIME: THE COMMON ELEMENT IN PERFORMANCE DEVELOPMENT

Another piece of common sense that is commonly lost on traders is that the development of expertise occurs over time. How much time does it take to develop expertise? Research tells us that a minimum of 10 years is required. Indeed, this "10-year rule" is one of the more durable findings in expertise research spanning sports, the arts and sciences, chess, and medicine. There is so much knowledge and skill required by most fields that elite performance necessitates years of development.

In an effort to create developmental shortcuts, traders attempt to jump-start their careers at the middle and later phases, only to encounter frustration. No doubt the young Eldrick Woods would have been discouraged as a child if he had prematurely entered the PGA tour. Given that frustration and its effect on motivation, he might not have gone on to become the Tiger of his field. Dan Gable's approach to college wrestling produced incredible success but would have overwhelmed middle-school students first encountering the sport. If there is a shortcut to producing elite levels of performance, research has not yet found it.

Very recently I had a long and most enlightening phone conversation with Linda Raschke, who has sustained a successful trading career over decades. Recognized as one of Jack Schwager's Market Wizards and long known for her live online trading room that mentors traders, Linda now also manages a fund that has performed admirably since its inception. When the conversation turned to longevity in the trading field, Linda remarked, "Experience counts for so much." It's not that she makes money every month—in fact, she mentioned that much of her profit may come from a couple of very good months out of the year. She says of her performance, however, "I know the cycles." She knows there will be lean times as well as good ones. Her experience provides her with perspective on these ups and downs so that she remains disciplined in the lean times and adds to her account in the good ones. Without time and experience, no performer could hope to internalize such perspective.

What makes an expert trader such as Linda? At the end of their research project, Bloom and his colleagues found that three factors distinguish high-level performance across the various fields they studied:

1. Strong interest and emotional commitment to a particular field
2. Desire to reach a high level of attainment in the field
3. Willingness to put in the significant time and effort required for this high-level achievement

To invest the great amounts of time and effort required for mastery, an individual must emotionally bond with the talent field, creating a long-term relationship. Our task, in the initial phase of development, is to forge an emotional bond so strong that it will survive the inevitable frustrations and opportunity costs of the learning curve.

> The greats do not become great by working hard; they work hard because they find a great niche: a field that captures their talents, interests, and imagination.

TRADING: A MULTITUDE OF NICHES

Your journey down the path of elite performance begins with self-discovery and the simple recognition that trading is not a single activity requiring a single set of skills and personality traits. There are many niches within the trading world, some of which might fit you well and others that will not. Some forms of trading will never be ones you could bond with. Others might fit your personality and talents beautifully. Consider four traders:

- *Sherry*, a graduate from a top MBA program, is a currency trader for a multinational banking organization. She takes long-term positions in the spot (cash) market based upon global/macro considerations. Much of her day is spent talking with knowledgeable bank and hedge fund traders and researching economic statistics from the major regions and countries of the world. Sherry can tell you shipping rates and volumes for most of the major world ports; equally readily, she can summarize each country's monetary policies, debt levels, and interest rates. Just a few good ideas per year account for much of her profit. Sherry trades infrequently, but takes large positions when she does, using day-to-day market movement to help her build positions at favorable prices. Over time, Sherry has built a network of colleagues who share information about large buyers and sellers in the marketplace. She considers this form of information gathering essential in a decentralized global market. Her network, she believes, is her edge. She would never consider making decisions from short-term price swings, and she doesn't view trading as a science. Markets, she believes, reflect capital outflows and inflows that result from decisions made by the largest banks, funds, and central governments. Her job is to track these in an environment with limited transparency. She sees herself as a jungle explorer on a continual safari, stalking for information.
- *David*, a former star athlete in college, works for a proprietary trading firm in Chicago, where he is the equivalent of a market maker in the S&P 500 (ES) electronics futures market. David is in the market at most times, generally working offers above the market and bids below. His goal is to profit from the bid-ask spread by buying bids and selling offers. Rarely does he hold a position more than a matter of seconds. Once in a while he gets "run over" when the market moves rapidly, but he can usually scalp ticks and earn a good living. David has no idea what is going on in the economy; nor does he care. He is an aggressive, action-oriented trader. His world is the moment-to-moment shifts of

bids and offers in the marketplace. David likens trading to playing poker: He watches what large traders are doing by monitoring volume on a trade-by-trade basis and tries to decide when they have strong or weak hands. His trading is punctuated by shouts of joy and frustration, and his cubicle—set near the trade stations of similar traders—seems more like a locker room environment than the office of a professional trader. Once he leaves his desk, his market day is done. He religiously avoids thinking about the market lest he become locked into opinions the next day. He thinks charts are a waste of time, and the only news he follows is economic reports released during trading hours. Markets move, he believes, because of the large locals and institutions that trade each day. His job is to read their actions and intentions the way a poker player reads the tells of opponents.

- *Pat*, a business development manager for a regional manufacturing company, is a moderately active, part-time trader of equities, relying on momentum patterns for trades that last three to four weeks on average. He reviews dozens of charts each weekend, scanning his microcap stock universe for relative strength information and volume trends. Few analysts cover the stocks he trades. This is fine by him; he doesn't want the opinions of analysts to interfere with his reading of supply and demand. Pat cannot give much of a description of what each of the companies does; he only knows their short-term trading patterns. He particularly gravitates toward stocks of companies with recent news events and price breakouts. His greatest success has come from capitalizing on the volume and volatility in individual small stocks following earnings reports and surprise developments. His stocks don't closely follow the major market averages, so Pat spends little time looking at economic reports. Instead, he tracks patterns of momentum with the Commodity Channel Index (CCI) using end-of-day data. He has developed a feel for the CCI's patterns and uses them to time entries and exits. During the day Pat focuses on his work in sales; at night he briefly reviews his charts and adjusts his portfolio as needed. Holding his positions for days or weeks at a time and limiting his screen time to evenings helps him separate his trading from his family and work obligations, but also provides him with supplemental income. He believes that charts capture the psychology of the marketplace and that small stocks avoid the noise created when large institutions trade in and out of the market. He views himself as a kind of psychologist: His job is to catch swings in market sentiment and profit from price trends.

- *Ellen* retired from her position as a software engineer following the buyout of her previous employer. Her cash-out from stock options allowed her to take up trading as a second career. She studied market patterns from historical data, testing these to determine whether it was profitable to trade them. Eventually she found a recurring pattern of trending price behavior in the fixed-income markets based upon early morning strength and weakness. Ellen developed automated programs to trade these patterns in the 10-year Treasury note and 30-year bond, freeing her from the screen as the trades unfolded over the day. Recently she hired a brokerage firm to trade the systems for her, providing her with more time to develop mechanical systems in other markets. Ellen's goal is to diversify her risk by trading a basket of commodities with her best-performing systems. Her research is filled with estimates of risk and evaluations of system parameters: drawdowns, profit/loss (P/L), and so on. She frequently tweaks existing systems and tries out new ones. She studies little of the fundamentals behind market movements and rarely interacts with others over their trading opinions. For Ellen, trading itself is an unemotional task best left to computers. System development is her first love, a source of continual challenge and fascination. She believes that markets are continually evolving, requiring constant evolution of her systems. Her job is to recognize when markets are changing and identify their new patterns as quickly as possible, before they become more widely known to traders. She views herself as a scientist, ferreting out patterns amid randomness.

These four traders are composite portraits of individuals I know personally and who are successful in the markets. As a psychologist, I find it interesting to see how each of them found a niche in the market that fits their personality and lifestyle. Pat is a consummate businessperson, with more than a bit of people skill. It is difficult to imagine him as a full-time trader; he enjoys the social process of business development far too much for that. It is also impossible to imagine Ellen haunting trading chat rooms. Truth, for her, is to be found in empirical research—not the randomness of people's impressions.

To look at him, David could be any kid off the street. He wears shorts to the office, with a baseball cap turned backward. When he is not trading, he is drinking with buddies over a poker game or playing basketball in a local league. He is clearly driven by the competitive element of trading and its nonstop pace. Over the course of any particular day, he may trade well over a hundred times. Sherry, on the other hand, is far more calculating. She divides the world into those people who have information and those who don't. Her skill, she believes, is the ability to assemble large amounts of information into a coherent picture. The upticks and downticks of the market, for her, are random noise hiding what is really going on among the market movers. She believes the real work of trading is extracting information from her network, just as Ellen believes the real work of trading is research and system development. For them, all the rest is merely placing orders. For David and Pat, reading the market is the essence of trading; everything else is extraneous.

We refer to Sherry, David, Pat, and Ellen as traders, *yet their careers barely overlap.* Each has found a niche, just as psychiatrists, surgeons, and radiologists find their niches within medicine. When my daughter Devon began modeling school, I always thought models were models. It turns out that very different talents and skills determine who will be successful as a runway model, a print model, or a hair model. Fortunately, trading—like medicine or modeling—is broad enough to encompass a variety of careers, each drawing on particular skill sets and interests. *This provides traders with the possibility of finding the kind of market and market activity that will prove personally as well as financially rewarding.*

> Success reflects the fit between the person and the performance environment.

Finding the right niche makes all the difference in the world when it comes to performance. A hall-of-fame baseball pitcher might well be a flop as a hitter; a punter in football rarely makes a good linebacker; commercial print models are not necessarily the ones who dominate the runway; the best medical researchers don't always make the best teachers: Over and over we see examples where the difference between success and failure is being in the right niche. Sherry and Ellen would fail miserably as scalpers; David would go crazy waiting months for his positions to work out. Pat actually did try trading full-time and lost his motivation as well as a fair amount of money; the experience was too isolating. Each of them, however, has found success through a meshing of who they are as people and how they approach markets.

All four traders work hard at what they do, but none of them really consider it work. Every single one has expressed a sense of wonder at getting paid for doing what they love doing. David is a gambler; Sherry is a huntress—they do what they do because it is who they are. The key step in their performance development was not the discovery of a great indicator or the exercise of some mystical knack for trading: It was simply finding, within the trading world, an activity that allowed them to express their talents and interests. For that reason, trading became intrinsically interesting and rewarding, sustaining their learning curves. One does not become a top gun without some click between personality, abilities, and the challenges of being a fighter pilot. That same click is found among trading's top guns.

HOW DO TRADERS FIND THEIR NICHES?

Oddly, this topic is almost never addressed in trading texts. In the medical world, niche finding is a paramount concern: Students participate in rotations covering each of the specialty fields to experience them firsthand. After six weeks of pediatrics, six weeks of general surgery, six weeks of radiology, and six weeks of psychiatry, students begin to gain a sense for the kinds of medical practice that speak to their strengths and interests. *Most of all, they learn which of the fields is fun.* Students destined for surgery and emergency medicine are a bit like David; they gravitate toward active practice fields. Research physicians are more like Ellen, finding their fulfillment in problem solving and the analytical process. Each group finds its own path through the developmental process, cultivating what comes naturally and most enjoyably to them.

Traders rarely have the opportunity to pursue fun and sample different specialties. How many of us have attempted position-trading volatile instruments like Sherry, and then scalped deep electronic markets like David? Imagine approaching trading as if it were medical education: trading baskets of stocks for 6 weeks like Pat, developing a trading system for precious metals futures over the next 6 weeks, and then spending 12 weeks building currency positions based on macro analyses. The odds are good that, like medical students, we would hate some of the experiences and love others. Those emotional responses would be informative, because they would start us on a track where we could then develop ourselves in our preferred areas.

This is precisely the first step to take on the performance path. Before committing to a market or style of trading, you need to experience what it is like to trade frequently and how that differs—cognitively and emotionally—from holding positions. You need to immerse yourself in different markets and feel the difference between trading such instruments as large-cap stock indices, microcap stocks, energy futures, Treasury notes, euro currency, and equity options. Such experience teaches you much about yourself—and about markets.

Without exposure to different trading activities, traders are a bit like partners in an arranged marriage. Maybe the arrangement will be a good fit; maybe it will be a disaster. It probably won't be fun. And, as Benjamin Bloom found out, it is difficult to sustain a commitment without that emotional bonding. *How many traders never progress through the stages of mastery not because they're lazy, but because they're simply in the wrong place?* If, even after a period of courtship and engagement, half of all marriages end in divorce, how can we expect to make better decisions about the markets we marry without so much as a few dates?

> It's not whether you can be a good trader; it's whether you can find the trading that's good for you.

We started by distinguishing experts from novices and found that experts are engaged in learning loops fueled by deliberative practice. The question then arose as to why more traders are not traversing these loops. Desire for an easy lifestyle and quick riches no doubt sabotages the pursuit of excellence for some traders, but Bloom's research suggests another possibility: Perhaps the initial focus on intensive practice is misplaced. Many traders have problems with their discipline for the same reason that young men have trouble committing to relationships: *They're just not ready.* If you're having performance problems in trading, instead of berating yourself with exhortations about discipline, perhaps we should figure out the answer to this question: What experiences will help you move through your developmental process, so that you'll eventually *want* to make—even crave making—a disciplined commitment to your work?

The famous American inventor Thomas Edison once noted, "Genius is one percent inspiration, ninety-nine percent perspiration." Many people missed opportunity, he said, because it dressed in overalls and looked like work. Yet he also claimed, "I never did a day's work in my life. It was all fun." That is the paradox of expertise: It is hard work—*and* it is fun. In fact, it is so much fun that we spend long hours at it and become highly skilled as a result. If you simply focus on the work part, you'll see nothing but overalls and miss life's opportunities. If you have nothing but fun, all the inspiration in the world won't make up for the absence of perspiration.

But to perspire at something that is all fun—*that* is possible only to those who have found their niche in life.

Does such a niche exist for you in the trading world? Let's find out.

CHAPTER 2

Finding Your Performance Niche as a Trader

Look, kid, don't ever—ya understand me?—don't ever let anyone monkey with your swing.
                    —Ted Williams to a young Carl Yastrzemski

ew major leaguers have wielded a bat like Carl Yastrzemski. Waving it high above his head, he created a huge arc with his swing to produce his power. For a coach and master batting technician such as Ted Williams, Carl's unorthodox stance should have been a nightmare. Never once, however, did Ted try to change Carl's style. He merely offered the advice that Major League pitchers would be quicker than those in the minor leagues, leaving no room for extraneous movement at the plate. The rest he left to Carl to figure out. Williams knew that Yaz had found his niche at the plate, and it was something to not mess with.

It would be wonderful if all of us found our "swing"—our natural place in life—in childhood. We would then have the luxury of pursuing our dreams and developing our potential from an early age. Mozart displayed interest in music very early, astounding observers with his precocious talent. Tiger Woods picked up golf clubs at one year of age and was putting shortly thereafter. Bobby Fischer first played chess at the age of six; eight years later he became the U.S. champion.

Most expert performers, however, do not start as prodigies. Some even have surprisingly modest early careers. Abraham Lincoln and Winston Churchill were undistinguished politicians until they found their leadership niches during times of crisis. Ray Kroc was an anonymous salesman of milkshake machines until he bought out his best customer, a hamburger restaurant owned by brothers named McDonald. Paul Gauguin began as a banker and stockbroker, only to transform his hobby of painting into a full-time pursuit in his mid-30s. Anna Mary Robertson, whom we know as the folk artist Grandma Moses, began painting in her 70s after arthritis prevented her from continuing her embroidery. Hall of Fame quarterback and kicker George Blanda was not a team starter for his first five seasons and actually retired before returning as a quarterback in the new American Football League. It wasn't until he was 40 years old that he joined the team that would provide his niche: the Oakland Raiders.

Would we remember Abraham Lincoln if there had been no War between the States? Would Paul Gauguin have achieved fame as a stockbroker? We like to think of greatness as a function of an individual's personal qualities, but reality is far more complex. *It is the fit between the individual and the performance environment that generates expertise.* As a Chicago Bear, George Blanda was a benchwarmer; as a Houston Oiler, he was a competent quarterback and kicker. As a Raider, however, Blanda was a one-man force whose last-minute heroics electrified the 1970 season.

So often, the difference between success and mediocrity is the difference from one performance setting to another. In one niche, an animal thrives; in another, it is threatened with extinction. *Unlike animals, however, we can select our niches.* We can find the environments that will nurture and expand our talents.

THE MULTIPLIER EFFECT

Is talent a matter of genes, or is it acquired? Perhaps no single question so dominates the discussion of performance. It is true that most elite performers display early talents. It is also true, however, that a sizable proportion of gifted youth never attain prominence and fall well short of their early promise. Recent research suggests that neither nature nor nurture is sufficient for the emergence of expertise. *It is the interaction between the two that supercharges development.*

Sandra Scarr's groundbreaking work on intelligence provides an excellent example of such an interaction. We know that IQ has a strong hereditary basis; that, all things being equal, high-IQ parents are more likely to have intellectually gifted children than low-IQ parents. Interestingly, however, by the time the children are well into their school years, the gap in cognitive functioning between high- and low-IQ children widens considerably. This is because children with higher intelligence tend to seek out peers—and environments—that are more intellectually stimulating than children with lower intelligence. Their *genotypes*—their inborn cognitive talents—help to determine their *phenotypes*—the environments they choose. Month after month, year after year of such differential stimulation allows higher-IQ children to develop far more rapidly than their less intellectually endowed peers.

A fascinating example of this genotype/phenotype interaction comes from the sports research of Janet Starkes and colleagues. They report that a significant proportion of skilled young athletes were born early in the calendar year. The reason for this is that, as very young beginners at their sport, the difference in their maturation compared to peers born late in the year was noticeable. This led parents and coaches to consider the early-birth children as talented, encouraging them to funnel those children to enriched performance environments. By the time the children were older, the gap between those with early and those with late birthdays was profound. The assignment of differential environments based on biology (month of birth) played a crucial role in shaping performance development.

Stephen Ceci and affiliated researchers from Cornell University refer to this phenomenon as the *multiplier effect*. Biological, inborn advantages—the basic strengths of individuals—steer them toward enriched environments, creating rapid growth. Imagine two young traders beginning at the Acme Trading Arcade in Chicago. One develops a quicker feel for the market than the other due to superior speed of mental processing. This trader is selected by a group leader within the firm for specialized training. The other, slower trader is not pulled aside for additional mentoring. By the end of the training program, the faster trader is profitable and reading markets with confidence thanks to mentorship and support within the group. The slower one, lacking such assistance, does not make money and loses his trading capital. Through multiplier effects, a small initial advantage expands exponentially, creating greatly enhanced outcomes. Ceci and colleagues conclude that even slight genetic advantages can snowball into significant differences in competency when amplified by superior environments.

The researchers explain that talents are necessary for success, but not sufficient. In that sense, abilities are like muscles. In the absence of exercise, a well-endowed musculature will not develop signficantly. With proper environmental stimulation, however, elite levels of strength and physique are possible. The proper environments exercise and develop our talents, paving the way for enriched settings that stimulate still further growth.

When traders find their niches, they open themselves to talent-environment interactions that create massive multiplier effects. This is why one sport can elicit hall-of-fame performance from an athlete, while another yields mediocrity; why we can trade some markets like market wizards and others like rookies. How many highly profitable tech stock traders in the late 1990s were unable to flourish once their niche evaporated? The difficulties of transferring skill sets from the pit to the screen are so legion that exchanges have established educational programs to aid in the transition. Multiplier effects that generate greatness need more than the right people: They require the right people in the right places.

> Multiplier effects are the difference between normal learning and the enhanced development that generates expertise.

MULTIPLIER EFFECTS IN TRADING

When I first came to Kingstree Trading as director of trader development, one of the first books that owner and founder Chuck McElveen recommended to me was *Good to Great* by Jim Collins. The book is an excellent illustration of performance concepts at a company-wide level, as the author explored what makes some good companies turn into great ones while others languish. Key to Collins's findings is the notion of the *Hedgehog Concept*: the idea that great companies simplify by focusing on their strengths. The three elements of the Hedgehog Concept are:

1. What you can be best at
2. Where you can be most profitable
3. What you are most passionate about

Good companies that never reached greatness, Collins found, strayed outside the circles defined by each of these elements. The great companies focused all their efforts at the intersection of those three circles. The flywheel principle described by Collins is akin to the multiplier effects described earlier: When companies blended passionate motivation with a focus on strengths, the result was hypergrowth. Success bred further success.

Kingstree itself experienced such a flywheel early in the company's history after it began as a good company in Evanston, Illinois, trading stocks. McElveen perceived the potential of electronic trading and became an early adopter of a new trading platform from Trading Technologies to trade the relatively new S&P 500 E-mini contract. The company quickly identified this as an opportunity, focused its efforts there, and recruited traders who were drawn to the new medium. Within just a few years, Kingstree became one of the volume leaders on the Chicago Mercantile Exchange. Trading individual equities, Kingstree was undistinguished; in the electronic trading niche, it found its way from good to great.

Traders with longevity in the industry have taken a similar flywheel course. They located themselves in the Hedgehog circles by discovering a style of trading that exploits their talent and so appeals to them that they stick with the intensive learning process. Consider two traders I will call Cindy and Joyce. Both participated in the training program I coordinated for Kingstree and were dedicated students. Cindy was highly intellectual and wanted to analyze trades exhaustively before risking money. She had difficulty adapting to the short-term trading style at Kingstree and eventually left the firm to pursue another opportunity. Joyce, however, had experience with competitive games and loved the process of making rapid decisions and putting herself on the line. She found a market that offered good movement and became profitable in her first year.

Scalping the markets did not exploit Cindy's strengths. She learned the market, but never experienced any multiplier effect. Joyce's growth curve, however, had a flywheel trajectory. From the start of training, you could see that she was having a good time with the learning. It was fun—it was taking advantage of things she could do well—and that prodded her to stick with it.

If your trading results have not been what you hoped for, you may have looked to new trading methods for your success. You may have looked to trading psychology for answers. The chances are good, however, that you haven't looked to the intersection of Collins's circles: the point at which talent meets opportunity and passion.

What are your talents? Where is there opportunity in the markets? What turns you on? There you will find your learning efforts turbocharged by multiplier effects, yielding not just competence, but expertise.

HOW DO WE FIND OUR NICHE?

Traders cannot afford to find their niches when they're in their 70s like Grandma Moses or even their 40s like George Blanda. Economic pressures—if nothing else—force traders into premature decisions about what and how they trade, reducing the likelihood that they will find multiplier effects.

If Scarr and Ceci are correct, the ideal niche will be one that matches your native abilities and traits to the specific opportunities in a given market and style of trading that market. Unless you know what your talents are and how they might interact with the many potential niches in the trading world, the odds of benefiting from snowballing multiplier effects are small indeed.

Alternatively, if we can clearly identify our strengths and market opportunities—and especially the overlap between them—we will be best poised to find the kind of trading that will sustain our passions.

With that in mind, let's go niche hunting.

An initial step in finding your distinctive place in the trading universe is self-assessment. Exhibit 2.1 offers a brief trading experience checklist. Take a moment and check "yes" or "no" for each of the items. We'll see how you respond, and then use the results to start you on your performance path.

We will take the first three questions first. These are the "dating" questions of trading: Have you played the field? Have you, like medical students, completed your rotations and sampled the many specialties in the field?

If the answer to any of these three questions is no, the follow-up question to contemplate is: *How do you* know *that you're trading the right way for your talents and personality?* Maybe you happened to stumble upon the right combination of time frame, market, and trading style. If so, you'll know you're graced with luck because you'll find it natural to trade in your chosen mode with your chosen market. Your trading will feel right, the way a good relationship or a career feels right. If, however, you're finding trading

EXHIBIT 2.1 Trading Experience Checklist

	Yes	No
Have you tried trading different time frames (intraday, swing, long term) on an ongoing basis?		
Have you attempted to trade different markets (stocks, futures, commodities) on an ongoing basis?		
Have you experimented with trading different styles (technical, tape reading, quantitative, mechanical) on an ongoing basis?		
Have you been trading on a regular basis for a year or longer?		
Have you made major adjustments in your trading approach after becoming dissatisfied with your results?		
Do you have a trading method that you consistently follow?		

frustrating and/or unprofitable, and if you answered no to any of the first three questions, perhaps the answer to your performance concerns does not lie in psychology. Perhaps you're like Ray Kroc selling Mixmasters or George Blanda relegated to kicking for the Bears. *Perhaps you're simply performing in the wrong niche.*

Now we get to the fourth question: Have you been trading regularly for at least a year? Once again, if the answer is no, the natural follow-up question is: *Have you truly had sufficient time and experience to try out different combinations of markets, trading styles, and time frames?* If my daughter had less than a year's worth of total dating experience and then told me she had found the love of her life, I would congratulate her. Then I would encourage her to cultivate the relationship for a while before making the commitment of a lifetime. My advice is the same for a trader who commits to a market or trading approach after a few weeks of training at a firm or after attending a great seminar. Sure, try it out, but keep your mind open. If you give it your best and it isn't working, consider alternatives. There is no sense losing 80 percent of your trading stake pursuing something that may not be right for you. If you're in the right niche, it will be like being in the right romantic relationship: It will capture you; it will fire you up; it will be all you'll look forward to. If the glow isn't there early, it certainly won't be there later on. *As in romance, never settle.* Commitment should follow falling in love; the latter never emerges from the former.

The fifth question assesses a different kind of experience. The best traders I have known and worked with are tinkerers. They have refined their trading over time, and failure has been their greatest teacher. Over time they become multidimensional, learning how to adapt to different market conditions. If you haven't traded a year or more and made adjustments in your trading approach, the chances are good that you haven't (yet) experienced dramatic market shifts. "Don't confuse skill with a bull market" is the old saying, and we saw what happened to too many "skilled" 1990s daytraders at the turn of the century. If you go to a clothing store, you may have to stay a while and try on many outfits before finding the right one. It will take repeated efforts and many adjustments to optimally tune your performance car. *You learn your ideal trading style by experiencing styles and market conditions that are less than ideal and then refining your approach.* If you answered no to the question "Have you made major adjustments to your trading approach after becoming dissatisfied with your results?" you may have found a comfort zone that is temporary—one that reflects the current market but not the general marketplace. The odds are good that what you think is your niche now may not be the niche you occupy several years from now. Your challenge may not be to learn markets, but to relearn them as conditions change.

That brings us to the final question: Do you have a trading method that you consistently follow?

We'll have to spend a little time on that one. It's actually a trick question.

WHAT WE CAN LEARN FROM INCONSISTENCY

Dale initially contacted me with a question about his trading problems. A career military officer, he appeared to be ideally suited for trading. He knew about discipline, and he understood the relevance of deliberative practice to performance success. Bright and creative, he led troops in the field and planned and executed numerous missions. He could think on his feet and had the ability to act quickly—and lethally.

Dale's problem, to hear him tell it, was inconsistency. Although he had a trading method that he had developed over the past year, he would have had to answer no to the last checklist question. He would repeatedly veer from his strategy, exiting positions before reaching his stop-loss and price target points. Other times, he failed to place trades that were practically begging to be taken. "My emotions are getting in the way," Dale explained. "I've been wondering if I have the right personality for trading. Do you have a personality test I could take?"

I would say this is the most common question I receive from readers. Traders hear that personality (and, more broadly, psychology) is important to trading success, so they naturally wonder if they have the "right personality for trading."

Hopefully by now you see the futility of that question. It's like a medical student asking if she has the "right personality" to be a physician. Well, maybe she has the right personality for emergency medicine, but not for medical research; the right personality for anesthesiology, but not for family medicine. The issue is not one of possessing a global "right personality" for trading, medicine, sports, or any broad performance field. Rather, it is finding the *right fit* between your personality and the specific type of trading, doctoring, or athletics that you might undertake. Dale had the right personality to be a leader in the Army infantry, but perhaps he would have failed miserably on a Navy submarine or in the cockpit of a fighter jet.

What happens when someone well suited to one specialization has to perform in another, very different one? *The result is inconsistency.* A few years ago, a medical student who was well suited to psychiatry was referred to me during her acting internship (AI) in surgery. It turned out that her family dearly wanted her to become a surgeon, and, under pressure, she signed up for the AI. What happened? The student spent too much time talking with her surgery patients and their relatives. Indeed, she actually missed two scheduled surgeries because she was busy consoling worried family members. She empathized deeply with their plight—a wonderful quality for a psychiatrist, but one that is not so helpful for a surgeon. I imagine that I would want my surgeon to be steady and unemotional when I'm awaiting the knife in the operating room!

The student was referred to me specifically for her "inconsistent" performance during the AI. Her lack of attendance at the surgery, they felt, showed a problem with "professionalism" and "commitment." They also felt it revealed a lack of respect for the surgery interns and residents who were trying to teach her. In fact, it signified none of those things. She was merely doing what came naturally and avoiding what didn't.

That was Dale's problem, as well. When I gathered the details of his inconsistent performance, I found that his chosen methodology involved spread trading. He had read about spreading and was drawn to the idea of limiting risk by buying something strong and simultaneously selling something weak. So, for instance, he might think that energy-related stocks would perform well in an inflationary environment and technology-related issues might lag. He might thus buy the energy sector exchange-traded fund (XLE) and sell the semiconductor sector (SMH). He liked the idea that he could make money even if the market plunged on unexpected news. As long as XLE outperformed SMH, he would profit.

A majority of his "lack of discipline" trades were ones in which he detected unusual strength or weakness on one side of his spread and pulled the other leg. For instance, he would see crude oil break to multiday highs and XLE catch a strong bid. If XLE's strength was reflective of firmness in the broad market—and if SMH was holding its own or rising—he would bail out of his short position and leave himself with the outright position in energy. Sometimes this would work; often it wouldn't. Once XLE was strong enough to make him want to lift the leg on the spread, its move—at least temporarily—was over.

My question for Dale was simple. "Suppose you were leading your men in the field on a reconnaissance mission. You saw a key enemy installation was nearby and lightly guarded. You wanted to engage, but didn't want to give away your company's position. When you tried to radio in to request engagement, you couldn't get through to headquarters. How would you feel about your commanding officer if he was hedging his bet and refusing to answer your radio call, forcing you to make the decision regarding the engagement? If your mission succeeded, he could take credit; if it failed, he could claim that you proceeded without authorization."

Dale, understandably, winced at my scenario. He made it clear that he would lose all respect for an officer who didn't take responsibility for decisions. "A leader doesn't hedge his bets," Dale insisted. "He won't have the confidence of his men, and he's not fit to lead."

It didn't take Dale long to recognize his problem. By spreading, he was hedging his bets in the market. Deep down, he didn't respect that as a trading style. Intellectually he knew that it's a fine and potentially successful trading methodology, but emotionally he responded to it as if it were gutless. When he actually had an opportunity to "engage the enemy," as in the XLE trade, he showed his true colors. He ditched his hedge and took responsibility for the attack. Like the medical student talking with the surgery patient's family, he did what came naturally—and felt undisciplined as a result.

The last item of the questionnaire is a trick question because it is assessing a potential strength as well as weakness. Many traders who veer from their trading plans recognize at some level that those plans don't fit them. *Their losses of discipline are intuitive gravitations to their natural trading styles.* The answer to their problems is not to blindly adhere to their methods and work on discipline, but rather to determine whether those methods are truly the ones to follow. *The first step in climbing a ladder is making sure it's leaning against the right structure.* Too many traders are like Dale, furiously climbing misplaced ladders and then blaming themselves for getting nowhere.

When you have found your niche, you don't need discipline to do the right things; you won't *want* to do anything else.

At the risk of repetition, allow me to be clear about this: *All things being equal, we will naturally gravitate toward those activities that we find fulfilling.* We will avoid tasks that do not engage our talents and interests, and we will seek out experiences of success and mastery. If you are in your niche, you will consistently do the right things, because those come naturally to you. If you are not consistently doing the right thing, perhaps you have not found that point at the intersection of the circles that blends talents, opportunities, and interests. What we do when we're inconsistent may just point the way toward our strengths by revealing what comes naturally.

CLIMBING THE RIGHT LADDERS

Nothing substitutes for realworld experience when it comes to determining the markets and trading methods that best suit you. Nonetheless there are a few guidelines that can help you get started. Based on our earlier discussion of Sherry, David, Pat, and Ellen, here are several considerations for a quick self-evaluation.

Do You Make Decisions from the Gut or the Head?

Think about how you typically make decisions. Don't just focus on trading or investing decisions. Consider how you chose your house, your car, or your last major purchase. Did you research the selection carefully, weighing the pros and cons? Did you spend a good amount of time making the decision? Or was the decision rather quick and from the gut? Did you make your choice based on what you fell in love with or based on what had the best combination of features on your list?

How we make decisions is an expression of our *cognitive style*; it reflects how we best learn and process information. Research in psychology suggests that such traits have a strong inborn component and are not easy to modify. We are much more likely to find success by finding trading methods that fit our cognitive style than by trying to overhaul the workings of our brains. Nietzsche's claim that people are either Apollonian or Dionysian—processing the world intellectually or experientially—reflects an awareness of our fundamentally different wiring.

Jim Dalton, author of *Mind over Markets* and *Markets in Profile*, recently stressed to me, "Traders need to understand how they arrive at decisions: the role the analytic and synthetic parts of the brain play and the merging of those two. You can't assess risk without emotion, but you can get too wrapped up in emotion." Each of us has a different way of merging the information from explicit reasoning and emotional experiencing in making decisions. It is when we fail to effect the merger—and when we attempt to operate outside our cognitive styles—that, in Dalton's words, we become our own greatest adversaries.

Among the traders we discussed earlier, Ellen and Sherry are "head" traders; Pat and David are more likely to make their decisions from the gut. Ellen and Sherry love the process of research: They spend more time generating ideas than actually trading. They are analytical in their approach: They gather information and rely on the data to help them make decisions.

Pat and David, conversely, are pattern readers. They make decisions based upon their perception of market action. David watches how markets trade tick by tick, closely monitoring when size hits bids or lifts offers. He has developed a feel for when large traders—the big locals and institutions—are shifting their sentiment from bullish to bearish or vice versa. Pat is a chart reader and uses key indicator patterns to provide him with a sense for when momentum is shifting.

As we can see from the traders in our example, *our cognitive styles dictate what we look at in the markets and how we look at them*. A psychiatrist does not view patients the same way that a radiologist or researcher does. Similarly, a military man like Dale approaches decision making very differently from a marriage counselor or a priest. While all of us combine qualities that are analytical and intuitive, emotional and intellectual, we each generally have a leaning—a dominant style. That style, properly applied to markets, becomes an important part of our potential edge.

Do You Emotionally Gravitate toward Stimulation or Stability?

Some of us are patient and deliberate. We methodically work toward a goal and reap rewards at the end of the process. Others need to see payoffs more immediately. We are easily bored by sameness and the routine of a patient, deliberate pursuit. As you can imagine, this difference of *emotional styles* plays an important role in determining a trader's approach to entering, managing, and exiting trades. Someone who craves novelty, excitement, and gratification will have trouble holding onto positions or staying out of slow markets. A patient trader who thrives on consistency and stability will become ruffled if required to trade in and out of the market.

As with decision-making modes, our emotional styles are reflected in daily life. Those preferring shorter-term gratifications tend to be stimulation seekers. They are more likely to be extroverted, and they are more likely to enjoy activities that involve a high degree of emotional involvement: parties, exotic vacations, and competitive sports. Such individuals also tend to be risk takers. Given the choice between a safe, known alternative and one that is unusual and unknown, they will lean toward the latter. David is clearly a stimulation seeker. He hates slow markets and will sometimes use large orders to prod other large traders into action. He is happiest when markets are volatile, moving freely between price levels. In a different way, Ellen is also a stimulation seeker. She works and reworks her trading systems, and she enjoys following them across different markets. It would never occur to Ellen to develop a single system and simply trade it. A large part of the gratification she derives from trading is generating new ideas, testing them out, and refining them.

Those who prefer stability are motivated by security. They are not risk takers and prefer safe, familiar alternatives to the unknown. Most of all, they don't require a high degree of novelty and stimulation. If you look at their daily lives, you'll see a high degree of uniformity: They get up at about the same time, have a common morning routine, take the same route to work, eat the same foods, and so on. They do not seek change and often do not adapt well to change. For that reason, the stability seeker—unlike the stimulation seeker—will tend to limit exposure to markets and will rely upon familiar, comfortable trading methods. David and Ellen tend to push the envelope of comfort, always trying new things in the market. Sherry, on the other hand, is a plodder. She will take long periods of time to develop market opinions and build positions. The short-term ups and downs of the market represent mental interference for her—not stimulation or opportunity. Where David can be impulsive and Ellen takes the stance "Let's throw lots of things at the wall and see what sticks," Sherry does one thing and does it well. She doesn't take a position in the market until she has built a body of evidence that makes the position seem risk free.

Pat represents a different kind of stability seeking, one that is not often appreciated among traders. He does not look to trading for his bread-and-butter income. Trading is more avocation than vocation for him because he enjoys the income, stability, and challenge of his career. He also has commitments to his family and the demands of maintaining a household. In order to accommodate these priorities, he manages his trading in a streamlined fashion at night and holds positions for days or weeks at a time. Many evenings, he simply reviews charts, reads news on the Web, and gets on with his life. He does not want to be emotionally involved in trading, and he is not looking for excitement in the markets. To hear him talk, he enjoys more than his share of excitement in the business world. Trading is an enjoyable challenge and a supplement to his income. The money in his trading account, however, is a small fraction of his net worth. "If I lose all my money trading," Pat observes, "it won't affect my family or my career one bit." Pat will never be a multi-million-dollar trader, but neither will he take multi-million-dollar risks.

Exhibit 2.2 is a graph displaying the intersection of cognitive and emotional styles. Each of the four traders occupies a quadrant of the graph, which tells us that they have very different ways of processing the world. Not surprisingly, this means that they approach trading very differently. By identifying our cognitive and emotional styles, we can better understand ourselves and begin the process of identifying potential market niches.

My own cognitive style, for example, is analytical. Even when trading short-term I am analyzing whether size is differentially lifting offers or hitting bids. At each point in the trading day, I am gauging the odds of market moves continuing versus reversing by monitoring baskets of leading stocks. I am also relatively risk averse. I am willing to lose only a small percentage of my account on any single trade and will not trade slow periods that offer little price-change opportunity. Not surprisingly, I trade a market (stock indices) that offers a great deal of analytical information, and I trade almost exclusively in the morning, trying to catch a limited number of short-term swings during periods of movement. A poster in my office depicts a military sniper in the field. That is my approach to trading. I survey the territory for hours, keep my exposure low, wait for the right moment to take my shot, and return to cover when I'm done.

Does this trading style work for me? Absolutely. Clearly, it would frustrate an active risk taker or someone who trades by feel alone. *There are no*

Emotional Style – Stimulation Seeking

Ellen—Developing new trading systems and trading new research	*David*—Trading short-term patterns and always being in the market
Cognitive Style Analytical	**Cognitive Style Intuitive**
Sherry—Developing and trading established methods over longer time frames	*Pat*—Trading longer-term market patterns with a diverse portfolio on a part-time basis

Emotional Style – Stability Seeking

EXHIBIT 2.2 Examples of the Combinations of Emotional and Cognitive Styles as They Relate to Trading

right and wrong trading strategies—only strategies that are right or wrong for us. Ask yourself if you would rather be Sherry, David, Pat, or Ellen. Who among them is *least* like you? Your responses will provide you with valuable clues about your ideal niche.

MARKET OPPORTUNITY: THE OTHER HALF OF THE EQUATION

Thus far we've been focusing on your talents and interests and their fit with what and how you trade. There is another factor in the equation, and it is tricky: the amount of opportunity that is in *your* market at *your* time frame.

It's tricky because opportunity changes—and requires that we change with it.

I recently wrote an article for the Trading Markets web site that described why so many short-term traders were struggling in the S&P 500 E-mini market. Going back 40 years, I investigated the proportion of two-day periods during a moving 250-day window that were either both up in price or both down in price. In other words, I was looking at the number of times a one-day move in the market carried over to a second day. This was a very simple measure of trending behavior.

If we assume that the market has a 50 percent probability of rising and a 50 percent probability of declining, then we should see approximately 125 occasions out of 250 in which the market is either up or down for two consecutive days. In the late 1960s and early 1970s, however, the number of trending occasions out of 250 was consistently above 140. This proportion steadily declined into 2006, where it has been hovering in the low 100s as I write. In other words, we have gone from market conditions in which markets were more likely to follow rises with rises and declines with declines to a situation in which rises are more likely to be followed by declines, and vice versa.

Moreover, I found evidence that this was occurring over multiple time frames. The Barchart.com web site has an interesting feature for subscribers that tracks the performance of each stock vis-à-vis a number of technical trading systems. These are trend following in nature, assuming, for example, purchase at moves above a moving average and sales below the average. Some of the systems are short term, covering trades and patterns lasting a few days on average, and some are longer term: up to 60 days. Looking back over a three-year performance period, Google (GOOG), a stock that had been strong during that period, was profitable on each of the systems. The S&P 500 exchange-traded fund SPY, however, was a loser on every system. In other words, Google was trending across multiple time frames and the broad market was not.

With the rise of automated trading and the increased program trading and arbitrage that it facilitates, trending movements in the broad market have become less common. Because this is occurring in very short time frames (intraday) as well as longer-term, it affects scalpers as well as active investors. Momentum trading (buying short-term market strength; selling short-term market weakness) and longer-term trend following have simply not worked in the S&P 500 market—and the proof is in the many proprietary stock index traders who used to make a living scalping that market and found dwindling opportunity.

It is interesting that some traders gravitate toward being momentum traders, while others are patient trend followers, and still others trade in a countertrend style, fading market movements. I've also noticed that many traders have a persistent bias, either to the long or to the short side. No doubt personality plays a role in such preferences. While I strongly suspect that flexibility of trading styles has advantages over such biases, I've seen traders succeed with a variety of idiosyncratic preferences. *When that success has been present, however, it is always because market opportunity has lined up with those biases.* Trend followers make money in trending markets; momentum traders profit when short-term moves continue into the next time period. Once market opportunity shifts, as I found, those biases leave traders at risk.

At that point, either they need to move to new markets (that accommodate their biases) or they need to cultivate a new trading style. Neither is an easy adjustment, and yet they are the kinds of adjustments required by markets that regularly shift their trending patterns. While it is important to match one's cognitive and emotional styles to one's style of trading, none of that will be helpful if there is not objective opportunity in the marketplace. Simple analyses like the ones I performed, such as looking across time frames and determining how often rises are followed by rises and declines by declines, will tell you quite a bit about a *market's* personality—and whether it matches your trading style.

Another facet of the market's personality is volatility. Some markets offer more movement than others, and this translates into greater potential risk and reward. I recently completed an analysis for my TraderFeed blog that looked at five-day periods of weakness in the market. The market forecast for the following five days was significantly bullish for both the S&P 500 Index (SPY) and the Russell 2000 Index (IWM) of small-cap issues. While the number of historical winning and losing trades was similar across the two indices, the Russell offered a 50 percent greater return on average. This was because of the greater volatility of the small stocks during the period covered by the study. One's profitability, in this case—as in most cases I've studied—was thus just as much a function of the market they traded as the pattern being traded. Once again, we can see that matching trading style to markets becomes key to trading performance.

> Markets, like people, have their personalities; our relationships with markets will profit to the extent that there is compatibility.

One of the trickiest aspects of trading is that volatility varies on an intraday basis, as well as longer-term. Just as bear markets tend to be more volatile than rising markets, we typically see greater volatility when markets open and close than during their midday hours. Currencies, for instance, will trade greater volume and display enhanced volatility around the London and New York opens than during the period in between or during the New York afternoon. A short-term trading style that makes money in the morning can struggle mightily at midday. The fit between trading style and market personality that was there at one time period is no longer present later on. Opportunity thus becomes a moving target for the active trader.

These are the three legs of the performance stool: (1) your talents and interests, (2) your trading style, and (3) markets and their personalities. The meshing of your qualities with your trading style will help determine your ability to trade that style with consistency and discipline. The meshing of your trading style and the features of markets will determine the degree to which you have a performance edge in the marketplace. The ever-shifting features of markets ensure that traders who are adaptable will be most likely to sustain expert performance over the course of a trading career.

PAPER TRADING AS A SELF-DISCOVERY TOOL

When you're starting your development as a successful market performer, you have a disadvantage relative to students of other disciplines. A body-builder can develop in the weight room; a dancer can practice in a studio. Trading, however, involves money and risk. By the time you figure out your trading niche and gain experience with it, you could easily run through your entire trading stake!

This is where paper trading is a helpful tool early in the development process. The fact that paper trading does not involve monetary risk makes it psychologically different from live trading. At an early stage of develop-ment, however, that is a plus. You are not trying to precisely simulate entries and exits, and your profit/loss (P/L) outcomes are not all-important. *Rather, you're using paper trading to get a feel for different trading styles and markets.* In a sense, during your early, initiation phase as a successful trader, you want to approach paper trading as a video game. See if it's inter-esting and challenging. See if it is just plain fun. See if it fits your cognitive and emotional styles. And, yes, see if it offers opportunity.

Many trading platforms offer paper-trading capability, including CQG, NeoTicker, Ninja Trader, e-Signal, and Trading Technologies. For our cur-rent purpose, bells and whistles are not important—all you need is a setup that enables you to practice trading and that will track your trades and their P/L. *You will want to paper-trade different markets and different trading styles.* The combinations of these will expose you to many poten-tial trading niches. If you find that you really dislike a particular market or style, accept that as useful information and try to figure out what turns you off and/or what is missing for you. If something feels right and comes natu-rally, that will also be instructive. The important thing is to be creative. Try to observe traders, read about them, and imitate them. Cover as many mar-kets and styles as you can. Explore. Play.

How much time will you need to get a feel for any particular trading niche? In the best of all worlds, it would be at least several weeks for active intraday traders and at least several months for those trading longer time frames. Medical students, as I mentioned earlier, take at least six weeks to complete their specialty clinical rotations. This is because they need to have sufficient exposure to a range of treatment settings and patients to truly appreciate what the specialty is like. Similarly, experiencing different kinds of markets—fast ones, slow ones, trending ones—helps you appreciate the nuances of each trading niche. Six weeks' experience at intraday trading provides you with about 30 days of exposure—probably enough to capture varied market action. Equivalent exposure with a swing-trading approach, where you're holding positions for several days at a time, might require the better part of half a year.

This may seem like a long preparatory time. The temptation is to short-circuit the process and jump into live trading and the prospect of making money. Such an attempted shortcut, however, is precisely what generates many emotionally driven performance problems. Look at it this way: Your cognitive and emotional styles will always win out in the end. *You will always gravitate to your natural style of processing information, and you will always gravitate to what you find most gratifying*. This gravitation will either be planned—taking you in the direction you want to go—or unplanned, subverting what you are trying to accomplish. *If you rush your trading development and enter markets without first finding your niche, your most fundamental traits are apt to work against the niche you (artificially) define for yourself*. Instead of a multiplier effect, you will generate a divider effect. You'll be telling yourself to trade one way, and your heart and head will be leaning a totally different way.

I recently interviewed a trader who wanted to come to work at my firm. He had started a training program at another trading house, which went out of business shortly thereafter. In that prior training experience, he was required to develop what he called a "business plan." Incredibly (to my way of thinking), he composed a 20-plus-page document detailing the market he would trade, how he would trade it, how he would measure his performance, how he would improve his performance, and so on. The idea was that he would then start to work his plan on the company's trading simulator.

It sounds logical: Develop a plan, practice it in simulation, and then take it live. By now, however, you can see that his firm had it backward. How can the trader develop the best plan for himself if he hasn't first tried trading (on a simulator or live) and discovered the kinds of trading and markets that best match his abilities and interests? Trading plans are well and good, and business planning is essential to success in any commercial venture. But if you were a bank loan officer or a venture capitalist, would you fund a 20-page business proposal submitted by someone who had no prior business experience? *Any plan you develop should emerge from experience—and the opportunities that you observe during that experience*. The kind of experience that will allow you to develop trading plans, Bloom found, is *play*: trying out different markets and trading styles and observing which ones feel right.

What kind of experience would be helpful in exploring market niches? If I were to recommend a few core experiences to start your paper trading and niche finding, these would be (1) fundamental, longer-term trading of individual stocks; (2) short-term momentum or countertrend trading of equity indices; (3) system trading of a basket of commodities; and (4) relationship trading between related trading instruments (stock sectors, fixed-income instruments of different duration, options of different expirations or strikes, etc.). Your fundamental trading would expose you to the process of researching stocks and industries and acting upon your judgment. Short-term index trading would provide you with experience in making rapid decisions based on shifting intraday supply and demand. System trading—even something as simple as trading moving-average crossovers on an end-of-day basis—would give you a sense for rule-based trading across multiple instruments. Relationship trading would introduce you to a different way of thinking about market movement and ways of profiting from it.

These are but a few common trading markets and styles, and there are many ways of blending them. For instance, you can engage in spreading on a long-term basis if you think that small-capitalization stocks are in a bull market relative to large-capitalization ones, due to a favorable interest rate environment. This would have you trading the relationship between the Russell 2000 Index and the S&P 500 like a fundamental trader. Alternatively, you could follow a price chart of the difference between these instruments and trade the spread like a momentum trader. There are system traders who engage in short-term momentum trading, and there are systems for implementing longer-term fundamental market ideas. The permutations of instruments, time frames, and trading approaches are near endless.

SPECIFIC PERSONALITY CONSIDERATIONS IN FINDING TRADING NICHES

Research on personality traits finds that a set of five traits—the so-called Big Five of neuroticism, extroversion, openness to experience, conscientiousness, and agreeableness—are remarkably stable over the life span. These traits help define the core of who we are. They affect how we process information, and they capture many of our deepest needs and interests. Exhibit 2.3 lists several trading niche considerations associated with three of those traits.

Remember: We're using paper trading as a tool for self-discovery. Trade the markets that you're following—and by all means try to improve your trading over time—but don't get discouraged if you're losing money. That's why we're doing the trading on "paper"! At this stage of your development, think of yourself as a high school student who participates on several different sports teams. After experiencing each fully, the decision to specialize will come easily.

Are you moody or even-tempered? This will tell you something about neuroticism. Are you sociable and fun-loving, or do you tend to be serious and keep to yourself? This will reveal your degree of extroversion. Do you like trying new things and enjoy new ideas and new places to visit, or are you a creature of habit? This informs you of your degree of openness to experience. If your paper trading is enjoyable, the chances are good that it fits well for you across these three traits. If you find the experience frustrating, it is probably frustrating those traits. Vary the frequency of your trading and your average holding times; vary the markets you trade and the style you use to trade them: fundamental, momentum, system, and relationship. When something clicks, you know you've found something special—something that can start you on the path to multiplier effects and the accelerated learning that generates expertise.

EXHIBIT 2.3 Personality Traits and Trading Niches

Three Key Personality Traits

- *Neuroticism* Someone who is prone to experience a great deal of negative emotion—anxiety, depression, guilt, or anger—will, on average, have more difficulty with a very short-term trading approach than with a longer-term methodology. A longer period between trades reduces the likelihood of impulsive decision making under conditions of emotional arousal. Traders low in neuroticism are more apt to tolerate markets that are higher in volatility, as these will not trigger mood swings and trading disruptions.
- *Extraversion* Risk takers tend to be high on the trait of extroversion and often gravitate to approaches where they can be aggressive, either through frequent trading or through approaches that allow them to move significant size. Introverted individuals are more likely to make decisions from analysis and study and will benefit from markets with good information flows (news, volume, market depth, etc.). Often, extroverted, risk-taking traders will express their aggressive tendencies through active trading; more risk-averse traders will limit their market exposure.
- *Openness to experience* Those who enjoy novelty and variety gravitate toward stock picking or other trading approaches that allow them to take a variety of positions at different times. Such traders often lean toward discretionary trading methods that exploit pattern recognition and other trader skills. More structured, rule-based trading is apt to appeal to the individual who prefers the security of predictable experience over the excitement of new experience. They are more apt to prefer system trading and trading fewer, rather than more, instruments at one time.

WHAT YOU REALLY DISCOVER FROM YOUR TRADING NICHE

An interesting book called *Now, Discover Your Strengths* by Marcus Buckingham and Donald O. Clifton, Ph.D., makes the compelling case that people develop their potential by building on their strengths, not by trying to overcome their weaknesses. Successful performers, they argue, work around their shortcomings, but achieve great things by making maximum use of their strengths. A baseball team could waste considerable time trying to turn a talented hitter into a skilled fielder, when the time would be better spent refining his batting—and then using him as a designated hitter. I have always been much better at big-picture thinking than at execution of details. Errands and tasks are frustrating for me, but I enjoy starting with a blank sheet of mental paper and developing and executing a plan of action. My wife, Margie, on the other hand, is probably the most organized person I know. No detail escapes her notice. For that reason, I take the lead in researching our family's investment strategies and Margie takes the lead in paying bills and maintaining financial records. Our marriage has lasted more than 20 happy years because neither of us tries to change the other. We play to our respective strengths.

When you are paper-trading different markets and trading styles, you really are scouting for your strengths. Your success as a trader will mirror success in other areas of life, such as careers or marriage, by emphasizing your distinctive abilities. If speed of mental processing is one of your superlative strengths, you might excel at short-term trading. If you are a whiz with mathematics and computers, you might find a natural fit in systems trading. Your ideal trading niche will be one that allows you to exercise your greatest talents while working around your weaknesses.

Here is an important performance principle. Please make note.

Whatever your distinctive abilities might be, you are already engaging in them.

This is exceedingly important in identifying where you will perform best. Someone who is going to excel at market research (to generate fundamental trading ideas or mechanical systems, for example) has already shown the ability to research—and is probably already doing some form of research—in a field other than trading. As a young child, I collected mounds of statistics on baseball players and used these to decide which cards I would add to my trading card collection. Now, as any visitor to my web sites knows, I collect mounds of data on markets and use these to trade my market. Organizing information for decision making is one of my strengths. It was a strength long before I placed my first trade. When successful short-term traders begin their careers, they frequently bring with them a history as competitive video gamers, gamblers, or poker players. They're accustomed to rapid decision making and risk taking: Those are their strengths. Quantitative traders at hedge funds often bring a very different background—one steeped in math, science, and other analytical pursuits.

I recently talked with Jon Markman, editorial writer for the MSN Money web site, professional money manager, and editor of the Strategic Advantage and Trader's Advantage stock selection services. He recounted to me that his start as a successful stock picker actually began in fantasy sports competitions. He decided to conduct statistical research on the players and found that it paid off, as he consistently did well in the competitions. Later, he applied his same love of research to stocks and was instrumental in developing MSN's StockScouter screening tool. Now he applies this research bent to finding highly successful companies that fly beneath Wall Street's radar, providing ideas for investors (Strategic Advantage) and traders (Trader's Advantage). Jon's core competence is digging deep: He approaches stock selection with the talents and mind-set of a financial journalist. That allows him to find opportunity where others don't think to look. His niche is off the beaten path.

> A formula for success: Find what you do well and then figure out how to do it in trading.

An interesting feature of Buckingham and Clifton's book is that it allows readers to take an online test to assess their strengths. The test is not exceedingly sophisticated—and as with most questionnaires, the results can be fudged—but it does identify the activities that people naturally prefer. There are a total of 34 strengths, each of which has a simple label. For example, the strength called "Woo" reflects the ability to persuade and influence others. That is an invaluable talent among leaders and sales professionals, not one that is so important to creative artists. Feedback from the test identifies an individual's five primary strengths. *While one's optimal trading style may not draw upon all five, it is difficult to imagine succeeding at trading (or anything else in life) if a majority of the top five are not actively engaged.*

My top five traits, for example, are achiever, learner, relator, analytical, and maximizer. The relator strength is one in which a person develops a limited number of intimate relationships rather than a broad social network. Deepening an existing relationship comes more naturally than forming a new one. The maximizer strength reflects an interest in making the most of one's own abilities and relating to others based upon their talents. Given those traits, is it so surprising that I am a psychologist who emphasizes the building of strengths through solution-focused counseling methods? Nor is it a coincidence that I trade markets by continually analyzing and learning new patterns—or that I start my day's work well before 5 A.M. My strengths also help to frame what I am not good at: rapid-fire scalp trading, large social events, and long-term therapy with patients diagnosed with significant emotional disorders. Whether I am socially successful or a miserable interpersonal failure depends upon whether I play to my relator strengths or try to become something I'm not, as a social butterfly. Similarly, the successful traders I've known and worked with have found market activities that fit them naturally. Perhaps that is why they—and other high achievers—seem to perform so effortlessly at times.

Although it can be informative, you don't need to take the book's test to identify your strengths. Following Buckingham and Clifton's discussion in the book, several factors will help you home in on your distinctive qualities:

- *What you naturally enjoy.* Given free time, what activities do you gravitate toward? What do you look forward to most each day? For reasons that we will explore shortly, our strengths are inherently enjoyable to us. If you have to summon all of your will to make yourself do something, it probably does not draw on your strengths.
- *What you naturally do well.* Most of us enjoy what we do well and what brings us success and recognition. Bloom's research found that an unusual proportion of the highly talented people studied began their development with a display of early skill. Most acclaimed medical researchers, for example, began by excelling in school, especially the sciences; most Olympians display early athletic abilities. Very successful traders display different talents—from mathematical analysis to intuitive pattern recognition—but all of these have been present from a relatively early age.
- *What significant others perceive in you.* Sometimes we are not the best judges of our own assets and liabilities. Others may perceive strengths in us that we take for granted. Bloom, for instance, found that talented performers were often singled out early on by teachers and coaches as "special." Sustaining this sense of specialness became an important early motivation. Long before I thought of myself as a professional writer, I had feedback from editors that affirmed their belief in me. If an experienced and perceptive mentor believes you're gifted in a facet of trading, the odds are good that this facet will contribute to the success of your career in the markets.

From the paper-trading exercises, you learn your distinctive strengths. You will know that you are close to your market niche when you develop a feel for market patterns quickly, find yourself fascinated by the patterns you see, and act readily upon your perceptions. If you don't find such a natural fit with a trading approach after giving it a fair test, move on. After all, when the first few dates with someone don't go well, you don't convince yourself to double your efforts and "work on the relationship." If it's work at that point, it's probably not drawing upon your strengths or the strengths of the other person. The same is true of trading styles. If at first you don't succeed, try, try again. *But if the trying becomes trying, try something else.* There are too many possible good trading niches—just as there are too many possible good relationships—to settle for a mediocre fit.

CAN ANYONE SUCCEED AT TRADING?

A while back I mentioned that the most common question I encounter is "Do I have the right personality for trading?" The second most common question is similar: "Can anyone become a successful trader?"

What most people want to hear when they ask this question is "Of course. With persistence and motivation, you can succeed."

That, however, is nonsense.

Does everyone have the strengths required to succeed in athletics, chess, ballet, military leadership, or poetry? Of course not; the proportion of people in *any* performance field who ultimately make their living from their performances is small. If everyone could be an elite performer, there would be no elite.

The question "Can anyone become a successful trader?" generally is framed within the contexts of weaknesses. The questioner feels that he might be too emotional, too undisciplined, or too cerebral to succeed as a trader. *My sense, however, is that it is not the weaknesses that keep people from trading success; it's their strengths.*

Allow me to explain. At the moment I am writing this, I am thinking of three highly successful traders whom I have known personally. All have made more than a million dollars trading for multiple years. Each of these expert individuals possesses just about every flaw you read about in trading psychology texts. They are hyperemotional when they trade, they become stubborn and hold onto positions when they shouldn't, and they rarely if ever engage in systematic planning before markets open. They succeed because their strengths overwhelm these weaknesses. Just as we saw earlier with Mick and Al, other traders who are less emotional, more disciplined, and more systematic may fail *because they lack strengths that readily translate into trading edges.*

Richie was a perfect example. A graduate of a well-known university and a varsity athlete, Richie might be the most personable trader I've ever known. With a winning smile, a warm personality, and good looks to spare, Richie was popular with women and others at the firm. As a developing trader, however, I found him frustrating to work with. He would sometimes spend more time talking with other traders about trading than he would spend actually trading. Half the time I would visit his office, he'd either have other traders in his room or he would be instant-messaging other traders about the market. The prospect of not making it as a trader upset Richie, but he was philosophical about it. He had already investigated businesses that he thought he could manage and had even thought through how he would manage them. Not surprisingly, all of the businesses were people oriented and involved hands-on interaction with customers.

When I heard Richie talk about his alternatives to trading, the immediate thoughts that went through my mind were: (1) He had invested more time into researching a future business than into researching any of his trades, (2) he sounded more excited about his future business than about trading, and (3) he was a natural as an entrepreneur. Richie was destined to fail as a trader, but not because of his weaknesses. *Rather, his strengths were in other areas.* He had skills as a leader, and he had prodigious people skills. I wouldn't be surprised to find him seeking elective office someday. He certainly wasn't built to sit at a computer screen all day and trade electronic futures contracts.

Recall that among my own strengths were relator, learner, and maximizer. Could I succeed at trading markets from open to close each day? Actually, I tried that a few years ago and found the process dull and meaningless. Without significant time devoted to learning and working with others, I felt that I was not fulfilling myself. My strengths, not my weaknesses, made me a failure as a full-time market participant.

The important thing in life is not to trade. The important thing is to find your niche: a field of work and a set of relationships that bring out the best in you. Too many traders find that trading brings out the worst in them. They're feverishly climbing a ladder that is leaning against the wrong building. If you're happier and more successful doing something other than trading, perhaps that's the ladder meant for you.

> The right ladders lean against our strengths.

THE ROLE OF MENTORING IN EARLY DEVELOPMENT

Bloom's research indicated that mentors play an important role in the development of most expert performers. Athletes benefit from coaching, pianists study under teachers, and accomplished researchers begin in the labs of senior investigators. As we saw, however, the role of mentors varies over the course of one's career. Early in the development of experts, they provide basic instruction, with a strong element of encouragement. This support is especially important in the initial encounters with a performance field, because those encounters so often lead to the frustrations characteristic of any early learning curve. The concern and confidence of teachers help budding experts sustain the motivation needed to progress to later, intensive phases of training.

Research also suggests that, early in the process of developing expertise, mentors play an important role in cultivating a work ethic among their students. Work demands expand with continued instruction, as students tackle greater challenges and cultivate increasingly complex skills. When my son Macrae began wrestling in junior high school, practices were after-school affairs during the season only. Now, early in his high school career, he is expected to attend practices during school vacations and engage in weight training throughout the year. Practice for the beginning pianist might be a few minutes a day of scales and arpeggios. Soon, however, the practice includes simple pieces rehearsed for an hour a day. Within team sports such as wrestling, peer pressure and support help to sustain the work ethic. "Not letting the team down" is a frequent refrain. When the performance field is individual, however—as in the case of most trading—the motivation is to not let the teacher down. *Good mentors become significant others.*

This has important ramifications for traders early in their careers. It is not crucial to find a mentor who is a master trader or who teaches master traders. Indeed, most mentors of elite traders will not spend their time with beginners, just as Olympic coaches won't teach lessons at the Y. *Instead, if you're a new trader, you want to find knowledgeable mentors who fulfill the role of significant others, providing you with a blend of basic instruction, structure, and support.* Within trading firms, those individuals may be leaders of trading groups or professionals specifically hired to facilitate trader development. Outside of such firms, mentorship is increasingly found within online trading communities.

The Trade2Win community is a good example. The site includes a wiki with basic trading information. There is also a separate knowledge base that consists of articles that have been submitted by recognized traders. Readers are encouraged to discuss the articles online, ask questions, and learn from each other. All of these conversations are archived in a forum. John Forman, until recently the content editor for the site, has encouraged dialogue and a mix of content relevant for a variety of traders. The policy appears to be continuing under his successor. As an author who has addressed topics pertinent to beginning traders—his text *The Essentials of*

Trading is an excellent resource—and a sports coach at the university level, Forman understands traders' mentoring needs. He realizes that it is not only the content but the off-line interactions among members that provide much of the supportive fuel for self-improvement. After contributing articles to Trade2Win, I consistently receive e-mails from readers with questions about their trading, asking advice to help them get to that next level. Like other contributors, I always respond to these e-mails. Sometimes they lead to extended interactions and collegial relationships; other times they enable me to point the writer to valuable learning and mentoring resources. Similarly, members frequently e-mail each other when they read interesting comments on the forum, creating new avenues for information and support. Just as senior members of an athletic team help develop rookies, experienced members of an online trading community are usually available to guide newcomers.

Perhaps the best example of such informal mentoring is Woodie's CCI Club, whose motto is "Traders helping traders." Woodie, aka Ken Wood, is an experienced trader who developed one of the first trading chat rooms utilizing hotComm. This allows traders to actually watch Woodie (and his accomplished students) trade in real time. Their comments on market action model a trading approach that others can integrate with their own style. Especially helpful within the club is the presence of a large community of traders eager to help newcomers. "A candle loses nothing lighting another candle" is one of Woodie's slogans. As a result, his example attracts a large number of traders who are willing to be candles by lighting the path for others. Sometimes their off-line help is as simple as assisting traders in setting up trading screens; other times it focuses on identifying market patterns and ideal time frames to utilize the CCI for various markets. Very often the interactions are about the joys and frustrations of the learning process. In this sense, the club is akin to Alcoholics Anonymous, in that it is a dedicated group of people who enjoy helping others. The great advantage of such a group is that all of the helpers have been there" themselves and have hard-earned experience to share.

> Your best mentors are the ones who have undergone their own learning curves trading your markets.

Woodie's CCI Club may seem like an anomaly in a trading world where people are hypersensitive about sharing proprietary trading secrets. I have not found that to be the case, however. For years, Linda Raschke has hosted an online trading room that allows traders to watch her and her protégés trade. The trades are accompanied by market commentary and helpful advice about trade management and trader psychology. Traders utilizing that service interact with each other in a separate online room and engage in mutual teaching efforts. This provides opportunities to model a variety of trading styles.

Many user groups associated with trading software platforms serve a similar function. TradeStation, for example, has a very active group of users who assist each other with programming, system development, and trade ideas. Groups using the VectorVest stock selection software meet in person in various cities and discuss ways to use the program and develop portfolios. Trading tools are offered to members of e-Signal's user community via bulletin boards. This includes file sharing, allowing members to exchange scripts and indicators that they've developed. I belong to forums for the Market Delta and NeoTicker programs, which allow users to quickly reach others with questions and suggestions. Many of these firms, such as Market Delta, CQG, and Ninja Trader, sponsor live educational programs. These invariably provide opportunities for networking and guidance as well as instruction.

Of late, we have also seen a large number of free trading blogs that provide useful trading information and opportunities for interaction. My own blog, TraderFeed, is geared toward analytical traders. Other blogs, including the Trader Mike site and The Kirk Report offer stock-picking guidance. Todd Harrison's Minyanville site covers a broad range of economic, market, and educational content. An increasing number of vendors are offering blogs to users to encourage mutual learning: Trade Ideas helps traders screen for stocks that meet their trading criteria; Market Delta's blog educates users of the program about its unique applications. Most of these blogs maintain extensive lists of links that enable you to find highly specialized trading resources—and the people who specialize in them.

Whatever you plan to do in the markets, there are others who have been doing it far longer, who have information to share, and who can help shorten your learning curve and make it more enjoyable. Look at the greatest actors and actresses, elite golf and tennis players, Olympic athletes, and top gun pilots: All have made it to the top with guidance and mentoring. Expertise begins with talents and strengths, but does not fully develop unless these are channeled properly. Your job is to figure out where your strengths might lie—and then find the mentors and resources that will help you make the most of them. At the end of this book I have compiled a list of trading resources that I have found particularly helpful and that might also help guide your development.

SELF-DISCOVERY: YOUR FIRST LEARNING LOOP

If you have been trading for a while and have not achieved desired results, this chapter is asking you to think outside the box. Perhaps your trading shortcomings are not the result of a flawed psychology or inadequate motivation. Rather, you may be trading in a manner that does not capitalize upon your specific strengths. *If you are on a normal learning path as a trader, you will not find expertise and elite performance.* The world's great performers ride multiplier effects that generate exponential learning: They exploit their talents and use early success to enter and benefit from enriched environments. If you know yourself, you're most likely to find the match between trading niches and personal strengths that will lead you to those environments—just as that unorthodox swing led Yaz to Ted Williams.

Early in the chapter we encountered learning loops. *Now you can see that the first learning loop of performance development is learning about yourself.* This is your chance to enroll in the college of market experience, take a variety of courses, experience different teachers, and figure out your major. If you do it right, it can be the start of a great adventure—and a phenomenal learning experience.

CHAPTER 3

Building Competence

Developing as a Performer

For the first lesson, I want you to play over every column of Modern Chess Openings, including the footnotes. And for the next lesson, I want you to do it again.

—Bobby Fischer's assignment to biographer
Frank Brady, who had requested chess lessons

What does it mean when we refer to someone in a performance field as competent? Surely it suggests that they possess basic skills and talents that separate them from beginners, enabling them to perform more successfully and consistently. It also, as Bobby Fischer realized, implies a certain degree of experience and an adequate fund of knowledge pertaining to the performance field. When we say that an individual is a competent physician, athlete, or chess player, we offer a compliment—and we withhold one. Competence is not the same as expertise: A NASCAR winner is more than competent; a competent singer is not one automatically destined for Broadway. Though competence does not imply expertise, it is impossible to consider someone an expert performer who is not also competent in his or her domain. Competence, from this perspective, is necessary but not sufficient for expertise. If we are going to master markets, we must first keep up with them. We become competent before we become expert.

DEFINING COMPETENCE IN TRADING

I have a very simple definition of competence in trading and an equally simple definition of expertise.

- A competent trader is one who consistently covers his or her trading costs.
- An expert trader is one who makes a consistent and acceptable living from his or her trading.

It is impossible to limit one's definition of trading competence and expertise to the possession of particular abilities, personality traits, and skills. This, as we saw in Chapter 2, is because there are many forms of trading requiring quite different strengths. I know many competent traders of stock index futures who are not competent in other markets, and I know many competent position traders who could never cover the costs of scalping. Defining competence and expertise by the consistent attainment of results provides the only yardstick by which we can gauge whether participants realize nonrandom edges in the marketplace.

The criterion of covering trading costs may seem like a modest definition of competence, but there is more to breaking even than meets the eye. The inexperienced trader looks at a trade as a 50/50 proposition: Either the market will move in one's favor or it won't. Even if we generously assume that traders will be equally good at harvesting profits and absorbing losses—something that does not come easily to human nature, as behavioral finance researchers have found—trading still is not an even bet. For traders to truly cover costs, they must recover the expenses of a real-time data feed, trading software, and other tools purchased to aid trading. Add to this hardware expenses for screen traders, the cost of an adequate connection to the markets, and the expenditures associated with maintaining redundant systems (in case of equipment or connection failure), and this overhead can add up quickly. Professional traders, who require very fast connectivity to exchanges, dedicated computer support, and state-of-the-art software configurable to their needs, can easily spend thousands of dollars a month on such overhead. If they are high-volume traders, they probably also have expenses associated with exchange membership fees.

What retail traders may save in overhead by trading from their homes is eaten up in other ways. For a frequent trader, retail commissions accumulate insidiously. Five dollars per round turn does not sound like a lot of money to a five-lot trader of the ES futures who might trade three times a day. At $75 per day, however, this expense easily tops $15,000 in a trading year. If our five-lot trader is trading an account size of $100,000, he needs to achieve a 15 percent return just to break even relative to commissions. Add in those equipment and other overhead costs and it's easy to see how the odds are loaded against the average trader.

In reality, the situation is much worse than I have just depicted. Suppose our five-lot retail trader enters and exits positions at the market. Doing so, he gives up a tick of execution with each round turn by buying the offer price and selling the bid. In other words, if he immediately exited every trade, he would lose one tick per trade simply as a function of losing the bid-ask spread. Trading three times a day with those five lots, this adds up to 15 ticks per day that must be overcome to break even. At $12.50 per tick, he is in the red $187.50 each day or more than $37,500 each trading year. Add that to the commissions and—incredibly—he has lost half of his trading capital in a year without a single blowup.

To cover costs, a trader actually must be at least modestly and consistently profitable. This requires appreciable skills at execution, risk management, and the reading of market patterns. While covering one's overhead is not an exciting goal, it is a necessary one along the path to greater success. When a restaurant opens, it can stay in business only by recouping its fixed overhead: the costs of equipment, real estate, personnel, food, taxes, and utilities. If it can do that in a reasonable period of time, it can then afford to wait for marketing and menu tweaking to build clientele. Your trading business will need to achieve competence long before it attains expertise. As with the restaurant, breaking even will buy you the time to survive your learning curve and reach that point where expertise can earn you a decent return on your capital.

What makes for trading competence, however? How does a talented novice become a competent performer? Can this process be accelerated? These are the questions to which we now turn. Fortunately, a sizable body of research lights our way.

THE COMPETENCE OF THE EXPERT AND THE COMPETENCE OF THE COMPETENT

My review of research conducted with expert performers (see the bibliography at the end of the book) leads me to advance an idea that will not seem obvious at first blush: *The path to competence for someone who eventually develops expertise is different from the path for those who remain competent nonexperts.* Most traders—and those who work with traders as mentors—fail to recognize this vital distinction.

Let's start with a simple example. I am a competent typist. I took a typing class during my sophomore year of high school, typed all my papers in college, and have continued to do my own typing over the course of my writing career. As a result, I've had a fair amount of experience at the keyboard. I am reasonably fast and accurate, but surely no court stenographer. Years of exposure have been sufficient to provide me with competence, but not expertise. In a similar way, most of us are competent drivers, but we are not experts who could execute daredevil stunts for action movies. Repeated experience produces learning, and this learning provides a measure of competence. It is competence, however, that rarely if ever blooms into expertise. I am quite sure that I could type or drive for 20 more years and still occupy no elite status in those fields.

When we look at the histories of truly expert performers, we see that they have achieved competence via a different path—not simply through the accumulation of experience. *This path has everything to do with why their competence blossoms and the competence of others does not.*

The developmental psychologist Howard Gardner, who has studied creative achievement in the lives of such luminaries as Einstein, Picasso, Stravinsky, Gandhi, and Freud, observed that—prior to their accomplishments—these talented individuals encountered *crystallizing experiences*. Those were the equivalent of "Aha!" experiences: emotionally powerful encounters with the fields that they eventually mastered. It wasn't merely that Einstein or Stravinsky became capable by performing many physics experiments or musical pieces. Rather, *something about those fields captured them*. They felt a *compulsion* to pursue the field, not just a desire to engage in it. Competent music students sit at a piano for an hour a day and practice their pieces before getting on with their lives. The budding expert, however, has to be dragged from the piano. The interest, born of that crystallizing experience, is all-consuming.

Walters and Gardner report crystallizing experiences among elite mathematicians, musicians, and visual artists. They cite the composer Debussy as a typical example. As a teen, Debussy was a talented musician, but showed little interest in composition. After starting with a new instructor, Lavignac, he discovered the works of Wagner and became enthralled, not leaving the music classroom until late at night. This was a major influence on his interest in composition and his eventual development of highly nontraditional harmonies. The developmental psychiatrist Robert Coles began the unusual course of his career by interviewing a six-year-old black child named Ruby, who was attending an otherwise all-white public school in New Orleans. Denise Shekerjian, who interviewed Coles and 39 other winners of the MacArthur Foundation genius awards for her book *Uncommon Genius*, notes that Coles was uncommonly drawn to the young girl, recognizing that he had found his life's work. Over the next 30 years, Coles and his wife traveled to remote regions of the world, from Appalachia to South Africa, to interview children and listen to their stories. The result was an unprecedented charting of the moral and cognitive resources of children and their responses to crises.

Coles told author Shekerjian that most people thought he was crazy to travel to the poorest regions of the country and forsake the comforts of traditional medical practice simply to talk with children. And yet, he said, he was convinced that he was on the right path. By his own account, Coles trusted his instincts, fueled by a sense of competence. At a deep level, he believed that this was the work he was meant to be doing.

Coles recognized that he developed competence, but his was hardly the path of my typing competence. He gained competence through an intensive pursuit of work that captured his imagination, not by taking classes or practicing skills in structured lessons. Learning by immersion is different from traditional learning, and it is a distinctive common thread among expert performers. That is why it is so critical to find one's performance niche and emotionally bond to it. *Only such a bond creates the immersion that leads one to internalize a field, not just learn about it.*

> Ordinary competence comes from familiarity with a field; the competence of experts is born of intimacy.

CRYSTALLIZING EXPERIENCES AND IMMERSIVE LEARNING

Without a doubt, my greatest talent as a therapist is reading what psychologist Lester Luborsky calls "markers" of emotional change that occur within sessions. It is a bit like poker players reading the tells of other players. A client might use one tone of voice to talk about her arguments with her husband, then another voice to describe her promotion at work. Later, she tells me that she might be late to our next appointment, returning to the voice that characterized her description of the troubled marriage. Immediately I know that whatever was going wrong between her and her husband was manifesting itself in the session with me. For all practical purposes, I had become her husband. By helping her see that and work out the issue with me, I can provide her with an experience that might aid her in dealing with the marriage.

There are all sorts of markers in a therapy session—some verbal, others nonverbal. The marker could be a posture, a figure of speech, or a particular gesture. Sometimes a simple shift of topic serves as a marker, as when an uncomfortable client crosses his legs, shifts his gaze, and turns from an anxiety-producing subject to a more comfortable one. From that point on, a good therapist makes note of every leg crossing and gaze shift, identifying themes that might be anxiety provoking.

My crystallizing experience in the markets came when I was watching a trading screen day after day, noting the various symbols and price levels. My attention was taken with something called TICK. As a rule, it would rise when the market moved higher and fall when the market declined. Sometimes, however, it would rise and the market would fail to move higher, or vice versa. Very often, these out-of-the-ordinary instances led to short-term changes in market direction. It was like a lightbulb going off in my head: *I had found a marker for trading; I could read the market like a person!*

From that time forward, I became engrossed in following the NYSE TICK. I was working full-time as a psychologist, however, and could not follow the market in real time. That did not deter me: I purchased a video recorder and recorded the financial news channel on television. Every evening I reviewed the recording and jotted down price and TICK values at five-minute intervals. My data collection was far from perfect, but over the course of many evenings I developed an intimate feel for the indicator. By the time I started formally collecting the data from a real-time data feed in late 1997, I already had ideas regarding short-term trading patterns. As I write this, it is eight years later and I have faithfully collected the TICK, examined it, and archived it every day over that time. I have customized the indicator to improve its accuracy, and I have acquired a variety of customized TICK measures for different market indices. Because of this intimacy, I can trade equity index markets competently armed with only my TICK indicators and one-minute price and volume data.

Is my evening-by-evening data collection from the VCR so different from the quirky quest of Robert Coles? I think not. Crystallizing experiences generate obsessions—desires to immerse ourselves fully in what is meaningful. Shekerjian relates the account of artist Robert Irwin, who withdrew from daily life to paint variations on a single theme—a color field with two straight lines running through it. In the process, he sustained concentration for 12 or more hours a day, seven days a week. At the end of two years of effort, he had completed 10 pictures—and achieved much more. As Shekerjian notes, his experiments with changes in the color field and placements of the lines altered his perception, sensitizing him to the subtle ways in which our surroundings shape our experience. This led him to environmental sculpture: creating works designed for specific sites. Irwin developed a perceptual competence—an ability to see art in the interplay between person and environment—but the acquisition of this competence was not through any typical learning mechanism. His development, like that of Coles, stemmed from an immersion so deep that it enabled him to

EXHIBIT 3.1 Learning that Generates Ordinary Competence and Expertise

Ordinary vs. Immersive Learning		
	Ordinary Learning	**Immersive Learning**
Motivation	Desire to build skill or obtain information for practical purposes	Crystallizing experience; fascination with the learning field for its own sake
Emotion	Effortful; very different from play	Absorbing in its own right; becomes a form of play
Process	Proceeds in discrete lessons, often from books	Continuous absorption in learning and doing
Outcome	Competence; replicating what has been taught	Expertise; novel performance

see what was not apparent to others. He came away from his learning with something new and creative.

Is this what separates the competence of the competent from the competence of the expert? An ordinarily competent person achieves a requisite level of skill through repeated, normal experience, the way I developed my typing or driving. The budding expert, immersed in nonordinary experience, learns to think and perceive in fresh ways, the way I learned to read the TICK like a client's communications. Stated differently, ordinary learning generates ordinary performance. *Immersive learning—sparked by the crystallizing experience—is the motive force behind Collins's flywheel, generating multiplier effects that build expertise.* (See Exhibit 3.1.)

Good performers do common things uncommonly well. But great performers do uncommon things. Their learning leads to novelty, not just the skilled replication of what has been taught. Might creativity—the novel seeing and doing born of unique, immersive experience—be the ultimate source of edge in the markets? Is it creativity that distinguishes great traders from those who are merely good?

A FRUSTRATED TRADER'S EXERCISE WITH CREATIVITY

Chad was frustrated. It seemed as though every time he took a position, the market jumped against him. At first he joked that the market had it in for him. Later it wasn't such a joke. For long stretches of time, he became so afraid of initiating positions that he would sit and watch opportunities pass.

When he finally became frustrated with his fear, he would impulsively lurch into large positions—only to see them promptly move against him. His winning days were far smaller on average than his losing ones: He was either too cautious or too headstrong. There seemed to be no happy medium.

What was perhaps most frustrating for Chad was that he often had a correct assessment of the market's general direction. He would see strength and buy the market, but he could not tolerate drawdowns. Sometimes he would even say, as he was "puking" a long position that had turned south, "Watch, it's going to go up now." Sure enough, the market would eventually rise to his initial target after the locals had played their games. Several times, however, when he tried to hold on after his position went into the red, the market broke even more sharply against him. The results were losses that wiped out days of profit, causing him to return to over-cautious trading.

I watched Chad trade and noticed a repetitive pattern. When the market became more volatile or when Chad was in a position, his rate of breathing speeded up. His body was noticeably tense, and he shifted a great deal in his chair. During quiet markets or if he was out of a position, he sat in a much more relaxed posture and breathed more deeply and slowly. These markers told me that Chad was experiencing market exposure—and market movement—as danger signs. His body was mobilizing in the classic flight-or-fight response. He was no longer trading to make money. He was trading to avoid danger, the way someone might navigate through unfamiliar and threatening terrain.

My first exercise with Chad was to have him follow the markets and make mental paper trades while keeping his posture relaxed and his breathing slow. We also made use of a portable heart rate monitor to keep track of his physiological arousal. We agreed that he would not take actual positions until he had mastered the art of keeping himself calm and collected when he watched the market.

Several times Chad told me he was ready to resume trading—especially after a mental paper trade that would have made him money—but those invariably were times when his heart rate had elevated. I encouraged Chad to be patient and stick to our plan.

So he watched the market. And watched. And watched. After a while, he settled into the watching, just like Robert Irwin staring at the lines on his painting. He was not simply looking at the screen; he was *seeing* what was there.

Irwin got to the point where he noticed a small crack in the wall of his studio. He observed that his perception of the crack influenced his view of the wall the same way his placement of the lines affected his experience of the color field. When he filled the crack with plaster, his view of the wall changed, *but so did his perspective on the picture he was painting at the time*. This piece of insight led Irwin from painting to sculpture, as art became something new for him: the generation of experience through actual environmental modification.

Chad's Robert Irwin experience came when he was calmly following the market, called out a trade to sell the offer, and then saw the market jump four ticks with barely a pause. I was pleased that Chad seemed to stay calm and was about to comment on that when he observed, "The market didn't trade!"

"What do you mean?" I asked.

"Look!" he said excitedly. "We barely did any volume."

Sure enough, only a few hundred contracts traded at each price level during the market's quick jump. This seemed strange, because there were thousands of contracts in the order book. When we reviewed the videotape, we saw what happened. Offers in the order book were pulled immediately before the sharp market jump, creating a temporary vacuum of sellers. The few remaining offers in the book were immediately lifted, creating the modest volume that we observed. Once no more buying entered the market, prices moved back down to their prior levels. It wasn't an abundance of buying that created the rise, Chad noticed; it was a temporary absence of sellers.

That is how he intuited, during those puking incidents, that price would eventually move his way. Now, however, Chad was excited. He saw the possibility that these short-term "vacuum" movements could be opportunities, not threats. He responded by wanting to enter the unfamiliar terrain, not tiptoe through it.

The key, he decided, was making sure that no other buyers or sellers would ride the coattails of the vacuum move. Chad agreed to scale into his positions, something he hadn't been doing. He would begin with a relatively small position and keep himself calm with our exercise while he focused on how the market was trading. If the market ripped against him, he would gauge the volume of the move and determine whether the move occurred because of an influx of supply or demand or because of a one-sided withdrawal from the marketplace. If the latter, he would briefly wait to see whether the move attracted new business. If not, he would add to his position at a better price. In the event that the move attracted further volume, he would exit his position and take a loss on his reduced position size. This, for Chad, became a win-win.

Chad eventually developed a very nice countertrend style of trading from this experience. Scaling into positions and staying calm during the trade greatly reduced his sense of danger. Equally important, like Irwin, *Chad shifted his perception*. What had been a threat was now a source of opportunity. Chad now began to scan the market for places where sharp moves left overexposed traders vulnerable. Once they had puked, he realized, the market would return to its equilibrium level, just as it had done when he was frustrated. Those returns to equilibrium provided him with several high-probability trades per day. Indeed, he became so adept at recognizing when others were trapped (as he had been) that other traders would immediately seek him out following sharp market moves to get his read on the market.

What was the essence of Chad's work with me? If I had merely taught him some relaxation exercises, Chad might have become competent at lowering his body's level of arousal and slowing down his thoughts. Chad, however, accomplished much more than that. He immersed himself in a state of focus and, while in that state, observed something he had not seen before. This new perception—his crystallizing experience—reorganized his views of the market. What was danger became opportunity; what was frustrating now was exciting; what was incomprehensible made sense. The competence he developed was not just that of self-control. *He developed new ways of seeing and doing.* His was an exercise in creativity, not therapy.

CALLINGS, TALENTS, AND THE PERFORMANCE HIGH

Chad sustained his excitement after his discovery. He loved exercising his new insight and catching vacuum movements in different markets. This excitement kept him glued to the screen, and this in turn helped fuel his growing competence at reading the market. To say that Chad was practicing a skill would be to miss an important element of his motivation. He felt driven to observe markets in the new light; it became more of a calling than a simple learning exercise.

We see this with Debussy, Coles, Irwin, and the many others whose competence develops into true expertise. *It's not so much that they select a niche as the niche selects them.* Something clicks that engages a sense of meaning and purpose well beyond the norm. What else could keep an individual traveling to poor regions of the country, secluded in a studio with a single picture, or staring at a market screen hour after hour?

This is one of the easiest ways of distinguishing competence that can lead to expertise versus normal competence building: The future expert becomes so immersed in the generation of new experiences that his or her efforts transcend normal work routines. What is work and what is play blurs: Free time is as apt to be used for work as for nonwork. *This is because the work no longer feels like work.* It becomes pleasurable in its own right.

Ed Seykota, in his *Market Wizards* interview, noted that it's not that great traders have talent; rather, the talent has them. This is exactly what we see with expert performers who find themselves ignited by a crystallizing experience. The flame of interest is generated by a kind of chemical reaction between one's talents and the opportunities experienced in a performance field. Sometimes this occurs at an amazingly young age, as when Tiger Woods began putting a golf ball at one year of age after watching his father. Bill Gutman, Woods's biographer, recounts that, even at that tender age, Tiger displayed real talent and couldn't get enough of golf. Tiger has described golfing as an addiction, with low scores providing the high. When Tiger's father, Earl, tried to encourage Tiger to simply enjoy himself on the course, Tiger responded, "That's how I enjoy myself. Shooting low numbers makes me happy."

One gets the sense that the thrill Tiger gets from the low score is not so different from what Coles must feel when he discovers something new about children or when Irwin crafts the sculpture that creates the quintessential experience of a particular site. The experience is not just fun; it is powerful and meaningful. It generates happiness.

The young Dan Gable did not start out as a wrestler. He tried swimming, but his success was temporary. When other boys experienced their growth spurt ahead of Dan, biographer Nolan Zavorel explains, Gable could no longer win his swimming competitions. He found, however, that wrestling came easily to him. It seemed as though he could control competitors with his grab. Energized by this fit between his athletic strengths and the field of wrestling, Gable obtained a key to the gym from his coach and began workouts far ahead of his teammates. Wrestling, young Dan found, was constant motion—an activity that kept him in a constant state of adrenaline rush. It was, he explained, a high that he couldn't get from any other workout.

The very successful traders I have worked with are as competitive in their own way as the great athletes. As a coach, Dan Gable would request permission to slap his wrestlers to focus their fighting spirit and would tape his hand before practice to prepare for his brand of motivation. Michael Jordan is said to have so despised losing that, after being defeated in a table-tennis game with a teammate, he bought his own table and practiced religiously until he could win. The hardest thing for the best traders is not to lose money; it's to stop trading when losing money. They are so competitive that they accept defeat only with the greatest of reluctance.

And yet, it isn't only about the money, just as cycling, for Lance Armstrong, is not only about the bike. I have asked many successful traders whether they would choose to change their trading methods if I found them a well-constructed mechanical system that guaranteed them a healthy, regular income. All said no. They did not want a system to beat the market; *they* wanted to beat the market with *their* skills. I can imagine that if someone gave Robert Irwin an art-generating computer program capable of museum-quality paintings, he would study it—and then resume his work. The competence that leads to expertise is not driven by acclaim or success alone: It stems from a drive to master a field and leave one's mark. Winning a lottery is not apt to generate the performance high. Chad, however, experienced that high before he had placed a single trade with his new approach.

> The expert's path to competence is the pursuit of the performance high. Performers don't work because they're motivated, but because they're captivated.

Where talents are modest, there can be no performance high. I am pleased with my typing and, yes, I do a competent job at it, but I will never, as a typist, experience what Tiger Woods experienced as a three-year-old golfer. The performance high stems from an indulgence in one's strengths. Without strengths, there is no high; without the high, there is no immersion; and without immersion, there is no creativity—no breakthrough of perception to take the performer to new heights. *Quite simply, if you do not experience the performance high, you are in the wrong niche.*

"Only those who have the patience to do simple things perfectly," the saying goes, "will acquire the skill to do difficult things easily." Chad's patience with the exercise transformed a difficult market situation into an easy one. And yet, it was not the mere patience of a person waiting for a bus. It was attention, rapt attention: the attention that can come only from complete absorption in what one is doing. Like all elite performers, Chad was not merely motivated; he was captivated.

WEAVING THE IMPLICATIONS: THE FUNDAMENTAL PERFORMANCE FALLACY

Exhibit 3.2 summarizes the differences between common competence and the competence of the developing expert. The most important thing to notice is that experts and nonexperts begin their development on very different paths, even though—at the time—they may be difficult to distinguish from each other on pure performance grounds.

What does this mean for your development as a trader? It suggests that hard work alone will not yield expertise. The idea that effort, by itself, will produce superior results is so prevalent that I call it the *fundamental performance fallacy*. Because we see expert performers working hard, we assume that hard work is responsible for their success. We thus believe

EXHIBIT 3.2 Differences Between Common Competence and Expertise Competence

	Common Competence	Expertise Competence
Nature of learning	Discrete lessons and experiences	Continuous immersion in a performance field
Mode of learning	Ordinary experience	Extraordinary experience
Result of learning	Enhanced skills	New, different skills
Emotional experience of learning	Satisfaction	The performance high
Impact on the self	Does not change self-perception	Greatly impacts and even dominates self-perception

that more of the normal, ordinary efforts—an intensification of the activities of common competence—will bring expertise.

If one class teaches us skills, the fundamental performance fallacy would have us believe, two classes will make us twice as skilled. Four hours of piano practice surely must bring us closer to virtuosity than two hours. Expertise, as we're seeing, however, is not simply more of the same competence-building experience. *Rather, it is a transformation of one's relationship to a performance domain.* Irwin painted *fewer* works during his transformative period than other painters, but came away with much more. Tiger became a tiger before his first golf tournament. There is a difference between hard work and immersion, and it gets at the heart of what competence means to expertise. It is the difference between painting and becoming a painter, the talent that you have and the talent that has you.

Ellen Winner of Harvard University's Project Zero, a research program investigating talent development and creativity, wryly notes that no one asserts that mental retardation is the result of insufficient effort, but we somehow assume that hard work will yield genius. Summarizing research on the visual arts, she observes that it is impossible to get ordinary children to work as hard at drawing as artistically gifted children. Those gifted children also demonstrate different kinds of drawing skills than ordinary children, not just more of the same skills. Because gifted individuals learn more quickly than others, they tend to put more effort into learning and are more capable of developing new ways of utilizing their artistic materials. For example, precocious artists quickly develop the ability to incorporate perspective into their drawings and do so without explicit instruction. They also display a more flexible and creative use of color and shape— talents that show up as early as age two. These findings suggest that their talent is, in part, perceptual: They see the world differently from their peers. An absence of such talent cannot be replaced by mere effort alone. Nor will mere motivation substitute for the performance high that comes from the exercise of talents.

It is the combination of effort and talent that defines the competence path of the expert. Winner calls this a "rage to master": a consuming motivation to extend and express one's capacities. She cites the case of Jacob, a four-year-old boy who immediately requested a guitar upon hearing heavy metal music. For two years his parents resisted this unusual request, but they finally relented. Jacob refused to leave his first music lesson and spent hours each day practicing the guitar. Winner reports that his parents never had to encourage him to practice; indeed, they had to pry him away from the instrument to do other things. The young Tiger Woods was very similar: His parents had to insist that he fulfill his home and school obligations before picking up the golf clubs. His rage to master the game was so strong that it obliterated the normal distinction between work and play.

The fundamental performance fallacy is a fallacy because it fails to account for the rage to master. Even if ordinary children could be compelled to practice as long as a Jacob or a Tiger Woods, they would not put as much of themselves into the effort. Nor would they necessarily be able to build upon the same perceptual, motor, and intellectual advantages as the gifted child. Effort without talent, Winner notes, produces a drudge, not an elite performer. Talent without effort, however, results in wasted potential. The rage to master yokes talent to effort, creating competence that is qualitatively different from that of the normal student.

DEVELOPING THE IDENTITY OF A PERFORMER

At some point in the development process, performers begin to integrate their activities into their identities. They are not just making trades; they are traders. Early in this development, the praise of teachers and parents is a crucial motivator. As talents find expression, however, the experience of competence becomes its own motivation. Lauren Sosniak, a researcher with Bloom's project, investigated talented young pianists who blossomed into successful artists. As they progressed, they realized that they were better than their peers and enjoyed being treated differently because of their talent. According to Sosniak, mastery becomes as stimulating as attention and approval had been for these early performers.

Competence-based motivation is important in fueling ongoing learning efforts. The more special pianists felt, the more willing they were to commit themselves to their musical education, Sosniak observed. *The rage to master is also a rage to experience oneself as masterful, transforming one's sense of self.* In the initiation years of expertise development, performance is play. With growing success and the exercise of talent, however, performance becomes self-enhancement.

The Israeli golfer Zohar Sharon is a dramatic example of the transformative power of competence. As reported by Aron Heller of the Associated Press, he recently shot a hole in one at the fifteenth hole at the Caesarea Golf Club, the only 18-hole course in Israel. He has also won numerous international golf tournaments—a notable accomplishment for a 53-year-old man who took up the sport only four years ago.

That, however, is not what makes Zohar Sharon unique.

He is blind.

Accidentally blinded during his service in the Israeli military, Sharon experienced a deep depression. "Everything I had before fell apart," Sharon describes. "All of a sudden, you are nothing, a 3-year-old is more productive than you." He tried a number of activities, from painting to a career as a physical therapist, but none stuck. Indeed, his initial attempt at golf failed and he gave it up for 10 years before returning with his closest friend as caddy and a determined sport psychologist, Ricardo Cordoba-Core, as a coach.

Cordoba, Heller explains, used unorthodox techniques to teach the blind man proper ways to swing the golf club. He instructed Sharon to sweep the floors at home, using the broom as a club. He also tied Sharon's arms to his body to force him to swing with his hips. These exercises proceeded for months before Sharon actually swung a real golf club—a vivid, real-life example of how those with the patience to do simple things perfectly acquire the skills to accomplish difficult things. Cordoba's feedback sustained Sharon during this early period; later, he received guidance and feedback on every swing from his friend and caddy Shimshon Levi. His development accelerated to the point where he is now the world's preeminent visually impaired golfer.

More important, however, Sharon is no longer a depressed man. He describes his experience on the golf course as one of freedom. Engrossed in golf, he doesn't have to dwell on his disability. Indeed, he experiences himself as a person of distinctive ability. His growing competence was not only a motivator, but an organizer of his identity. He is no longer merely a man playing golf.

Now he is a golfer.

Normal competence extends who we are by building skill; the competence of experts redefines who we are by exploiting talent.

THE TRADERS' KISS OF DEATH

Prior to my coming to Kingstree Trading, I was contacted by a small group of traders who were trading the euro currency. They were not experiencing success and asked for my help. I asked a variety of questions, including how their results broke down as a function of time of day. Were they more or less profitable around the European open compared with the New York open? A pause greeted my question. The traders, it turned out, were not trading the London open at 2:00 A.M.

I responded with shock. My current daily routine has me waking at 4:00 A.M., exercising, and watching the European markets, the Asian closing prices, and the overnight trade in the ES futures. After the commute from Naperville to Chicago, I generally arrive at the office between 6:30 and 7:00 A.M., plenty of time to prepare for the release of 7:30 A.M. numbers. It would never occur to me to miss the opening of my market.

After talking with the leader of the currency group, I raised the question with several colleagues: How can you trade a European currency and not be there for the European open? In my usual way, I conducted a statistical study and found that the periods of greatest volatility and trending price behavior occurred near the times of the London and New York opens. To not be present when the European markets opened, it seemed to me, was like stock traders not being at their screens when trade began for the day on the NYSE. It was missed opportunity.

My question, however, was not exactly the right one. Yes, missing periods of opportunity and missing screen time are not the way to build profits and trading expertise. The more critical question, however, is: *How could an expert trader* bear *to be away from the markets when they opened?*

Would Tiger Woods not show up at the first hole because tee time was too early? Would Dan Gable miss morning practice? If someone has the rage to master, you'd have to physically restrain them to prevent them from being at their screen at the open. They *want* to see how the market trades; they've been thinking about it in the evening, mulling ideas from the previous day.

The kiss of death for expertise is comfort. The comfort of the bed on a cold Chicago morning keeps the trader away from a London open. The comfort of a long lunch with buddies is the price one pays for missing an early afternoon breakout. There is nothing comfortable about the training regimens of Bobby Fischer, Lance Armstrong, Dan Gable, or Bob Knight. I wanted to reach out and shake the currency trader: How in the world can you possibly trade your way through the much greater discomfort of an adverse market move when you can't even muster the will to show up on time for the open?

The point is not to motivate yourself to be there from open to close, to be there for early economic reports, to review markets even when they're not trading. Like prima ballerina Wendy Whelan, expert performers *love* to do those things. Set loose in their performance domains, they are like Weimaraners romping in the park. That isn't to say there isn't discomfort associated with practice and even a dread of exhausting efforts to come. In the end, however, there is a performance high that makes all that effort pale by comparison.

Those currency traders lacked the performance high and thus lacked an emotional reason to be there for the open. Without the rage to master, they did not master—and did not last for long.

It's a little after 6:30 A.M. as I write this at my office at Kingstree. We're due for a potential market-moving economic report in less than an hour. Pablo Melgarejo walks by and waves as I refill my coffee. He's already checked out trading in the Bund and the S&P and formulated his ideas for how those markets will move under different news conditions. Pablo has been with Kingstree from the start and has been consistently profitable throughout. When you talk the markets with him, his eyes brighten just a little and his tone becomes a bit more animated. Pablo doesn't have a trading career. It has him. And that makes all the difference in the world.

FLOW: THE DRIVING FORCE OF COMPETENCE

It is difficult to appreciate what could motivate a man like Robert Irwin to spend day after day recreating lines against a colored field or what could lead Zohar Sharon to spend months practicing strokes with a broom. The rage to master leads performers to spend hours at tasks that others would find mind-numbing: replaying one chess game after another, poring over months' worth of TICK data, or rehearsing a particular gymnastic exercise. Writing of his cycling experience, Lance Armstrong describes being "clamped" to the bike pedals for hours and days on end, burning 6,000 calories a day and losing up to 12 liters of fluid during all sorts of weather conditions.

No one can sustain such activity unless it is not only intrinsically rewarding, but also intrinsically *meaningful*. Armstrong explains that the Tour de France is not about the bike. It's a metaphor for life; an overcoming of mental, physical, and spiritual obstacles.

This sense of participating in something larger than oneself is a common theme among highly successful individuals. Psychologist Mihaly Csikszentmihalyi refers to this as the *flow* experience: the performer becomes so absorbed in the performance that it seems to flow effortlessly. In my book *The Psychology of Trading*, I describe the performer in flow as operating on a high bandwidth of consciousness, a nonordinary state of awareness.

Csikszentmihalyi's research supports this notion. Obtaining reports of experience from a variety of performers, from rock climbers to violinists, he found that they entered into states where they lost track of time and became fully absorbed in their performance. These were pleasurable states—so much so that they became motivators in and of themselves. Mountaineers do not climb to reach the top of the mountain, Csikszentmihalyi observes, but pursue the summit in order to climb. This dynamic very much characterizes the successful traders I have worked with. The profit and loss of trading is important, but only insofar as it is a scorecard in the quest for mastery. Trading provides a performance high that they do not find elsewhere; the same high that Dan Gable finds in wrestling and Lance Armstrong in cycling.

Csikszentmihalyi's important observation is that the flow experience occurs only when there is relative balance between the demands of a task and the talents of the performer. Exhibit 3.3 depicts this relationship: When task demands greatly exceed the ability of the individual, the result is anxiety. If task demands fall well short of a person's capability, boredom is the consequence. The flow state occurs between boredom and anxiety, at that optimal state of arousal in which tasks are challenging without being overwhelming.

The late bodybuilding champion Mike Mentzer came to an important insight regarding a weight lifter's experience of his routine. If the weights are set too high, he will be unable to lift them and the workout will be frustrating. If the weights are insufficient, he will lift them with ease but experience no test of his strength. Eventually, this would be dull and get him nowhere. When the weights challenge the lifter and he "trains to failure"— keeps lifting until he can perform no further repetitions—he builds muscle strength *and* creates an absorbing, challenging workout. Regular lifters know the feeling of being "pumped up" after a good workout, the muscles engorged with blood and the lifter both exhausted and energized by the challenge. That feeling becomes an important reward of hitting the gym, one component of the lifter's flow experience.

The flow state that sustains performance development requires challenges that match skills.

Boredom   **Flow**   **Anxiety**

Absence of Challenge	Match of Skills And Task Difficulty	Task Difficulty Exceeds Skills

EXHIBIT 3.3   Flow And Optimal Arousal

In most performance activities, it is possible to titrate the level of challenge so as to create the optimal balance for developing performers. Earl Woods used to adjust par for his young son Tiger so that the budding star could experience shooting par or below. Similarly, a music teacher assigns pieces of varying complexity to a student, creating a match between task demands and the student's skill level. This is difficult in trading, however. There are no separate exchanges for easier and harder trading: Trading always pits one against experienced locals, fund managers, and speculators. Even paper trading is trading in the big leagues when it is from real-time price feeds. For this reason, it is easy for developing traders to become mired in frustration and anxiety. Instead of affirmations of competence, they eventually internalize the sense of "this is impossible." Then, in the parlance of traders, they "lose their mojo," their drive and desire to compete.

And, as it turns out, there is no flow without mojo.

TIM, THE DEPRESSED TRADER

By the time I began working with Tim, he had lost most of that mojo. Once a reasonably successful trader, he found that the kind of trading that had made him a living was no longer profitable. In the late 1990s, there was a tendency for momentum in the stock indices—especially the NASDAQ—to persist in the short run. If you could get in on a market move early, it was usually possible to ride it for at least a few ticks if not points. As volatility came out of the market in the first part of the new millennium, however, those momentum effects disappeared. Traders accustomed to buying upside breakouts or selling weakness suddenly found that they were buying highs and selling lows.

Tim's first response to this situation was frustration and then anxiety, as Csikszentmihalyi would have predicted. "What the hell is going on!" became replaced by "This market has become a lot harder to trade!" Much of Tim's casual conversation about markets centered on the question "When is volatility going to come back?" Tim's expressions of hope eventually became an office joke: The market will pick up after the holiday, after the Federal Reserve announcement, after we break a particular price level. His greatest fear was that the market had become too difficult to trade, that his skills were no longer matched to the demands of the task. This was especially threatening to him because he was engaged and his wedding was quickly approaching. With that, he knew, would arrive added responsibilities and expenses.

The market didn't pick up after the holiday, however, nor did it pick up after economic reports or price breakouts. Volatility, in fact, lurched to multiyear lows. The thought that "this market has become a lot harder to trade" shifted to "this market is impossible to trade." Realizing that he could not buy strength or sell weakness, Tim tried to pick highs and lows and fade them. This worked at times, but would leave him with large losses when markets did make sudden, extended directional moves. As a result, he would make small profits most days of the week, but give them back during occasional market breakouts. He knew that he could not afford to sustain large losses, and he knew he needed time to figure out the new market environment. Reluctantly, he dropped his size, trading so small that he struggled to cover his costs even when he was profitable.

Facing a crumbling career and a worried fiancée, Tim felt increasingly desperate. His anxiety gave way to outright depression. At times he would let promising trades go by, convinced that the market would move against him no matter what he did. Perhaps most important of all, he no longer enjoyed trading. He dreaded coming in each morning.

What emerged from our counseling sessions was that Tim had mixed feelings about learning a different way of trading. He held out hope that either his market would return to form and let him make money by momentum trading or that he could find a related market to trade with his momentum style. He knew the learning curve for a wholly new market would be extended; this was unacceptable to him, given his mounting personal expenses. When he tried to trade differently, he became frustrated by those occasions when momentum did follow through, creating what would have been profits had he stuck to his old approach. More than once he voiced the concern—sometimes jokingly, other times less so—that the market would revert to its old form once he had mastered a new trading style. Murphy's Law, he was convinced, was out to get him. A sure sign that he was torn in his change efforts was that he took frequent time away from trading, leaving whenever he was up a modest sum. At the very time he should have been immersing himself in the learning process, he found himself withdrawing.

I would like to report that I helped Tim regain his former market glory with just the right insight, technique, or advice. That was not meant to be, however. Tim left trading for the business world, where he could support a family with a stable income. For quite a while I wracked my brain to identify what more I could have done to aid Tim. I wasn't so concerned about Tim's future—he actually seemed happy in his new career—but I knew I would face many more Tims in my work with traders.

Could I have done more to show him a new market? A new trading method? Should we have taken a more extended time away from trading?

Frustrated, I realized that we had tried all of those things, with no appreciable results.

The sad truth was, Tim had lost the path to expertise and neither of us could figure out a way back.

WHY TRADERS FAIL: SELF-AWARENESS, COMPETENCE, AND MOOD

Let's try to figure out what happened with Tim. Social psychologists Shelley Duval and Robert Wicklund discovered that when people were made objectively self-aware—that is, when they were placed in situations that made them self-conscious (such as seeing themselves in a mirror)—they displayed a more negative mood than when they were not self-aware. The researchers concluded that self-awareness makes individuals aware of discrepancies between their real selves and their ideals. For instance, let's say that you give research subjects a task that is supposed to measure creativity and then inform them that they have an average level of creativity. Self-aware subjects would focus more on the distance between their actual creativity and their desired creativity level than would non-self-aware subjects. This would influence their mood negatively.

Obviously, this objective self-awareness effect is more likely to manifest itself if people are focused on aspects of themselves that are important to them. If you make an athlete self-aware and she notices her reflexes slowing, this would generate significant negative mood, because it poses a threat to her identity. The same perception might not generate drops in mood for an accountant. Self-awareness became painful for Tim because he was continually confronted with a discrepancy between his real results as a trader and his ideal. Tim wasn't just responding to the day's losses; he saw this as a threat to his career. Not surprisingly, he behaved as Duval and Wicklund would have predicted: He avoided self-awareness. He took breaks from trading whenever those could be justified. It wasn't simply that he lost motivation; it was just too painful to stay self-focused and experience the chasm between real and ideal.

David Aderman and I, during our research days at Duke University, tried a variation on the objective self-awareness theme. We gave subjects negative feedback on a task and made half of the subjects self-aware, while the others focused outwardly. The wrinkle, however, was that we told half the subjects that they could readily improve their performance. The other half we told that the results reflected inborn traits that could not change. As we hypothesized, the group that believed they could change ("competent" group) did not experience a diminished mood in response to self-awareness. Only the "noncompetent" group—the group that received negative feedback and believed they could not change—felt worse when they focused on themselves.

The implications are important. *There is nothing inherently aversive about being far from our ideals as long as we believe that we can achieve these.* As I am writing this book, I am only a fraction of the way through the manuscript, but this doesn't trouble me. I know that I can finish it by the editor's deadline and have a plausible plan for doing so. If, however, my computer's hard drive were to fail and I had not backed up my files, I would feel quite differently. Faced with a looming deadline and lost efforts, I would become anxious like Tim. I would no longer be confident that I could reach my goal.

If we combine the objective self-awareness research with Csikszentmihalyi's work, an important conclusion emerges: *Our ability to sustain the immersion that generates multiplier effects depends upon the experience of competence.* Without the perception of mastery, there can be no learning that generates expertise.

> To a large degree, our moods are moderated by our perceptions—and especially our perceptions regarding our own competence.

Tim's experience was bounded by the emotions of boredom, anxiety, and depression. We are bored when we feel excessively competent for a particular task—when the demands of the situation do not actively engage our talents. We are anxious when we experience ourselves as inadequately competent for a task that we need to perform. Depression, however, results once we appraise ourselves to be incompetent to meet the demands of an important task. Certainty of success leads to boredom, and doubt creates anxiety. *Depression results from certain doubt*: the assessment that the gap between real and ideal can never be bridged.

Think, for example, of a man who is told that he has a Stage I skin cancer that is easily operable. The survival rate after the operation is extremely high, though not 100 percent. One can easily imagine this situation producing anxiety. Bridging the gap between sickness and health— real and ideal—has been placed in a modest degree of doubt. However, what if the man is told that he has an advanced cancer that has so metastasized that it is inoperable? Chemotherapy, he is told, will slow the progression of the cancer but cannot eliminate it. Now the prognosis is bleak indeed. Real and ideal cannot be bridged; there is now certain doubt. Depression rates among such patients are understandably high.

Tim fell into an emotional trap in which doubt spiraled into the certainty of failure. Anxiety became frustration, then depression. He could not turn his trading around because part of him was working at avoiding self-awareness while part of him was working on his trading. In a very real sense, he was a divided human being.

Why is this important?

We cannot be divided and also immersed in the flow experience that generates expertise.

FIRST- AND SECOND-ORDER COMPETENCE

Flow, we have seen, results when individuals are immersed in situations where their skills are evenly matched to the demands of situations. At this optimal state of arousal, the performer is divided by neither the understimulation of boredom nor the overstimulation of anxiety. Nor is there a divide between real and ideal that cannot be bridged. Flow occurs when there is a perception of likelihood of success at an important task, but not certainty. Flow activities provide *worthy challenges*.

Csikszentmihalyi observes that attention is intensified during the flow state. This is a large part of the absorption that makes performers lose track of time during the flow experience. *It is also what makes flow a state of enhanced learning.* Under conditions of undivided attention and enhanced cognitive bandwidth, performers process information more efficiently and more deeply than during normal learning. In the normal classroom, students may be bored if the material is repetitious, or they might tune out if they realize the material is over their heads. Their attention divided, they are far less likely to acquire and retain information than the rapt learner. Learning research finds that when learners have to perform a distracting task while they are exposed to information, their recall of the material is significantly poorer than it is for nondistracted learners. Boredom, anxiety, and depression interfere with learning because they are distractions: They divide attention. Positive thoughts born of overconfidence are equal distractions. Interestingly, we need to feel competent to develop competence: *The perception of competence generates the flow that enhances concentration and learning.*

Tim's case is interesting because he had the motivation, skill, and talent to succeed as a trader. We know this, because he had been a successful trader for a sustained period. He found a niche and bonded to it: He made it his own. When the markets changed, however, that emotional bond worked against him. He was reluctant to give up what had worked. Unable to wipe the slate clean and begin as a new trader, he experienced frustration, anxiety, and depression. Thus divided, he never picked up new market patterns the way he picked up the earlier momentum ones. When he was in his niche, he sustained flow and his trading came naturally to him. Once that niche changed, however, he could not recapture the flow state. He was like the ordinary student, trying to build competence through normal efforts and practice. He could not immerse himself in markets to achieve the competence that leads to expertise.

> Divided attention is the source of most performance shortcomings.

Surely this is one of the great challenges of trading. Imagine mastering a domain such as bowling and then having the Pro Bowlers Association change the length, width, and surface of the lanes. What used to break sharply now moves in a straight line; a straight release now hooks sharply left. Velocity and pin movement are different owing to the longer length of the lanes; scores plummet as the greater lane width allows for less interaction among the pins. It is not difficult to imagine frustration and anxiety setting in among even the best performers. *In fact, the best performers— those who are intensely competitive and most accustomed to success— might be just the ones who experience the greatest disruption of mood, as we saw with Tim.* Garry Kasparov found the rules of his game changed when he lost his chess match to the IBM supercomputer Deep Blue; the normal bluffs that might unnerve a human opponent now had no effect. Moreover, thanks to improved programming, his electronic rival now could execute moves with an element of novelty. Kasparov, a consummate champion, found his concentration broken and made uncharacteristic mistakes that hastened his loss.

Markets continually change. The high volatility and bear market trend of the early to mid-1970s were very different from the low-volatility environment of the early to mid-1990s. Morning markets do not trade the same as midday or afternoon markets; holiday periods trade differently than other days. The expert trader doesn't merely master a market, as Tim did. *The expert must master changing markets.* We normally think of the development of expertise as a linear process: A student becomes competent, then becomes expert. Trading, however, requires that this be a circular process: a continuous learning loop. We are always learning— and relearning—markets.

This brings us to an important distinction: between first-order and second-order competence. *The performer with first-order competence has a sense of skill at a task. The second-order performer has a sense of being able to obtain the skills needed for any foreseeable task.*

The performer who demonstrates first-order competence feels able to make money in the market. The performer with second-order competence feels able to make money in *any* market. First-order competence is optimism about doing; second-order competence is optimism about competence building itself. A first-order performer feels competent to navigate through New York City but not London. A second-order performer feels competent to quickly learn the layout of any city.

First-order competence among market performers is necessary but not sufficient for expertise, as we've seen with Tim. He felt confident in high-volatility markets, bull and bear, but could not adapt to slow, rangebound markets. Once conditions changed, he could not regain the enhanced learning state—the flow bandwidth—that had fueled his earlier development. If, however, he had achieved second-order competence—if he had felt competent to achieve competence across market conditions—the market change would have been a doable challenge, not an overwhelming threat. He could have stayed in flow once he saw the changing market as a worthy challenge for his skills and talents. The first-order performer will be vulnerable to objective self-awareness effects and cognitive interference whenever conditions change. The second-order performer is like the subjects in my study with Aderman. Once they realized they could bridge the gap between real and ideal, they could face their shortcomings without fear or distraction.

RESILIENCE AND COMPETENCE

I know of no trading approach that works equally well (and is profitable) under all market circumstances. The best trading systems encounter periods of drawdown. Eventually they must be tweaked to adapt to shifting market conditions. I have been privileged to work with—and personally observe in action—a number of highly successful traders. Every one of them goes through lean periods as well as highly profitable ones. Even the best of traders occasionally wonder if they still have it in them to sustain success.

In *The Little Book That Beats the Market,* author Joel Greenblatt describes a deceptively simple—but effective—system for stock picking. He counsels investors to concentrate on firms that have an above-average return on capital and an above-average earnings yield. That's it: Invest in companies that earn more on their money—and earn more as a fraction of their stock price—than other firms. He even provides a free web site for investors to screen for stocks that are likely to outperform: www.magic formulainvesting.com.

Greenblatt is not worried that publicizing his stock selection criteria will ruin his approach. He knows from his historical studies that his stock-picking criteria work only over the long haul. For periods of months and even years, the solid companies will not outperform the stock prices of lesser companies. During these lean periods, would-be value investors lose their faith. They grow frustrated and anxious, just like Tim. Eventually they stray from the discipline or abandon self-directed investing altogether. Lacking emotional resilience—unable to access the second-order competence that turns setbacks into worthy challenges—they never participate in the benefits of the approach.

Vendors of mechanical trading systems observe the same thing among their purchasers. When the system goes through a period of drawdown, users tinker with the system parameters or abandon the system altogether. The losses create a chasm between real and ideal that is simply too painful for the average trader to tolerate.

Imagine a trading method that is profitable 60 percent of the time and unprofitable on 40 percent of trades. Over time, one would think that such a method would be highly profitable. This same method, however, has a 2.5 percent probability of generating four consecutive losses. A 2.5 percent probability sounds quite small, until you think of the active trader making hundreds of trades in a year. Just one trade a week will produce a likelihood of incurring four consecutive losses at some point every year. Without proper money management, those four consecutive losses could easily wipe out months of profit—or even obliterate an entire account. Equally important, the string of losses could wipe out the confidence built over many months and years of trading. Most athletes know the experience of entering a slump. Once athletes think of themselves as being in a slump, they become self-aware—no longer in the state of flow. They begin to make changes in parts of their game that aren't broken. This creates further slump, which creates further deterioration of confidence and performance.

Changing markets and the law of averages dictate that slumps will occur. A historical look at even the best-performing hedge funds, for example, will reveal periods of significant drawdown. Resilient hedge fund managers, confident in the validity of their methods, view such drawdowns as inconveniences, not as threats. Not all their investors, however, share this resilience. Losses, for them, are too painful to sustain.

The idea that great performers always perform greatly is romantic, but it is rarely true. Indeed, Dean Keith Simonton's research suggests that the ratio of successful to unsuccessful performances among elite scientists, artists, and scholars does not differ over the course of a career. We remember Edison for his inventions, not his duds; no one gives much thought to Shakespeare's unsuccessful writings. Yet elite performers such as these have a relatively fixed ratio of success to failure. The difference is productivity. The elite performers generate many more works than their nonelite colleagues, guaranteeing that they will leave behind a body of significant creations. Such productivity requires a very high level of resilience: an ability to keep going in the face of setbacks and frustrations. The investor who sticks with the good companies through thick and thin is the one who receives the payoff of Greenblatt's approach. Those who bounce from strategy to strategy are apt to pursue each one until it produces failure, leaving behind a string of disappointments. *The resilient performer has cultivated enough second-order competence to stay in the zone even when the inevitable strings of setbacks occur.*

Perhaps the most dramatic example of resilience is Lance Armstrong. Diagnosed with testicular cancer that spread to his brain, he underwent a grueling regimen of chemotherapy treatment that, according to his book *It's Not About the Bike*, left him in a fetal position, retching. Almost from the start, Lance treated cancer as he had treated his cycling foes: with a powerful competitive drive to win. "You've picked the wrong person to mess with" was his way of talking to the cancer. When his nurse tested his lungs for strength, he blew with all his force and told her to never bring the device to his room again; his lungs were fine. He insisted on walking the floors of his hospital rather than accept a wheelchair. He began biking as soon as his treatment allowed, despite his greatly weakened state.

In his book, however, Armstrong reveals an important secret about his ability to overcome this late-stage and often-fatal cancer. He explains that cancer gave him "a new sense of purpose" (page 151), replacing biking as his reason for being. He would start a cancer foundation and help others fight the disease. His role was no longer cyclist; he now defined himself as a survivor who would help other survivors.

Interestingly, Armstrong came to this realization at the end of his chemotherapy, but before he was assured a healthy recovery and survival. His new goal—and his redefinition of who he was—no doubt contributed to that recovery.

The lesson we can learn from Lance Armstrong is that the competence of expertise is more than skill building. It is the cultivation of a particular kind of relationship between performer and performance field. Lance was always a competitor, and his book makes it clear that one of his great strengths has been to channel his anger and energy competitively. *His greatest competence, however, was resilience, and this stemmed from his ability to define setbacks as challenges.* When his market—his health—changed on him, he did not wilt, as Tim had. He took it as a further challenge and defined a goal—and identity—for himself that was great enough to embrace this challenge. "I like the odds stacked against me," he explained to his riding coach. " . . . It's just one more thing I'm going to overcome" (page 119). *This* is the essence of second-order competence.

The relationship between performer and performance field that characterizes expertise begins with the meshing of talents and performance challenges. Under proper conditions, it blossoms into a feeling of specialness that supports a higher-order form of competence. This pervading sense that one is competent to master changing conditions allows performers to develop resilience to setbacks that would overwhelm their peers. Very often, as with Armstrong, this resilience is fueled by the performer's creation of a new identity—one that redefines the challenge ahead. Zohar Sharon did not overcome blindness merely by learning skills to navigate. He overcame blindness by becoming something more than a blind man. He became a golfer.

Teaching traders to enter and exit trades properly, to read charts and indicators, to manage risk, and to research winning trade ideas—all of these are important, and yet all fail to get at the heart of developing performance expertise. Reading 100 trading books and taking 100 trading seminars will produce a knowledgeable amateur, not a trading expert. It's not about the trade, just as, for Lance Armstrong, it's not about the bicycle. The competence that distinguishes the path of expertise from the path of normal capability is one that transforms the individual. This is what Robert Pirsig meant when, in *Zen and the Art of Motorcycle Maintenance*, he declared that the real cycle you work on is yourself.

> Your goal is not just to learn to trade, but to become a trader.

The rage to master is fueled by the sense of self-mastery, and that is generated by experiencing and overcoming changing conditions. Recall Linda Raschke's observation: "Experience counts for so much." The learning process that generates elite performance exposes traders to continual challenges, initially building first-order competence but then, over time, fueling the second-order sense of ability to master any challenge.

COMPETENCE AND MODELING

There is no better way to internalize the thinking of expert traders than to spend time with expert traders—online, in books, and live. In observing their resilience, you become better able to find your own. Hearing their words, you begin to see the world through their eyes, linking observations in new and meaningful ways.

I invite you to try a small experiment and visit the Daily Speculations web site of Victor Niederhoffer and Laurel Kenner (www.dailyspeculations.com). There you will find a summary of posts to the Spec List, a long-running online forum for traders with a scientific bent. It is rare indeed to not be able to find a unique observation on the site or a fresh perspective from which to view markets. I date my coming of age as a trader to my participation on the Spec List and the lessons I learned from those more accomplished than I.

One common theme on the list, also found in Niederhoffer's book *The Education of a Speculator* and his later effort with Kenner, *Practical Speculation,* is the notion of markets as ecosystems. There are food chains within ecosystems, and there are roles for each of the species. Ecosystems also undergo change and species either adapt to these or face peril. Thinking in terms of systems, predators, and prey helped me crystallize my ideas about tracking the behavior of the market's largest participants and developing trading methods based upon these. While I have spent considerable time refining the ideas through research, the basic notion that ecosystems are dominated by the most powerful species provided me with the insight that I could filter out more than 90 percent of market activity and, in the short run, feed from the scraps left behind by the predators.

In a recent post to Daily Speculations, Niederhoffer mentions that he and his traders pose and test approximately 100 hypotheses a day. Consider the multiplier effect generated by such activity: the cumulative knowledge gained of markets and their tendencies. Equally important, however, is the modeling effect generated by such activity. Not only do participants learn about markets, they also learn to think like disciplined speculators.

To work in a setting where such modeling is the norm is a tremendous personal and professional boon. What if we do not have access to such resources? Can traders guide their own learning processes and cultivate flow, mojo, and the second-order competence that will support them through shifting risks and uncertainties? The answer is yes, and—once again—research lights our way.

CHAPTER 4

Strategies for Cultivating Competence

*On the mountains of truth you can never climb in
vain: either you will reach a point higher up
today, or you will be training your powers so that
you will be able to climb higher tomorrow.*
                                        —Friedrich Nietzsche

In 1940, the Viennese psychiatrist Viktor Frankl began writing his book *The Doctor and the Soul*. He married in 1942, but later that year was separated from his wife when they were taken to Nazi concentration camps. His book manuscript, sewn into his coat, was discovered by the Nazis at Auschwitz and destroyed. During his three years in a concentration camp—years of starvation, illness, uncertainty, and the experience of seeing others die—two things kept him alive: piecing together his book on scraps of paper and holding out hope for a return to his wife. Those who did not survive the experience, Frankl observed, did not have either hope or purpose. He had a reason to surmount adversity, and—paraphrasing Nietzsche—this *why to live* provided him with the courage to bear the *how*.

From a performance perspective, there is an even more compelling facet to Frankl's history. After his release from the camp, he was devastated by the news that his wife had not survived her internment. He remained steadfast to his purpose and finished his book. Then, in a nine-day period, he wrote *another* book—the one that would be his best-known work: *Man's Search for Meaning*.

Who writes a book—not to mention a profound and important one—in nine days? How is this possible? Clearly, Frankl "wrote" the book during his three years in the camp. He did not memorize every phrase and page, but his reflections on his experience were so keen that they cascaded from his pen upon his release. Incredibly, Frankl found a flow state under the worst of human conditions. He remained a psychiatrist even as he was a prisoner—*and he made his wretched life situation a patient that he would study for years*. By the end of his ordeal, he was a different psychiatrist: a logotherapist, one who emphasized the pursuit of meaning as central to mental health.

In Chapter 3 we saw how Lance Armstrong redefined himself in the face of advanced cancer. Frankl maintained—and extended—his identity throughout captivity, hunger, and typhoid fever. Each found in adversity a worthy challenge; each displayed an indomitable second-order competence. If cancer and concentration camps cannot keep the human spirit from mastery, no challenges in markets, careers, or relationships are too great to overcome—*as long as you have the why*.

There is no performance without purpose.

FROM FINDING A NICHE TO CULTIVATING COMPETENCE

Hopefully the book thus far has clarified why it is so crucial to find your trading niche. If you do not find a style of trading and a trading market that match your talents and interests, you will not spend enough time in the state of flow to supercharge your learning efforts. Nor will you cultivate the second-order competence that will allow you to weather inevitable trading storms. Finding a niche means so much more than simply making money or having fun. It is the discovery of that worthy challenge that energizes you, tapping into your deepest sense of meaning.

What do you discover when you're energized in this manner? You realize that you're still a beginning student of the markets—a motivated and talented beginner, to be sure, but still a beginner. You will make many of the beginner's mistakes. You will start out by not even covering your costs. At times, competence—not to mention expertise—will seem dauntingly far from reach.

How do you learn trading basics, undergo the beginner's frustrations, and still sustain the ability to perform in the flow state? *This is the central challenge of performance development.* You will not master trading by desiring to make money. You will master it because it becomes a challenge worthy of your talents *that just happens to rely upon money as a score-card.* How you structure your learning, however, will determine whether trading becomes the worthy challenge or a frustrating obstacle.

Take the example of Ralph, a new trader at a proprietary firm trading individual equities. Upon his hiring, Ralph was given basic instruction regarding his trading software and the placing of orders. He was told to follow the market on his screen and enter trades in simulation mode. He would then report back to his mentor at the end of each day to discuss his results. As you might guess, day after day Ralph lost money on the simulator. His mentor gave him general advice about limiting losses, watching for price levels, and so on, but Ralph was not able to translate this advice into usable real-time strategies. He did not understand his mentor's brief demonstrations with market maker screens, nor did his classmates. As his frustration mounted, his simulator performance declined. His mentor dismissed him from the firm, convinced that he lacked potential.

Ralph seemingly had the ingredients for success. He was motivated. He was given access to realistic market simulation and a concerned mentor. The advice he received was sound, and he started with a genuine interest in his market. Nevertheless, his training could produce neither competence nor expertise. *Quite simply, his learning experience was not structured for success.* In an important sense, his learning was not structured at all.

THE STRUCTURE OF LEARNING: CREATING MIRRORS

What does it mean to structure learning for success? Csikszentmihalyi outlines several preconditions of the flow experience in his book *Creativity*:

- Clear goals at each step of the learning process
- Immediate feedback regarding one's actions
- A balance between challenges and skills

It is easy to see why Ralph could not achieve the flow state and never developed trading competence. He gained exposure to the markets, but did not have clear goals or immediate feedback. Working in a relative vacuum, he could not perceive a balance between his skills and the challenges he faced. Rather, he saw himself as hopelessly overwhelmed with the task of learning a complex market dominated by professionals.

Let's return to Zohar Sharon, the blind golfer introduced in Chapter 3. Recall that his coach, Ricardo Cordoba-Core, required him to practice his golf swing for months before Sharon ever stepped foot on the golf course. Cordoba emphasized coordination and encouraged Sharon to utilize his lost faculty to visualize his shots. During one exercise, Sharon had to swing the club while standing near a pole. If his swing was off, he would smack the pole. That is immediate feedback!

Going to the golf course at the outset of training would have merely frustrated Sharon. He could not have experienced himself as competent. The coordination exercises, visualizations, and practice sessions for his swing, however, allowed him to master basic skills and develop a sense of confidence and ability. Cordoba's feedback was essential to this process. He helped his student feel like a winner, and his student responded.

When they finally did begin work on the golf course, Sharon's caddy and friend, Levi, guided him from hole to hole. Levi would stand near the hole and clap his hands so that Sharon could aim his shot. As a result, a visual task was converted to an auditory one. Armed with the ability to estimate distance from sound and a well-honed swing, Sharon was able to play well enough to beat sighted competitors. With Levi providing feedback about each shot and Cordoba working on skill development, Sharon internalized a sense of expertise. His learning was structured to generate flow and, from that, he developed mojo.

Two criteria best capture your initial goals in structuring your learning:

1. Does your exposure to markets provide flow?
2. Does your market experience generate mojo?

Do you experience immersion and the sense of can-do, or do you find the essential tasks of trading to be boring, frustrating, and self-diminishing? The best exercise you can perform after each practice session of trading is to look into a metaphorical mirror and create the self-awareness described by Duval and Wicklund. If your experience of yourself as a trader makes you want to turn away, you know that it has provided neither flow nor mojo. If you like what you see and find it energizing, it's your best evidence of mounting competence.

The structure of practice provides us with a mirror by which we experience ourselves. We experience ourselves through our work just as we experience ourselves through relationships. Abraham Lincoln once described tact as the ability to describe others as they see themselves. All good mirrors are tactful in this way. Studying successful marriages, psychologist John Gottman found one common denominator: Each partner provided the most charitable explanations possible for the other's flaws. Poor marriages, in contrast, were not so tactful. Spouses used each revealed flaw to confirm their worst possible views of each other. Good marriages are good mirrors, reflecting the best of who we are.

A while back I learned of a trading shop that tried to teach new traders to limit their risk. They did this, incredibly, by limiting daily losses to $200. Traders who lost two points (eight ticks) on a one-lot in the S&P 500 E-mini (ES) market were done for the day. Because the traders were being taught to scalp the market, it was inevitable that they would go down eight ticks at some time during the day. The traders, in essence, were trapped. If they did not trade continuously, they were criticized for not being active learners and market participants. If they competed in the marketplace and lost money, they were turned off and left with a failure experience. Over time, the new traders learned to trade scared; they never developed the confidence to put on large positions and act upon their edge. Fearful of doing the wrong thing at all times, they never reached the flow state. One of the traders related to me that he made money for three straight days and proudly showed one of his mentors the results. The mentor seemed unimpressed and commented that the profits were not even sufficient to cover costs.

Think about the mirroring effect of such a statement. It convinced the young trader that, even if he tried his hardest and did his best, he wouldn't be able to cover costs. His motivation so deflated, he lost his sense of flow and began taking imprudent risks to increase his profitability. When he went into the red as a result, he was terminated by the firm. The negative mirroring provided a self-fulfilling prophecy.

Your structuring of your learning experiences will provide your mirror. That mirror will either affirm your growth or highlight your weaknesses. It will leave you feeling either increasingly competent or increasingly frustrated. Too often the latter is the case. After all, when you delve into a market, you are trading against pros—the very best Wall Street, Chicago, London, Tokyo, and Zurich have to offer. How can you possibly cultivate and sustain a sense of competence when you're struggling against larger, more experienced competitors? If your practice is not structured to keep you in flow, how can you possibly hope to find mojo?

> The best learning experiences are structured to mirror competence and sustain flow.

HOW TO STRUCTURE LEARNING: DIVIDING TASKS INTO COMPONENT SKILLS

Let's return for a moment to our blind golfer. His path to mastery is an excellent example of how learning can be structured to generate experiences of competence.

Cordoba's genius in working with Sharon was his breaking down of complex tasks into component skills that could be rehearsed with clear goals and feedback. This is close to a universal principle in performance development: Wherever we encounter expertise, we see the intensive rehearsal of component skills. Not only does this *drilling* build performance to the point where it becomes automatic, it also cultivates the sense of mastery by creating positive mirrors.

Dividing performance into component skills that can be drilled and mastered is common in the athletic world. In his book *Coaching Wrestling Successfully*, Dan Gable explains how he consistently elicited excellence from his teams. He broke each skill into several segments and then demonstrated each with a clear explanation. These demonstrations were conducted several times, from different angles in different ways, before wrestlers attempted to execute the skill themselves. For instance, the first demonstration might be by the coach alone; the next one by the coach against a passive opponent. Repetition and explanation preceded actual doing, so that performers began with a vicarious experience of mastery prior to their skill practice.

Celebrated tennis coach Nick Bollettieri, who has mentored a number of collegiate and professional champions, also advocates "drilling with purpose." Each drill has a specific goal, a skill to be developed. He begins by explaining the function and importance of the drill and the expectations of the student. The skill to be practiced is then demonstrated by the teacher, providing a model for execution. Students observe each other's successes and mistakes, creating multiple learning opportunities prior to actual skill execution. Key to this mentoring is the pacing of practice. The drills move quickly enough to sustain learning, but not so quickly as to overwhelm learners. In this way, Bollettieri keeps his students in that sweet spot of flow where challenges and tasks are evenly matched.

What does this breaking of skills into components accomplish? *It takes complex performance demands that might be daunting for a beginner and makes them manageable.* Having a coach repeatedly explain and demonstrate a skill—and then provide rapid feedback when the student attempts the skill—maximizes the likelihood of achieving a learning experience that supports the sense of competence. The divide-and-conquer approach to instruction creates favorable mirroring experiences for developing performers, allowing them to see that they are progressing toward their goals.

Remember, if you are guiding your own trading development, you are both coach and student. You will create your own mirrors through the structuring of your learning. The specific component skills that you will rehearse will depend on your trading niche. In my work with new traders, several skill components have preceded actual practice:

- *Learning the hardware.* Becoming proficient with the computers; building a workspace to optimize real estate on the screen; implementing redundancies at the hardware, online connection, and brokerage account levels—along with emergency procedures—in case of equipment or connection failures.
- *Learning the software.* Becoming proficient with charting, analytic, and order execution applications; learning to use these in combination to read multiple markets and time frames.
- *Learning market basics.* Becoming proficient with reading patterns among different markets and in different time frames; reading short-term supply and demand to aid order execution; learning specific trade setups and identifying them in real time.

Later in this chapter, I will outline a sample set of skills for a trader's curriculum. For now, the important thing to realize is that you can break trading down into bite-size pieces, rehearse those, develop mastery, and keep yourself in the flow state. Drilling is fun once we get it, and we are most likely to stick with something that feels good. The perfect practice that makes perfect develops performance-specific skills but also cultivates the conditions for sustained concentration, enhanced learning, and increased confidence.

HOW TO STRUCTURE YOUR LEARNING: CREATING VARIED PRACTICE CONDITIONS

David Lavallee and colleagues recently summarized research in sport psychology, identifying features of the learning process that enable athletes to acquire sport skills. Some of their key findings are summarized in Exhibit 4.1.

One of the most important conclusions of the research is that varied practice conditions are more effective than uniform conditions. To illustrate this, let's return to the practices structured by Nick Bollettieri. He will illustrate proper backhand form for players and initiate rehearsals by hitting one ball after another to the players' backhands. He'll hit to a variety of areas of the court, however, so that players also must work on their foot speed and anticipation of the ball. He might also mix in forehand shots to keep players honest and make the drills realistic. This might seem less efficient than simply hitting one ball after another to a stationary player's backhand, but such a strategy would not integrate skill development in one area (backhand) with other skills (ball anticipation, foot speed). Varying skills within practice sessions creates a realism that allows skills to more readily transfer to real-life situations.

Similarly, the research of Lavallee and colleagues suggests that it is

EXHIBIT 4.1 Research on Acquiring Sport Skills, taken from Lavallee et al (2004).

Structuring Practice for Success: Research Findings

- Practice of varied skills is more effective than concentrated practice of a single skill.
- Mixing skill practice in a random fashion is more effective than practicing skills in uniform blocks of time.
- Qualitative feedback is helpful for beginners, but very specific quantitative feedback is more useful for experienced learners.
- Frequent feedback is helpful for beginners; not as helpful for experienced learners.
- Practice that encourages implicit learning is more resistant to emotional interference than practice that facilitates explicit learning.

helpful to mix skills throughout the practice rather than practice a skill for one block of time, a second skill for a second block, and so on. For instance, a therapist could teach a relaxation skill for one block of time, then a cognitive skill (such as thought stopping) for a second block. This would be less effective, however, than integrating the skills within practice blocks. Thus, a client would be encouraged to interrupt negative thoughts and initiate progressive muscle relaxation as a single practice module. This would facilitate the integration of skills in actual stressful situations, ensuring a transfer of learning from the therapy room to daily life.

Interestingly, the research suggests that initial learning is hampered by the mixing of skills in practice, but that learning is more durable under mixed conditions. That is, learners are less likely to forget skills when they've drilled them in a varied way—but it might take more drills to bring performance to an acceptable level. Someone practicing their backhand while standing stationary in front of a ball machine could get the backhand stroke down quickly, but then would lose performance in game situations where the backhand had to be coordinated with ball anticipation and other skills. This is a common concern in the therapy world, where overly rapid learning is often followed by high rates of relapse. More learning trials under realistic conditions are generally preferable to fewer, less varied trials.

Feedback is another area in which variation pays off. Research suggests that beginners benefit from frequent feedback and that qualitative feedback ("Reduce your size in a thin market so that you won't get filled at bad prices") is as helpful for new learners as detailed, quantitative feedback ("You held your losing trades 30 percent longer than your winners when you were short."). As performers become more experienced, however, frequent feedback can actually be harmful, as it makes the learner dependent upon the instructor for a sense of competence rather than being able to gauge performance independently (as is required in real-life situations). The feedback that is helpful for the experienced performer usually needs to be detailed, capturing a nuance of performance that can be targeted for intensive work. Information that would not be useful to a beginner—the specific quantity of volume hitting bids that might make one exit a long trade at a given price level, for instance—might be essential to the experienced trader.

> Effective practice targets specific skills, mixes them for drilling, and provides constructive feedback geared to the performer's stage of learning.

The review of Lavallee and colleagues also indicates that there are advantages to implicit versus explicit learning strategies. Explicit approaches to learning rely on rules that can be verbalized. For example, "Exit a trade when it goes more than a full point against you" is an explicit strategy. After providing such a strategy to a student of trading, an instructor might then generate random entries for paper trading and observe the student apply the rule. Implicit learning approaches, in contrast, rely on the student to develop a feel for performance, rather than using an explicit set of rules.For instance, the instructor might provide a very general guideline—"If volume is not expanding in the direction of your trade, get out"—and then generate the random entries with the simulator set to double speed. The rapid movement of price does not allow the student to generate explicit rules for exiting. Instead, over time, he or she develops a feel for when volume and volatility are moving with the trade. *The interesting conclusion of the sport psychology research is that implicit learning strategies are more resistant to emotional interference—such as from anxiety—than explicit strategies.* Thoughts of fear or greed interfere with the cognitive processes needed to implement explicit strategies, but they do not get in the way of intuitive learning. This is a primary concern for the training of SWAT teams, for instance, where the development of "muscle memory"—creating automatic skill performance—is necessary in rapid-fire, risk-laden situations where there is neither time for explicit analysis nor room for emotional interference.

What does this mean for trading? *It suggests that there is much more to the development of competence than simply sitting behind a screen, turning on the paper-trading feature of your platform, and putting on trades.* If we apply the research to our trading curriculum, we would structure learning in the following ways:

- *Rehearse skills in realistic combinations.* We would not simply learn to build charts or place orders in the book, but would drill placing orders based upon what we see in the chart. We would follow the market on different time frames with different applications to obtain more complete pictures of trending or rangebound behavior.

- *Set goals for each practice session to generate immediate feedback.* Each practice session's objectives would be based upon progress from previous sessions. Goals would be specific, to track gains in learning.
- *Drill skills to promote implicit learning.* We would make skills automatic through rapid repetition, solidifying learning, and providing resistance to emotional interference.

What we see is that training is not simply an activity; it is a program that requires a curriculum—no less than the education of physicians or the training of athletes. Much that you will encounter in the coming pages will be designed to help you create your own trading curriculum.

Competence requires curriculum: a systematic approach to learning.

HOW TO STRUCTURE YOUR LEARNING: REASSEMBLING SKILLS INTO SIMULATED PERFORMANCES

Once a skill can be performed in piecemeal fashion, it is important to integrate it into a full, simulated performance. Performance simulations for the practice of skills create opportunities for extending learning to real-time environments without incurring the losses associated with errors. Swinging the broom in his house helped Zohar Sharon develop excellent form on his golf swing, but eventually he needed to leave house and broom behind and integrate his skills to the golf course. *Effective learning is accomplished by progressively approximating the conditions of actual performance.*

In wrestling, for example, after illustrating specific skills, Dan Gable encourages practice with wrestling dummies and against passive partners to achieve skill integration. As always, this is undertaken with the oversight and feedback of the coach and with rapid correction of errors. Wrestling dummies and passive partners provide a relatively safe but realistic context for practice, continuing the learner's internalization of skills. Bollettieri progresses from fed ball drills—where the coach can control how balls are hit to students—to fed ball drills with target scoring, where students receive a score for how they hit the fed balls. SWAT teams practice raids the way basketball teams learn new plays: first walking through them, then rehearsing at half-speed, then at full tilt. This crawl-walk-run process builds familiarity and confidence among performers and allows mentors to identify problems before they impact real-time performance.

Consider the developing trader who is learning her trading platform and individual applications. At first, as we've seen, she will learn to use these in combination, guided by goals and feedback. Once she can recognize trade setups in real time, she will make the transition to simulated trading using historical data. This enables her to pause and replay segments of trading, review her actions, and absorb the immediate feedback. Only later, after her skills develop in this controlled environment, will her training proceed to simulations with live data and then actual trading.

> Simulation provides the missing link between knowing and doing.

As skills are brought to increasingly realistic performance settings, coaches generally advocate working thoroughly on one cluster of skills before starting others. Chris Carmichael and Lance Armstrong, detailing performance programs for cyclists, use the analogy of painting a house. Painting a wall of one room, then going to the ceiling of another, and then to a hallway would be inefficient. It makes more sense to complete one room at a time. Similarly, performers integrate one cluster of skills (timing of market entries and execution of orders) before working on others (scaling in and out of positions once entered). This is known as *periodization*. Carmichael and Armstrong describe four-week blocks of practice for each skill module before working on subsequent modules. Thus, for example, a cyclist may spend four weeks working on sprinting, the next four on climbing. Within each four-week block, the skills are integrated into increasingly realistic performance settings. The cyclist might start on a stationary bike, for instance, and then progress to short runs on easy terrain, and then move to longer and more challenging runs.

A skilled trading mentor functions very similarly to the athletic coach. The difference is that the trading mentor utilizes historical and live simulated markets—not stationary bikes or punching bags—for the realistic rehearsal of skills. *Simulated trading is the market learner's equivalent of a football practice field, the body builder's equivalent of a weight room.* Trying to jump from initial learning of trading skills to actual trading is like making the transition from diagramming a pass play on the blackboard to running it in a football game. *Graded simulation, progressing from more controlled environments to more realistic ones, fosters the internalization of skills.*

If you are serving as your own trading mentor, the need to bundle skills into modules for simulated performance—and the blocking out of time for modules via periodization—requires that your curriculum be supported by an overall training plan. (See Exhibit 4.2.) Certain skills are more basic than others and need to occupy the first training period; others will build on these basics. As a rule in athletics, for instance, strength training and physical conditioning precede the rehearsal of tactical skills. This is why, for instance, elite military training programs begin with a phase of conditioning before teaching such specialized skills as shooting or parachuting. In the electronic trading world, knowing your machines and trading applications must precede the effective reading of markets, which—in turn—must precede the placing and managing of trades. If you look at any formal training program—whether in the military, medicine, or tennis—you will see a plan for development that can be diagrammed with timelines, activities, and goals. When you are both mentor and learner, you create your own training curriculum—one adapted to your pace of learning that enables you to tackle and master skills in increasingly realistic situations.

To reemphasize: The specific content of each curriculum will vary with the trader's niche. A curriculum for the spread trader of options would look different from that of the system trader of stocks. Each trading niche embodies its own skills. Mentorship and peer guidance are invaluable early in the learning curve simply in helping to identify key skills and break them down for drilling.

The pacing of this entire structure—the learning curriculum— ensures that there is a match between student capabilities and task demands. It facilitates clear learning goals as a part of each training session

---

EXHIBIT 4.2   The Structure of a Training Program

Creating a Training Plan

- Divide overall performance into a set of skill modules that include the processes of monitoring markets for favorable trading conditions, researching/identifying trade ideas, working orders/entering positions, managing trades, and working orders/exiting positions.
- Assign time periods to each module to create a curriculum, with the most basic skills preceding more specialized ones.
- Within each period, break each module into component skills and mix the drilling of these skills to create realistic enactments.
- Within each period, move from slower and less complex skill practice to faster practice that integrates skills.
- Establish explicit, challenging, but attainable training goals for each practice session and period and collect feedback about performance to track progress toward goals.
- Utilize feedback to set goals for the next practice sessions.
- Utilize feedback to make changes in the pacing of the curriculum, extending periods if progress is slower and moving ahead if progress is rapid.

and incorporates rapid, relevant feedback at every level of learning to sustain the flow state. If the training is successful, it will be demanding—but motivating and empowering. It will build the sense of competence so that training becomes motivating in its own right.

> How you practice is every bit as important as what you practice.

THE PROFESSIONAL AND THE AMATEUR

I hope by this time you can see that there is a huge difference between the learning of professionals and the learning of amateurs. The amateur golfer learns golf by playing rounds with buddies; amateur tennis players get on the court and hack around. Amateurs learn by performing, creating repeated experience without structure or feedback. Professionals learn by drilling, progressing through structured sequences of skills with the assistance of feedback and mentoring.

Nothing is more common than the notion that you learn to trade by trading. I humbly ask that you check that premise. You would not learn to fly a plane by getting in the cockpit and flying a jumbo jet, nor would you learn surgery by taking a knife to a patient. Why should trading be any different? Every performance field I have researched progresses from knowledge acquisition to skill drilling to simulated performance to real-time rehearsals. *Despite this seemingly obvious truth, we see few traders attempt to learn through training. Instead, they approach trading in the amateur mode, only to lose money and court frustration.*

That's not to say that traders can't learn trading through dedicated screen time. Later in the book, we'll see how concentrated screen time can greatly shorten a trader's learning curve. When I talked recently with Pablo Melgarejo, a trader who has sustained success throughout his history with Kingstree, he shook his head and said, "I can't appreciate when people hit their loss limits and go home. I always watched every open, watched every close. I may not be trading, but I'll be there at 3:15 P.M." Indeed, I can always count on Pablo being among the very first to log on to his machine in the morning and among the last to log out. He is not in front of the screen for enjoyment, for thrills, or even necessarily to trade. He is always in the mode of observing and learning.

Pablo's secret to longevity as a trader? "I know when to say when." When he loses the maximum amount allotted for that day, he puts the mouse down and calls it a day. He doesn't brood—"Tomorrow's another day" is his motto—but neither does he forget about the market. He will stay there until the close, figuring the market out. *That* is the mind-set of a professional. Pablo recognizes that many core trading skills boil down to pattern recognition. The trader who spends high-quality screen time is more likely to internalize patterns than the trader whose market contact is intermittent.

Some of the best examples of professional training can be found in the sport of boxing. Mark Hatmaker emphasizes in his book *Boxing Mastery* that the expert boxer progresses along a training continuum. The first phase in this continuum is mirror training: practicing footwork, upper body movement, handwork, and defense while watching oneself for feedback and correction. Next comes equipment training, using such tools as the heavy bag, speed bag, and jump rope. Equipment training provides opportunities for drills under the watchful eye of a trainer. Drills with the trainer or partner follow work on the equipment, rehearsing specific maneuvers apart from actual sparring. Only once there is mastery of the drills do boxers progress to situation sparring (simulating specific fighting situations) and actual sparring.

Recall the 10-year rule mentioned in Chapter 1, which suggests that expertise in any performance domain generally takes 10 years of dedicated practice. When you see how much has to be put together for the boxer—strategy, footwork, hand speed, punching power, and accuracy—it is easy to see why training lasts at least this long.

This is not a perspective that most traders possess. And yet there is no reason to believe that trading is any easier or less complicated than boxing or any of the other performance domains we've touched upon. Traders are eager to trade, and they fool themselves into the notion that their trading provides learning experience. Yet we can see clearly that a novice boxer would not learn from getting in the ring with a champion.

He would get knocked out.

TRAINING AS TRADING PSYCHOLOGY

When traders serve as their own mentors, they fill a leadership function. Accordingly, they are tasked with sustaining their morale and motivation. Chris McNab, author of the *SAS Mental Endurance Handbook*, quotes Sun Tzu's classic text *The Art of War*: "If officers are not thoroughly drilled, they will be anxious and confused in battle; if generals are not competently trained, they will suffer mental anguish when they face the enemy." Sun Tzu's is an important insight: Much of the emotional pressure felt in performance can be traced back to inadequate training. The anxiety, boredom, and frustration described by Csikszentmihalyi are not merely causes of trading problems, they are the inevitable consequences of being out of the flow state. *Proper training is trading psychology, sustaining the mindset as well as the skill level of the performer.*

McNab describes a variety of training strategies that thoroughly and competently train ordinary soldiers and bring them to the elite levels of Special Forces troops. The key to such strategies, he emphasizes, is realism. For example, soldiers must be exposed to the sights and sounds of the battlefield—the blasts and noise of artillery, for instance—or they will become disoriented under actual wartime conditions. A fascinating study cited by McNab found that only 15 percent of Allied troops in World War II who were in battle actually fired their weapons. Without prior exposure to the intense fighting conditions that they encountered, they froze under pressure. This is highly relevant to trading, where the real-time conditions of risk and reward create their own battlefields.

> When emotions interfere with performance, you'll often find evidence of inadequate training. Psychological assistance can aid the performance of a well-trained professional, but does not substitute for thorough trianing.

McNab describes the process of exposing soldiers to the stresses of war as "battleproofing" and "battle inoculation." For instance, SAS soldiers aren't just instructed in ways to handle being captured by the enemy—they are actually captured by soldiers who role-play the enemy in realistic detail, including harsh physical treatment. Ranger training places soldiers in intense simulations demanding immediate decision making so that leadership skills will transfer to real-time battlefields. Raids never take place until SWAT teams have engaged in live fire and full-speed rescue or capture operations. Traders progress from simulating skill modules—entries, risk management, and so on—to placing and managing trades, then trading full days in simulation mode, and eventually putting money on the line with one-lots. Facing—and mastering—challenges time after time creates the battle inoculation that allows traders to keep their cool under the most pressured circumstances.

It is the role of the mentor to ensure that the increasing demands of training build the confidence of performers, rather than defeat them. Although we stereotypically think of drill sergeants as people who tear recruits down, the reality is that leadership requires a complementary process of building up. "Courage is fear holding on a minute longer," General George Patton observed. Training provides that extra minute.

If you are mentoring yourself, you are your own leader. Your greatest challenge will be to create learning conditions that test you but do not break your spirit. If you are not adequately tested and battleproofed, you will wilt under the stress of real-time performance. If you overwhelm yourself with demands, you will lose the motivation and mojo to power your learning curve. As your own mentor, you provide that competent and confident leadership by creating a steady stream of challenging goals that build upon one another. After struggling with one goal after another and succeeding, you will face the markets with a reservoir of confidence unknown by most market participants. Like the soldiers, you will be battleproofed—the hallmark of true competence.

WHAT ADVANCED STUDENTS NEED TO FIND IN A MENTOR

Let's step back and summarize. When we look at the training of athletes, professional musicians, therapists, physicians, soldiers, and chess players, we see the same three-step progression:

1. Breaking performance into component skills
2. Assembling modules of skills into simple simulations of performance
3. Requiring skill enactment in simulations of gradually increasing complexity

Moreover, we see a progression from more basic skills to more specialized ones over an extended period of time. The purpose of training is to produce a performer who is capable of utilizing skills effectively and who has a high degree of confidence in employing those skills. This is not just because confident performers will be more motivated than less confident ones. Confident performers will also derive a sense of intrinsic reward from their efforts that will spur them to greater multiplier effects. One needs mojo for flow and flow for mojo—and both require the experience of ongoing success and mastery.

The implications for mentorship at this phase of expertise development are far-reaching. Early in the developmental process, as we noted earlier, mentors provide basic instruction and a healthy measure of support and encouragement. A beginning piano teacher needs to know the piano, a golf instructor for novices needs to know golf, and so on—but it is not essential that these early mentors be masters of their craft. More important is their ability to nurture students through early frustrations and help them find their performance niche.

In this middle, competence-building phase of development, however, it is not good enough for a mentor to provide basic instruction and support. A mentor must have intimate content familiarity with the specific trading niche in which the student is seeking competence. *This is why surgeons teach surgery, soldiers teach soldiers, and basketball coaches invariably have played the game themselves.* It is not necessary that mentors be world-class performers themselves—some of the best coaches of college basketball, such as Dean Smith, Mike Krzyzewski, Jim Boeheim, and Bob Knight, have been competent players but not dominant professionals. They must know the "Xs and Os" specific to the performance domain, however. Without such content knowledge, there is no way that they could break down performances into component skills and know which skills to drill first, second, and third. It is impossible to set specific goals and provide detailed, meaningful feedback to a performer if you have not engaged in the performance yourself. If asked to mentor a budding psychotherapist, I could readily set up a series of exercises and simulations and provide useful feedback at each step. If asked to provide the same experience for a budding ophthalmologist, however, I would be stymied.

> Find a mentor who is steeped in your particular market niche. The best mentors have solid experience doing the kind of trading that is right for you.

I have heard individuals who advertise themselves as trading mentors assert that they are not traders themselves. They work, they claim, on the mental aspect of trading to build performance. As we can see from this chapter, however, the way you work on the mental aspect of performance is by performing under increasingly realistic and challenging conditions. There *is* no mental performance building apart from performance: No amount of talking or self-analysis will battleproof a soldier who will face artillery fire or prepare a cyclist who will have to cope with rainy, mountainous conditions. For that reason, it is always preferable to train with a mentor who has intimate experience with the kind of trading you will be doing. If you are going to be trading currencies based on fundamental, macro factors—like Sherry in our example in Chapter 1—you would do well to enter a training program at a bank where currencies are actively traded. If, alternatively, you hope to scalp the stock indices, you might look for training at a proprietary trading firm in Chicago that has a clearing relationship with the exchange(s) you'll be trading. Your chief goal in searching out these firms is to find mentors who will facilitate your professional development. The right kinds of firms will invest in such mentorship and will have experienced mentors on board.

That having been said, content expertise is not sufficient for successful mentoring. All good coaches consider themselves teachers first and foremost—and the people skills that make for teaching competence are as important as the content mastery. Mentoring, after all, is a performance field just like trading or playing ball. The factors that make for successful mentoring are no different from the factors that lead to success in those other fields. A good mentor has an intrinsic love of teaching and finds it inherently rewarding. *Excellent mentors work on their game as obsessively as their students.* They review past performances—think of the hours coaches spend watching videotapes of their own teams and their opponents—and they intensively monitor practices for teaching opportunities. Most important of all, they possess the keen sense of judgment needed to find that balance between challenging and supporting learners. In my earlier book, *The Psychology of Trading*, I mentioned that the therapist's role is to "comfort the afflicted and afflict the comfortable." The same is true of capable mentors. They provide enough praise, feedback, and support to build the sense of confidence among young performers, but they also know when to deliver a needed kick to the pants. Coaches realize that, left to their own devices, performers will rarely coax from themselves that extra minute that separates fear from courage.

> Mentors can never elicit greater expertise in others than they develop in themselves.

CAN TRADERS TRULY MENTOR THEMSELVES?

A look at the requirements of competent mentorship raises a difficult question that many readers will be asking themselves: "Can a person achieve competence without formal mentoring?" Does a trader at home, for example, have a chance to achieve the same learning as the trader who enters a training program at a professional firm?

Self-trained experts are not unknown in the performance literature. Such highly skilled performers as Bobby Fischer and Louis Armstrong achieved expertise with a minimum of formal mentoring, and I know several successful traders who found niches and developed competence and expertise with only minimal guidance from senior traders. Nevertheless, there are many indications in the research literature that mentorship is an important component of expertise development.

Bloom's work with expert pianists, sculptors, swimmers, tennis players, mathematicians, and research neurologists, for example, found that mentorship was central to the development of talent. This is because mentors imparted very specific knowledge and skill development strategies, not just generic advice. The pianists in the study, for instance, reported that, as they progressed, lessons became very long and detailed, with a minute focus on technical excellence. A look at the training manuals assembled by Chris Carmichael (Lance Armstrong's performance coach), Nick Bollettieri, Dan Gable, and elite military organizations reveals a similar focus on detail: how to pedal the bike for maximum efficiency, how to swing properly for optimum tennis serve velocity and placement, how to escape an opponent's grasp from the down position, how to assemble and disassemble a weapon in a matter of seconds. It is difficult to imagine obtaining such information and cultivating such skill entirely on one's own. It is equally difficult to imagine being able to consistently generate the matching of skills and challenges and the level of feedback needed to keep one in the flow state of enhanced learning.

Deakin and Cobley, summarizing research literature in sport psychology, found that even very skilled performers, left on their own, spend more time practicing maneuvers that they are good at than ones that need work. This is understandable in that performing old activities successfully has to be more enjoyable than struggling with new ones. An important role of coaches, according to the research, is to structure practice time in an efficient manner to ensure that effort is placed where it is most needed. Indeed, in one study of performance among fencers, the two most important factors contributing to success were coaching and time spent in solitary practice. Teaching specific techniques and setting the conditions for the rehearsal of those techniques made coaching central to the acquisition of competence.

In a separate research review, Janet Starkes and colleagues reported that expert skaters and wrestlers rate coaching as highly relevant to their success. Interestingly, both coaches and skaters rate coaching as the number two factor responsible for success, behind the desire and motivation of the performer. Given the early age at which many skaters and wrestlers begin their training, it is not surprising that mentors play an important role in their development. Indeed, one *cannot* play many sports at a serious level without the presence of coaching.

Other fields, however, such as chess and bridge, less commonly employ mentors throughout the development process. Neil Charness and colleagues refer to these as "entrepreneurial" skill domains, because expertise can be achieved through solitary pursuit aided by less formal mentorship. They find a modest correlation between the formal training of chess masters and their tournament ratings (.26), with coaching yielding an advantage of roughly half a standard deviation. Surprisingly, however, when the authors developed a regression equation to predict player ratings, coaching did not appear as a significant predictor. Instead, the cumulative practice hours of the players and the number of chess books that they owned were the two best predictors of expertise.

This is an interesting finding, because it suggests that coaching may be most important in disciplines where solitary practice is difficult or impossible. For instance, wrestling must be practiced in a team environment; skating requires a well-maintained facility and competent choreography. It is impossible to imagine learning surgery or psychotherapy in isolation, which is probably why the mentorship process of professional education is required for licensure. Disciplines where individual resources for practice are abundant, however, may not rely as exclusively upon mentorship for expertise development. Chess is a perfect example of such an entrepreneurial field: Books detailing expert performances are widely available, and sophisticated computer programs can provide competent competition for skill practice. It is not inconceivable that a highly self-motivated and talented young person, such as Bobby Fischer, could acquire competence and even expertise through a disciplined use of these resources.

Trading is similar to chess as an entrepreneurial performance field. Most of the highly successful traders on the floors of the exchanges and behind the screen received basic instruction from a senior trader but did not participate in long-term formal programs of expertise development. The reason for this, Charness and colleagues suggest, is that such entrepreneurial activities provide—by their very nature—a plausible set of goals, rapid feedback (winning/losing), and the ability to use simulations to match talents to learning tasks. Poker is a perfect example of an entrepreneurial performance field. Players typically learn from card-playing experience, with each hand providing feedback about skills and strategies. While books, computer programs, and courses can aid the poker player's development, direct experience is typically more important to success than formal training.

This doesn't mean that traders would not benefit from formal training. Russia, for example, cultivates chess players from a young age and provides them with extensive mentorship. This no doubt helps to account for the fact that a large proportion of grandmasters come from Russia. Recall that research suggests that coaching is most valuable in structuring the learning process for students. When learners begin their performance careers at very early ages—such as gymnasts—and when performance occurs within complex team environments—such as crew, soccer, football, and rugby—mentors are essential to the structuring process. When learners start later in life and performance is largely an individual affair—as in poker or trading—much training can be self-structured. Classical music training, for example, universally relies upon ongoing mentorship; more entrepreneurial musical training, such as we see among jazz musicians, is typically acquired through individual experience.

Self-mentorship occurs when performers have frequent opportunities for practice and feedback and structure their own learning.

MENTORSHIP RESOURCES FOR BUILDING COMPETENCE

In the first chapter I mentioned Web-based mentoring resources, including informal mentoring from peers on forums and discussion groups and more formal teaching efforts in online trading rooms. While the former are sufficient for the earliest phase of development, the requirements of competence development dictate that traders engage in live exercises. Electronic trading rooms are ideal for this purpose. These allow for the introduction and demonstration of skills, and they enable traders to observe how those skills are utilized in actual trading situations. As mentioned earlier, Linda Raschke has one of the longest-running rooms where traders can watch her and her protégés analyze and trade markets utilizing short-term, technical methods. Woodie's CCI Club models an indicator-based approach to technical trading in real time and is free of charge. John Carter's Trade the Markets service calls out short-term trades in real time, permitting students to see how traders utilize a variety of pattern-based setups in a variety of markets. Several experienced market teachers, such as Don Miller, offer specialized training videos and live courses through the Trading Markets site. The Minyanville site includes a promising Minyanville University feature that helps users model the thinking of trading experts. Many more online mentoring services can be found through simple Web searches or that partner with particular trading software firms. Due diligence is always needed to ensure that the services offer what they claim and that they provide mentorship for the kinds of trading you ultimately wish to be doing.

The value of the electronic trading rooms is not simply getting trade ideas from a guru. Instead, you are learning from the mentor his or her particular style of trading. Bloom's research found that during the middle phase of expertise development, students learn to mimic their teachers. It is only later in the development process that students incorporate the learning from several teachers and cultivate their own style. When you are building competence, you need mentors who show you, step by step, what they do and why, with opportunities for you to apply the knowledge and skills on your own. I find that Ken Wood's group, Woodie's CCI Club, is quite good at this. Woodie jokes, "We don't need no stinkin' prices" and encourages his traders to simply trade from the recognized patterns in the Commodity Channel Index (CCI). This forces traders to watch unfolding patterns day after day and become keen scouts of these patterns. The electronic trading room enables traders to observe these patterns under a variety of market conditions and compare their trade ideas to those of mentors.

A very different avenue for developing trading skills is through formal education. There is a growing tendency for graduate schools to incorporate trading rooms as part of their training curricula, allowing students to learn trading in highly realistic environments. Kent State University in Ohio, the Massachusetts Institute of Technology, the University of Northern Colorado, and the Illinois Institute of Technology are but a few of the programs that actively teach trading in simulated environments. The great advantage of these programs is that they teach marketable skills related to specialized areas of trading, including programming and quantitative analysis. These skills, crucial to systems trading and the trading of complex market instruments and strategies, are impossible to obtain informally on the Web. I find they are becoming increasingly important even in the daytrading shops that used to rely exclusively upon discretionary traders and methods. The other great advantage of pursuing trading through higher education is that the programs structure the curriculum for you. This is invaluable, because you may not know the specific skill sets that are required for success in particular trading niches.

There are continuing-education opportunities for mentorship as well. The excellent training facility mentioned earlier, the Globex Learning Center (GLC), is housed in the Chicago Mercantile Exchange for traders who take their courses and/or work at member firms. The education staff provides oversight and guidance, helping students with all facets of simulation. Through the Merc's education department, for example, one can take a course on electronic trading and then try out the various strategies in the GLC using state-of-the-art software commonly used by professional traders. Both the Chicago Board of Trade and the Chicago Mercantile Exchange conduct live and Web-based seminars delivered by industry leaders; many are archived on their sites and are available at no charge. Some of the most valuable programs, I believe, are those that allow you to watch experienced traders trade in real time and explain what they are doing and why. John Conolly's site, Teach Me Futures, archives many such programs and offers free access to a trading simulator through CQG. This allows traders to actually test out strategies that they learn through the online seminars.

Your best mentorship resources will be among people who are trading markets and styles similar to your own.

While none of these options offers a comprehensive package of mentorship services, they do achieve many of the goals we've seen to be necessary for competence development: introduction and demonstration of skills, rehearsal of skills in simulations, and the opportunity to set goals and receive feedback with instructors. What we've seen is that you will know that a mentorship process is working for you if you truly become absorbed in your learning and find yourself increasingly motivated to tackle new challenges. If mentorship adequately balances challenges with skills, learning will be neither boring nor frustrating. On the contrary, it will provide you with an ongoing sense of growth and mastery. Although you may pursue self-mentoring, you need not operate in a vacuum. A broad variety of electronic and live resources can hasten your learning curve and facilitate the structuring of your curriculum.

THE MOST IMPORTANT RESOURCE FOR COMPETENCE DEVELOPMENT: SIMULATION

If most of your development as a trader will be self-directed, as I suspect will be the case for the majority of readers, your number one resource for the development of expertise will be access to realistic, user-controlled simulations. Let's go back to the research reported by Neil Charness and his colleagues. The two factors that most accounted for success in the entrepreneurial domain of chess were the number of books owned and the amount of time spent in solitary practice. What that tells us is that knowledge and its application are keys to success. In other fields, knowledge is acquired directly from coaches and mentors, as documented by Bloom. This knowledge develops into competence when it is implemented in practice. This is why every single elite training program I have been able to find—in sports, chess, health care, and the military—emphasizes progressive skill building through a structured program of practice.

Research and experience suggest that the single most important investment you can make in your trading development is the acquisition of software that will allow you to develop your own training program and drill the skills that are central to your trading niche. Whereas any paper-trading functionality was sufficient for an exploration of niches, the requirements for competence development are more stringent. You will need simulation capability that gives you a high level of control over the simulation so that you can obtain quick feedback and readily adjust the difficulty of exercises to your skill level. Ideally, the simulation platform will allow you to rehearse component skills and modules of skills by replaying past markets prior to actual simulated trading of live markets. This allows you to start, stop, and replay simulations for maximum learning impact. As with tennis, wrestling, or boxing, you first want to isolate and drill basic skills and then rehearse those in increasingly realistic simulated trading performances.

A simple example from my own training will illustrate the use of simulation for competence development in trading. I mentioned earlier that I have long followed the NYSE TICK as a measure of buying and selling pressure in the market. The TICK is actually tracking the number of NYSE issues that are trading at their offer prices minus the number that are trading at their bids. When stocks are trading offer, it means that buyers are particularly eager and aggressive to own the issues. When they trade bid, it means that sellers are in a hurry to exit and will accept the lower, bid price in order to get out. In that sense, the TICK is a very short-term measure of market sentiment.

One problem with the TICK, I found, is that it is relatively slow for a short-term trader. Many NYSE stocks trade infrequently; hence, they do not contribute to the TICK for long periods. Another problem is that the TICK monitors the broad NYSE, not the stocks in the index one is trading. The TICK may move to extremes because of strong buying or selling among small-cap issues, fooling a trader of S&P futures.

My approach to this issue was to use a version of the TICK that only incorporates upticks and downticks from the 500 stocks in the S&P index. This Tick16 Index, developed by Tickquest, Inc., and implemented in their NeoTicker program, moves more quickly than the traditional TICK and is more faithful to the movement of the ES contract. Because it moves differently from the TICK, however, with a different range for high and low values, it takes a bit of adjustment. The NeoTicker simulation is perfect for this purpose. I create a chart that monitors ES price and volume, with the Tick16 displayed in a window just below. This allows me to see the movement of the Tick16 as I track ES price and volume change. On an adjacent screen is the Market Delta program, which graphically displays the proportion of volume in the ES that is traded at the bid and offer prices. This provides a ready measure of the degree to which participants are committing themselves to the long and short sides of the market.

At the start of my learning process, my goal was to identify occasions in the market where there was pronounced selling that was drying up or persistent buying that was fading. My reasoning for this was that the ES market is dominated by locals who utilize far more leverage than their accounts can reasonably handle over the long run. (This is where knowledge of your particular market and its trading characteristics is central.) When I see on Market Delta that the market is loaded up with traders leaning one way—they've been getting long and can no longer push the market higher, or they're short and the market is no longer breaking—I track the Tick16 to see if the underlying stocks are displaying similar lack of follow-through. If so, this provides a potential countertrend trade idea that takes advantage of the price movement caused when overextended traders need to exit their positions. My initial work on the simulator was simply to replay past markets and call out loud spots where I thought buying or selling was drying up. When I got it wrong, I used the replay feature of the simulator to review what had happened and where I might have made a mistake. Later, I followed live markets on the simulator along with the Market Delta and called out the spots of waning buying or selling at points of overextension. Only once that had gone well did I actually place practice trades on the simulator utilizing this core skill.

You may trade different markets and styles than I do, but the underlying process of structuring training for success will be quite similar. You begin with a talent—in my case, the ability to read the TICK like the markers of a client—and knowledge of a market. You add to those basics informational edges such as the Tick16 and Market Delta for decision support and pattern recognition. Once these are in place, simulation provides a means for drilling these skills until they become automatic. *The idea is to spend so much time on the simulator that the trading skills become second nature by the time you begin live trading.* At that point, you are battleproofed.

> Your initial goal in simulation is consistency, not profitability.

In the beginning, you can obtain performance feedback from the market itself as you see whether or not you were successful in picking spots where buying or selling was turning around. Later, with simulated trading, your software can provide detailed feedback about the profitability of your trades, how long you held them, and so on. I've found the Ninja Trader program to provide a particularly effective integration of simulation and the collection of performance metrics. As of this writing, the company is offering the simulation version of their trading platform free of charge. Company founder Raymond Deux recently told me that this was his company's effort to increase the longevity of traders' careers. Too many traders, he was finding, were not surviving their learning curves, losing their market stakes before they could develop competence. His idea for Ninja Trader's simulator was to provide a trading gymnasium in which skills can be practiced during and outside of market hours, accelerating traders' development.

As mentioned, another company that has made simulation free for the trading public is CQG, Inc., through the Teach Me Futures web site. The simulation permits paper trading of live markets, but also has a "training mode" in which traders can review the market day one bar at a time to aid pattern recognition. The simulator will also accommodate trading systems, enabling systems traders to see how their systems trade in real time before they risk money. One of the features I particularly like is the order display, which marks entry and exit points on the chart, as well as points of working orders. This allows for quick visual inspection of whether you are entering and exiting at good prices and whether your orders are well placed. Notes can be typed on the chart displays, creating a visual journal for end-of-day review. Such tools help provide the feedback needed to supercharge learning.

WHAT TRADING SKILLS SHOULD I REHEARSE FOR COMPETENCE DEVELOPMENT?

While it is impossible to catalog the skills basic to each trading niche—trading, as we've seen, is like medicine in that it embraces a variety of specialties, each with its own distinctive knowledge bases and skills—there are several fundamentals that I have emphasized in my own trading development and that I offer for your consideration. (See Exhibit 4.3.)

- *Flexible, organized use of trading software.* I would estimate that the average trader utilizes less than one-quarter of the functionality in his or her software. It constantly amazes me that traders will utilize standard, out-of-the-box settings for their displays rather than customize each screen to their trading needs. This problem is not solved by adding more monitors to the trade station; rarely have I found traders to make efficient use of large numbers of monitors in short-term trading. The key is to put as much of the information that is central to your trading decisions in front of you on as few screens as possible. If information can be delivered audibly—via a squawk box, for instance—this is preferable, because it saves your visual information-processing resources for other data. Every time you shift your attention, you lose potential attention and concentration. This may seem minor, but such small drains on energy add up. Lance Armstrong, for instance, improved his performance greatly by learning to stay seated for a longer proportion of his riding time, reducing wind resistance. Each time he stood, he faced a little more resistance and experienced a bit more fatigue. Draining your attentional resources has a similar impact. Practicing the use of your

EXHIBIT 4.3	Examples of Skills that Can Be Drilled and Resources for Guidance

Skill Drills for Competence Development in Trading

- Creating customized data displays to track specific markets across different time frames and track sets of indicators; see your data vendor for tutorials.
- Conducting stock screening or screening of other trading instruments to aid in the generation of trade ideas; see programs such as Trade Ideas for mentoring via their web site and user groups.
- Conducting historical analyses of market patterns ("We've made a 20-day low on high volume; what has happened in the past after this has occurred?"); see my Trader Feed web site for illustrations.
- Conducting backtests of specific trading ideas; see Trade Station and Wealth Lab for active user communities and examples.
- Reading supply and demand in the marketplace; see Market Delta and the various implementations of Market Profile for strategies that track volume and to join user groups for mentoring.
- Tracking the buying and selling among various sectors in the marketplace; see the Tick specific and NeoBreadth indicators within NeoTicker.
- Placing various kinds of orders and scaling in and out of trades; see Ninja Trader's order entry features that accompany their simulation program and the innovative chart trading feature developed by CQG, which allows you to track markets and trade directly from chart displays.

software enables you to quickly access crucial information on the fly with a minimum of effort and delay.

- *Reading the tape.* This is obviously most relevant to short-term traders but is also valuable to the position trader who needs to get good prices to maximize profits. There is no sense losing execution ticks when you can, with a bit of patience, buy the bid or sell the offer. Traditional charting programs, which display prices in bars along with volume, are of minimal help in tape reading. Instead, you will need applications that allow you to see how much volume is being transacted at particular prices, so that you can track whether price is being accepted or rejected at each level. Longer-term traders can utilize the Market Profile for such analyses; the WINdoTRADEr program is an excellent implementation. WINdoTRADEr allows traders to monitor volume and price developments at multiple time frames, flexibly chart these in real time, and replay market days for practice in interpreting market-generated information. Shorter-term traders can rely on a program such as Market Delta, which breaks volume down into the amount transacted at the bid versus offer, so that you can see whether buyers or sellers are more aggressive at given price levels. Scalpers will employ depth-of-market (DOM) information, such as the ladder displays pioneered by Trading

Technologies. These depict the shifts among quantities being bid and offered, so that traders can track the flow of potential buyers and sellers in and out of the marketplace. Initial exercises should be devoted to simply reading supply and demand at a given price and time by calling out whether buyers or sellers are in control (or whether control is evenly divided between them) and whether you think the next ticks will be up or down.

- *Historical pattern analysis.* This skill is most relevant to quantitative and systems traders, but I have also found it to be a helpful supplement for discretionary traders who seek a source of edge in trading apart from their tape-reading skills. Examples of historical trading patterns can be found on my research blog, TraderFeed, and on the Market History web site. The very creative SentimenTrader service developed by Jason Goepfert also provides useful models for historical pattern analysis. The idea behind such analysis is that you identify distinctive features of the present market and then see when those features have occurred in the past and what the market has characteristically done following those occasions. Large databases of historical market information can be acquired from such sources as Tick Data, Pinnacle Data, and real-time data vendors such as CQG and RealTick. These data can be easily transferred to spreadsheets, databases, or analytical programs to explore patterns. Many of my analyses simply sort and filter data in Excel to pull out my sample, so that simple analyses are completed in a matter of minutes. While this may seem daunting at first to those unaccustomed to spreadsheets, the process of picking through a historical sample of data becomes near automatic once you develop a routine. Requiring yourself to perform simple data sorts in simulation ("What happens the day after a market rise or decline?") and then working toward more complex analyses ("What happens three days following three consecutive drops in the market?") builds one's confidence with analytics.

Your reaction to the preceding may well be "I can't do all that on my own!" You're right: Most traders—including myself—need help before becoming proficient at using their software, reading the tape, or identifying historical market patterns. And these are only a few basic skills. (See Exhibit 4.3.) There are many skills specific to trading styles—spreading, options analysis, fundamental and econometric analyses—not included in the preceding. Utilizing the resources mentioned here and in the appendix to this book will be important to getting started. My personal web site now includes a section entitled Trader Performance that explains nuts and bolts about moving forward as a trading performer. It also includes a Trader Development page that updates links to helpful learning resources. Others can be of tremendous help as well. Software firms and their help desk staff are invaluable in learning to master the functionalities of your trading platform. The purveyors of high-quality simulation programs—NeoTicker and Ninja Trader come readily to mind—also have helpful user groups and support staff to aid you in setting up simulations.

Even if you are serving as your own mentor—and perhaps *especially* if you are mentoring yourself—you can't afford to go it alone. It is important to reach out and find traders who can assist you in learning. Online trading rooms, seminars/courses, user groups, electronic forums, and bulletin boards—the resources are considerable. The right kind of trading books— those that explain and illustrate specific trading methods—are also quite valuable by providing methods that you can practice, and eventually modify, on your own. (Jim Dalton's work on Market Profile, Thomas Bulkowski's work on chart patterns, and the trading patterns described by Linda Raschke, James Altucher, and Larry Connors come to mind.) Finally, make liberal use of sources from the appendix that can help you learn how to identify and track market patterns. Your best start is to subscribe to an order execution platform that fits your style of trading, allows for detailed simulation, and includes an active users group that addresses questions similar to your own. That base alone will provide you with many tools for self-mentorship.

> Network, network, network if you are your own mentor: Many people and resources can light your performance path.

MAKING YOUR START: THE BEST ADVICE DR. BRETT HAS RECEIVED

The fundamental skill of trading is pattern recognition. This is true whether you are a short-term trader or a longer-term one, whether you are discretionary in style or mechanical, whether you trade beans or bunds. You are trying to anticipate future market movement, and you are looking for patterns in supply and demand that will guide your decisions. Later in the book, we'll break down trading into mechanics, tactics, and strategy and explore how you can work on each. As you develop competence, however, you don't want to become so inundated by possible patterns that you become the master of none.

One of the best pieces of advice I ever received as a developing trader was something Linda Raschke wrote quite a few years ago. She suggested mastering just one pattern before tackling others. I took that advice to heart and never regretted it. Linda believes that every trader needs some way to "frame" the market: make sense of patterns that present themselves. Technical analysis is one way to frame patterns; historical pattern search, Market Profile, and fundamental analysis are others. When you have a frame for markets, you have a basis for making decisions and for knowing when you're right and wrong. Over time, you are apt to modify your frame—it will no doubt become more elaborated as you gain experience—but it will always serve as a compass, a way to orient yourself during market hours.

The best start you can make in developing your trading competence is to look among the resources presented and find just one that seems to speak to you. Utilize it to identify one or two trading patterns, and then track these patterns in past markets via simulator and in real time. Don't even worry about trading the patterns; simply focus on identifying them as they are occurring. For instance, if your pattern is a breakout from a consolidation range, train your eye to find all such consolidations and breakouts. Participate in online trading rooms that can model the pattern search for you. Only once you are proficient at identifying the patterns should you attempt to find prices to enter the market and take advantage of the breakouts. Review by simulator will help show you when you're right and wrong and, most important, will show you why. For instance, during your reviews you may discover that breakouts are most likely to occur in the direction of the longer-term trend—a key piece of information that would aid your future pattern search.

Your exercise is to find your frame and just one way of trading it. Keep it simple. Become good at one kind of trade. That will provide you with a foundation for further development. If your goal is expertise, you're in this for the long haul. Make it a memorable journey.

CHAPTER 5

From Competence to Expertise

The Development of Highly Successful Traders

Expert performance should thus be viewed as the results of a natural experiment, where some individuals give their maximal efforts to reach their highest level of performance within the task constraints imposed by representative tasks in their domain of expertise.

—K. Anders Ericsson,
The Road to Excellence, page 43

What is this "natural experiment" that generates greatness, expertise, and elite performance? An experiment, after all, is a procedure by which we introduce variables into a controlled situation and observe the consequences. Somehow highly successful performers begin with a set of talents and a sequence of learning activities and emerge with levels of performance that distinguish them for a lifetime. To paraphrase hockey great Wayne Gretzky, they don't just react to the puck's position; they learn to anticipate it. They don't merely jump aboard a trend or breakout; they're already riding the move as others pile in. What are the variables that account for the results of such natural experiments? What changes occur in performers as they move from competence to full-fledged expertise? Most important of all, can we conduct our own natural experiments and gain control over the development of trading success?

The theme of this chapter is that the leap from competence to expertise is not merely one of degree. Greatness is not simply a higher level of competence, more of the same skills. *Rather, the natural experiment that generates elite performance transforms the performer physically, cognitively, and emotionally.* After long, continuous months of drawing lines on colored backgrounds, Robert Irwin forever altered his perception of the environment. Lance Armstrong, drawing upon years of training to enhance his aerobic efficiency, improve his pedaling technique, cut his wind resistance, and focus his competitive drive, experienced a looming mountain differently than he did as an amateur cyclist. Like all experts, he radically and creatively shifted his perception and experience. This shift is the outcome of Ericsson's natural experiment, an example of evolution at the individual level.

THE EVOLUTION OF EXPERTISE

Evolution is the most basic of natural experiments. Imagine an environmental change that results in a massive drop in temperature and precipitation. Plants rapidly die off and, failing to reproduce, approach extinction. Animals living off those plants similarly meet their fates as species. Cold-blooded predators, facing a food shortage and unable to sustain their body temperatures, also perish. Mammals, however, regulate their internal environments and face less threat from predators. Their population expands, especially among species able to hunt for food. Over time, those species able to create tools and modify their environments fare best in the new environment; their reproductive rates expand. As these successful species migrate to new environments with different demands, their best-adapted individuals survive and multiply, generating new and distinctive populations. *At each phase of the evolutionary process, environmental constraints select for particular adaptations.* The result is a world that is transformed from one ruled by dinosaurs to one in which humans are dominant.

Imagine, however, that we speed this process tremendously by conducting natural experiments with individual human beings. New environmental constraints are introduced daily. The majority of individuals cannot adapt to these changing conditions and drop out of the experiment; from the scientist's perspective, they become extinct. Those who remain in the experiment begin with certain advantages that permit resilience in the face of changing environments. They subsequently develop adaptations that improve their fitness in the face of changes yet to come. At the end of a long selective process, a relative handful of unusually well adapted individuals remains: the elite performers in the game of natural selection.

To no small extent, expertise development is an evolutionary process. Many children start out in Little League baseball; fewer take up the sport in a more rigorous way in high school and college. Those who star in the sport at school continue to minor league organizations and, of those, only a fraction make it to the Major League. I recently talked with an executive of a well-known brokerage firm. He indicated that the average time from a customer opening a trading account to closing it was a little over six months. This was not due to lack of satisfaction; their surveys reported general approval of the firm's service. Rather, it took only half a year or so for new traders to blow through their accounts. These were evolutionary casualties, dropouts from the natural experiment.

What makes our speeded-up version of natural selection different from the evolution of species is that *we can control many of the variables that affect survival.* Imagine if dinosaurs had training programs that taught the great beasts to control their internal environments, adapt to new diets, migrate and forage, and so on. The elite performers in the dinosaur training program would have had a better chance to survive changing conditions than program dropouts. In the world of human performance, we create extreme environmental conditions—competitive sports, games, warfare, and finance—and then generate training programs to evoke superior adaptations to these conditions. *Training for performance is the evolution of the individual.* The modifications resulting from such training create, in a sense, new species—ones as different from their predecessors as humans are from dinosaurs.

> Training creates the conditions by which performers evolve; expertise is the result of individual evolution.

FROM COMPETENCE TO EXPERTISE

Recall our definition of trading competence: the ability to consistently cover one's trading costs. Expertise connotes something greater: the ability to sustain a living from one's trading. Given that the majority of traders are running through their accounts in a matter of months, it follows that both competence and expertise are the exceptions in the evolutionary world of trading. If each trader is a mutation—a particular combination of trading "genes"— we find that, as in the natural world, few mutations are well adapted to the environment. Trading is no different from other performance fields in this respect. There are relatively few competent musicians and athletes, but only a subset of those sustain a living from their performance. For every rock star or NBA legend, there are many competent musicians and athletes playing anonymously in their communities—and many more people who long ago put aside any dreams of concert halls or sports arenas.

In the previous chapters, we saw that competence begins with a constellation of inborn talents and a set of personal interests that encourage the development of those talents. Guided activity in the form of training and mentorship challenges the performer and builds the sense of competence, sustaining a flow state of high motivation, concentration, and learning. In this state, growth proceeds rapidly: *Mere skill development becomes evolution through continuous multiplier effects.*

As competent performers pursue expertise, there is an important shift of the training focus, one that radically alters the selective pressures on performers. Recall that as learners gain skill, simulations become increasingly realistic and demanding. Among athletes, simple drills give way to intrasquad practice games and then to preseason contests. Actors and actresses first read scripts, then practice scenes, and eventually hold dress rehearsals. Simulations, we've seen, are effective in generating competence by reproducing the realities faced by performers.

When it comes to expertise development, however, simulation takes a very different cast. *To facilitate expertise, simulations become* more challenging *than the performance conditions they are intended to model.* This is extremely important. If you want wrestlers to be supremely conditioned for weekly matches that last three rounds, you have them wrestle every day for multiple rounds. If you want Special Forces troops to survive and function in hostile terrain, you create *months* of hostile conditions in a training program. To battleproof performers, put them in more strenuous battles than they're likely to face in the real world. Many of the performers will drop out—the dropout rate from Special Forces training exceeds two-thirds—but the remainder will be the fittest of the evolutionary breed. *This is because extreme training creates radical adaptations, accelerating expertise development.* The more people sweat in practice, to paraphrase Navy SEAL Richard Machowicz, the less they'll bleed in performance.

Tiger Woods's father, Earl, resorted to tactics that seemed almost cruel to aid his son's development. He would purposely make noise and distract Tiger while he was preparing to hit the ball, forcing the frustrated youngster to develop mental toughness and superior concentration. Only a strong bond linking parent to child, mentor to student, can ensure that such challenges do not backfire and contaminate the learning process. SEAL instructors routinely tempt their recruits to abandon their training programs and the restriction of food, sleep, and comfort in favor of a warm meal and bed. Some soldiers, unable to tolerate the discomforts of training, capitulate and drop on request. Those who graduate emerge with a confidence that they can face any challenge because they have already mastered the toughest possible conditions thrown at them.

> Extreme challenges, once mastered, create extreme confidence.

To prepare for extraordinary performance, performers tackle extraordinary demands. Recall Bobby Fischer's chess lesson advice to his biographer: Play all the games in the chess book—then do it again. The cyclist who wants to master climbing cannot stay on flat land or even small hills. The steepest mountains prepare one for the terrain of the actual race. This is because tackling the steepest slopes forces the cyclist to develop muscles and aerobic conditioning that otherwise would never evolve. An actress required to convincingly pantomime a scene with no props will develop expressiveness that might never emerge under normal conditions of acting. Bodybuilders always set weights just beyond the level where they can sustain multiple repetitions. One must tax muscles—not merely exercise them—to generate growth.

IN THE OFFICE OF AN EXPERT TRADER

At my trading firm, Kingstree Trading, LLC, I am blessed twofold: I have access to real-life expert traders—ones who make their living from day-to-day trading year after year—and I work in an environment that supports the development of expertise. From the first day I came to the firm to deliver a talk to the traders, owner/founder Chuck McElveen emphasized to me that the firm's mission was to grow large traders. For that reason, Kingstree spends far more time—and money—developing traders than the average trading firm. Many times the investment doesn't pay off, but when it does, the rewards are substantial. From the start, Chuck understood that you could not develop highly successful traders by keeping them on a short leash. A former trader himself, he knew that you learn to trade by immersing yourself in markets. You learn to trade size by raising your size. Developing traders cannot rise beyond the goals they set for themselves and the challenges afforded by their environments.

Before I take you into the office of an expert trader, allow me to illustrate what expertise truly means at a proprietary trading firm. The traders at the firm trade actively, in and out of the market all day. Fifty or more trades per day and thousands of round turns are not unusual. Imagine the commission overhead on so many trades, even given the favorable rates available to professional firms. Imagine the slippage involved in 50 or more entries and exits a day. Add to that the overhead of fees that pay for comfortable office space, dedicated computer and network support, direct lines to exchanges, and the latest software, and you can see that competence alone—breaking even with respect to expenses—requires immense skill. Against that backdrop, imagine the skill of traders who make six and seven figures a year, year after year. To be in the presence of such talent is an inspiration.

In his late 20s, brash and outspoken, Marc Greenspoon moves and talks with energy. While he is trading, he talks, fidgets, shifts in his seat, and occasionally bursts out with expletives. But his attention rarely wanders from the screen. His focus while trading is palpable, not unlike that of a surgeon intent on a procedure. Ask a casual observer to describe Marc and you might hear words like "cocky" and even "hyperactive." My image of Marc is far different. I see him in front of eight screens, intently watching each tick, asking, "What do you think here?" even as he's preparing his next trade. I recall him phoning me at home to talk about his goals for the new year—after making millions of dollars the previous year. Trading, social life, vacationing, conversing: There is little that Marc does that is not high octane. My word for Marc is "committed": He pours himself into what he does.

This morning he is down tens of thousands of dollars. He is near his drop-dead point—the level at which he and risk managers have agreed that he should stop trading for the morning. Hitting a drop-dead level is a bit like pitching a poor game of baseball: Eventually the coach will come out of the dugout, signal to the bullpen, and take you out of the game. No real competitor is going to eject himself, so the coach makes the call. Thus it is with risk managers. They are the ones who take the traders off the mound.

For many traders, having to stop trading is worse than sustaining the losses of the drop-dead level. Perhaps you've watched professional boxers get pummeled in the ring, barely able to lift their gloves, absorbing punch after punch. At that point, the concerned referee stops the fight. What is the defeated fighter's response? He protests to the referee! He doesn't want the fight stopped. He wants a chance to win. The punches don't matter at that point; only the desire to stay in the fight. So it is with many elite traders. It is difficult to find a highly successful trader who accepts the stopping of the trading fight with equanimity. They will cajole risk managers, accept smaller size limits—anything to stay in the fight.

Marc is one trade away from the coach's visit to the mound. I visit his office to see if he can pull this one out. Understandably, Marc is frustrated. "Can you believe this market?" he says as soon as I enter. "Have you ever seen anything like this?" He doesn't wait for me for reply. "It's trading thousands at every level, but it's not moving." He pauses for a second, eyes still intently on the screen. "I can't believe how badly I'm trading." Another pause. "I know if I'm just patient I can bring it back."

"That's the key," I reply. "Piece by piece. You don't have to get it all back at once." Marc knows that I'm merely repeating something he had written at the start of the year. He is a piece-by-piece trader, making his money with one good trade after another—not by sitting in a single trade for hours at a time.

I return to my office where I can watch Marc and the others on my screen. Risk management software allows me to see their positions at all times and the orders the traders are working. I also have real-time profit/loss (P/L) calculations for the traders updated tick by tick as trades move for or against them. This information allows me to see when traders are trading well and poorly; when they're trading in their usual style and when they're out of their groove. My challenge is to identify problems—and help traders—before initial losses reach the dreaded drop-dead point.

The market has indeed been trading in a narrow range, as Marc has noticed. Each time it climbs to its highs on good volume, it swiftly reverses. Similarly, at lows, the market suddenly finds bidders. Not a few of the firm's traders have incurred losses by buying highs and selling lows, looking for the breakout move that seems right around every corner. Many of them have pulled in their horns, waiting for the move before trying to jump aboard. They know that one or two more whipsaws will take them out of the game for the day.

The market is trading near its highs and, sure enough, sellers start hitting bids. This time, however, the reversal itself reverses and the market bounces a couple of ticks. Then it sits there.

And sits.

Intently, I shift my gaze between my screen of traders and my market screens. I'm as focused as Marc, watching for the traders' next moves.

The market trades at the offer. Marc doesn't wait; he lifts the next 600 from the book. A few more orders hit the market, lifting offers. Then a pause, then more volume at the offer. Suddenly it's as if a tipping point has been reached: Buyers enter the market in full force, propelling the ES contract to new highs for the day. Some traders are quick to take profits, and the futures pull back a couple of ticks, but Marc stays in the trade. By the time it's over, he's up two full points on his 600 lot. That's $60,000—more than enough to turn his P/L green on the day. He participates in two more upthrusts and, by the end of the day, has added six figures to his account.

I congratulate Marc at the end of the day on his turnaround. "I should have taken more out of the trade" is his characteristic response. "I'm just mad that I let myself get down so much. I'm digging a hole for myself every morning and it's killing me." To hear Marc talk, you'd think he'd just lost a lot of money.

But that's Marc. He'll come in the next day trying to figure out how to not go down money in the morning. The memory of getting close to the drop-dead level will be stronger than the memory of the comeback—and that will provide the next day's motivation.

Like I said: committed.

LOCATING THE SOURCE OF TRADING EXPERTISE

Where do we begin in locating the source of Marc's expertise? Is it his ability to read a market so well that he barely takes heat on a well-placed trade? Is it a capacity to accept the risk and reward of large size and stay in a trade with conviction? Or maybe it is the competitive drive that leads him to raise the bar each time he experiences success. All of these contribute to Marc's performance, and yet none of them was what I found most impressive during his morning turnaround.

What I saw was simpler, but no less remarkable for the fact. Marc's trade, placed at the edge of a range while he stared straight at his drop-dead level, *was automatic*. It was the same trade I had seen him place dozens of times before. He saw market activity, an important price level, and a trading range. The experience of hundreds of market days—and long days of intent staring at the screen—made the scenario familiar to him. He calls it a "feel" for the market, and that's exactly what it is. There are many traders who know more about the stocks in the S&P than Marc, and there are many traders who can run rings around Marc with their talk of technicals, fundamentals, and macroeconomics. The vast majority of them, however, don't make in a year what Marc made in that single day. They know a great deal about markets, but Marc *knows markets*. His familiarity with trading patterns is such that he can place a trade flawlessly even when he is frustrated and on the verge of leaving the mound. Only a deep level of knowing could allow him the conviction to enter and ride his trade.

Marc has followed the market closely for years, but has undergone no formal training. His friend and fellow successful trader Pablo Melgarejo brought him to Kingstree and served as an early mentor. But Pablo is not one to tell people how to trade. He provided advice and encouragement to Marc—as he has with other traders—but most of Marc's learning came in front of the screen. Indeed, when I first came aboard Kingstree and guided the training program, I was horrified to learn that Pablo was encouraging the trainees to trade hundreds of times a day on the simulator. I was convinced that this was wrongheaded, that it would only teach traders to over-trade. Now, a bit older and more experienced, I see the wisdom of Pablo's advice. The way you become automatic in your trading is to do it so often that it *becomes* automatic. Tiptoeing in the water never taught anyone how to swim. Marc followed Pablo's example and traded so often in practice—and immersed himself so much in market action—that he developed the "muscle memory" of a rifle marksman. When the heat was on and he was about to hit drop dead, his performance didn't waver.

Expertise, I would argue, is not merely skillful performance, *but the ability to replicate skillful performance over time and across challenging conditions.* We remember a Babe Ruth for a career full of home runs. There are many one-hit wonders, but how many Mozarts, Shakespeares, or Einsteins sustain lifetimes of achievement? Dean Keith Simonton has it right in his book *Greatness*: Elite performers are distinguished by their productivity. Given enough cracks at the ball, they hit their share out of the park. I doubt that the ratio of winning trades to losers is all that different for Marc than for many less successful traders. His success comes from knowing when he's right and making the automatic trade with size even when the chips are down.

> Expertise is skill internalized to the point of habit.

But where does the automaticity of expertise come from? For the answer to that question, we must return to our first chapter, deliberative practice, and learning loops.

DELIBERATIVE PRACTICE: THE COMMON DENOMINATOR OF EXPERTISE

Janelle and Hillman, summarizing research concerning expert performance in sport, refer to practice as "the common denominator." Ericsson, studying three groups of violinists of different performance expertise, found that all of them spent similar amounts of time with their music. The most accomplished violinists, however, spent the most time in solitary practice. The best musicians spent over 10,000 hours in such practice, compared to 7,500 hours and 5,000 hours for the middle and least accomplished groups. The same pattern—expertise accompanied by extensive practice—has been found among other performing artists, as well as chess players and athletes across a variety of disciplines.

The key to the idea of deliberative practice is that it is both the quality and the quantity of rehearsals that generate expertise. We saw earlier that mere exposure to a performance field is not sufficient to yield elite performance. As Exhibit 5.1 summarizes from Ericsson's research, the practice

EXHIBIT 5.1 Deliberative Practice vs. Normal Exposure to a Performance Field From Ericsson, 1996

Characteristics of Effective Deliberative Practice		
	Deliberative Practice	**Normal Exposure**
Tasks	Well-defined	Unstructured
Difficulty level	Matched to performer	Not controlled
Goals	Specified	Not present
Feedback	Immediate, detailed	Delayed, general
Repetition	Emphasized	Avoided
Performer aims	Self-improvement	Enjoyment

that facilitates expertise is very different from normal exposure to a performance field.

Let's compare two developing traders, Chris and Pete, to illustrate the difference between deliberative practice and repeated exposure to a field. Chris follows the market for a few minutes before the open and makes trades mentally as a way of preparing himself for live trading. He enjoys seeing whether he's right or wrong and likes the fact that he's using live market data for his practice. This keeps the learning interesting and relevant. If he makes mistakes during trading, he writes them down in a journal at the end of the trading day for review the following morning. That way, his learning doesn't prevent him from losing trading time.

Pete, however, engages in deliberative practice on a simulator. He works on specific skills outlined by a mentor, such as learning to identify market transitions in which a correlated, leading market begins moving size at the offer while his market continues to trade at the bid. When he detects such transitions, he is expected to work an order to take advantage of the shifting supply/demand situation. Periodically, Pete pauses the simulator and replays market moments when he finds his timing off. He continues the replays until he identifies what he might have missed in detecting volume shifts. This exercise will continue for a period of time before Pete shifts to a new drill.

Chris has structured practice for enjoyment and action; Pete emphasizes the drilling of skills. Over time, Chris will make many fewer self-adjustments in response to his practice experience than Pete. The planful nature of Pete's practice—its deliberative aspect—makes the experience less fun than Chris's, but more effective as an engine for learning.

Ericsson's research suggests that the concentration of the performer is an essential element in deliberative practice—another factor that distinguishes it from playful experience with a performance field. This means that the duration of effective practice sessions must be limited to allow for rest and recuperation of attention and focus. Naps and rest periods are common among elite performers, reflecting the intensity of activity during practice. In addition to recuperative breaks, the presence of concrete goals and immediate feedback help to keep performers focused on learning during practice sessions. Good mentors—think of coaches during football practices and scrimmages—know how to keep players on task during practice.

Janelle and Hillman observe that competitive activity itself may serve as a form of deliberative practice. This is because many sports require strategy (goals), generate rapid feedback, and provide repetitive experience. For this reason, they—as well as Ericsson—note that deliberative practice does not always require formal mentoring. Self-taught jazz musicians play in clubs each night, receive feedback from listeners regarding their improvisational skills, and work on those skills between gigs. We saw earlier that a chess expert can play practice games against opponents, record the moves, and review these for learning. Such practice is different from mere play: It is self-directed learning.

This brings us back to Marc Greenspoon, our expert trader. Consider my observations of Marc while he is trading:

- He is highly focused and rarely takes his eyes off his screens.
- He trades actively, following market activity very closely.
- He typically takes a midday trading break to renew his concentration.
- He keeps a journal of his trading, records his P/L, and writes comments, including goals for the next day.
- He follows his intraday P/L meticulously and focuses on the success of each individual trade.
- He tries new trading tactics based on market conditions and trading results.

Clearly Marc is engaged in a process of deliberative practice, even though he is not formally structuring the learning with a mentor. *The active nature of trading is itself an incubator of learning, because it sets Marc up for clear expectations and goals, rapid and detailed feedback, and ever-changing challenges.*

One of the conditions of deliberative learning that is also central to generating the flow state is the matching of performance goals and learner skills. Marc is a highly skilled trader, as his results attest. The only way for him to build his performance is to set goals that extend his skills. By definition, these must be prodigious goals, the kinds of extreme challenges that generate extreme confidence. When I first met Marc, for example, he was trading the DAX in the morning and the S&P E-mini (ES) futures in the afternoon. When he saw changing trading patterns in the DAX and greater opportunity in the S&P during the morning, he switched to trading the ES all day long. This was during a year in which he made significant money. Marc knew that he would not extend his performance unless he tackled a new challenge. To reach expertise means that we demand of ourselves performance beyond competence, beyond what we can readily accomplish.

PERFORMING OUTSIDE THE COMFORT ZONE

Ericsson makes an excellent point regarding the development of skills. When we first learn a skill, the process is effortful, requiring considerable attention and thought. With repeated experience, however, the skill becomes natural and automatic. We no longer need to direct full attention to driving a car under normal conditions; performance becomes comfortable over time. Once it becomes comfortable, however, it no longer facilitates learning. *Automaticity is the result of effective learning, but it is also the enemy of new learning.* Elite performers are thus challenged to continually move themselves beyond what is automatic, beyond their comfort zones. This can be accomplished only by demanding the extraordinary of oneself.

> Evolution occurs when we are so taxed that we must make fresh adaptive efforts. The expert is one who continually adapts to extraordinary performance demands.

Nowhere is this better seen than in elite military training. What possible purpose is served by having Ranger School candidates engage in strenuous conditioning, repetitive drills of battle skills, and difficult leadership exercises in a variety of terrains—all while receiving at most one meal a day and a couple of hours of sleep? This goes on for 61 days, causing most trainees to lose 30 pounds. During the Hell Week of BUD/S (Basic Underwater Demolition/SEAL) training, recruits spend 132 consecutive hours in intense physical labor, braving wet, cold, sandy conditions. For $5\frac{1}{2}$ days, they engage in one strenuous activity after another: running, swimming, carrying heavy boats, rolling in sand, jumping in freezing water, carrying more heavy boats . . .

Eventually you could do those things in your sleep. In fact, given the frequent occurrence of hallucinations among sleep-deprived recruits, there's a sense in which they *are* doing it in their sleep—which is the whole point. *Through repetition, even extreme challenges become automatic.*

This ensures that elite soldiers will function effectively and maintain discipline during the normal conditions of battlefield hunger, fatigue, and uncertainty. It also ensures that traders like Marc Greenspoon can make the automatic trade, even as they are one trade away from the sidelines.

The elite in any field move from competence to expertise by creating performance challenges more demanding than anything they're likely to experience day to day. We evolve by creating and adapting to challenges that lie outside our comfort zone.

EXPERTISE AND IMPLICIT LEARNING

Observation of Marc and other expert traders has shown me that *expertise is the result of implicit learning under highly challenging performance conditions*. While performance can always be described as a series of steps, as in a standard battle drill, the expert's performance is always something more than a faithful and competent replication of the steps. The battle-hardened veteran develops a feel for when to advance and when to take cover, when to lay down fire, and when to observe enemy behavior. Similarly, expert traders develop a feel for handling situations in which their orders are unexpectedly hit. They do not merely ape standard operating procedures. I have asked the expert traders at Kingstree how they knew when to attack a market and when to reverse their positions, and the responses have been similar: "They couldn't get 'em down, so I decided to buy," or "It was just like last week; you just knew they were going to take them down once everyone was long." These traders have seen so many markets and market scenarios that they develop an anticipatory sense—a conviction that something is likely to happen because it has happened so many times before.

Research reported by Axel Cleeremans and Luis Jiménez supports this notion. Their studies investigated sequence learning: the ability to anticipate the next item in a series. This is relevant to any performance activity, such as sports or trading, in which the ability to anticipate the behavior of a competitor is key. They conclude that implicit learning results in a deep understanding of the statistical structure of event sequences. That's a mouthful; let's unpack what the researchers are revealing about expertise.

A good illustration is research reviewed by Curran that investigates serial reaction time (SRT): the ability to respond quickly to items in a series. Participants in the studies are shown a cursor on a screen that appears at one of several locations. They press a button corresponding to a location to indicate where they see the cursor. Researchers measure the reaction time of subjects under two conditions: when there is a pattern determining the location of the cursor and when the cursor location is determined randomly. The pattern is not a simple one. For instance, if there are four possible locations for the cursor (designated as 1, 2, 3, or 4), the pattern might be 4–2–3–1–3–2–4–3–2–1. This pattern would repeat many times over blocks of trials.

Several results emerge from the SRT studies. First, reaction times improve over the blocks in which the cursor's location follows a pattern. This means that subjects are learning to anticipate where the cursor is going to appear. Second, reaction times do not improve for the random blocks. This indicates that the improvement in reaction time is not just a function of familiarity with the task. Third, although it is clear that subjects are learning to anticipate the pattern, they cannot verbalize what that pattern is. Their learning truly is implicit.

Curran cites a large body of neuroimaging research that finds differences between implicit and explicit learning in terms of the brain regions that are activated. Specifically, the SRT studies appear to draw upon the brain's motor cortex: areas involved in the control of our bodies. This makes sense, given the intimate connection between pattern recognition in the studies and rapid responding to the patterns.

Cleeremans and Jiménez observe that implicit learning occurs during noisy sequences (ones in which random elements are mixed into patterns), indicating that subjects can pull patterns out of streams of data—a skill that sounds very similar to the activity of short-term traders. The authors conclude that subjects in the SRT experiments become sensitive to the statistical regularities in the data—that, over time, certain cursor locations are more likely than others to follow an appearance at one portion of the screen. In essence, the subjects act as neural networks, using new data to update the estimates of an event occurring.

Note that implicit learning occurs only after many learning trials. In essence, the SRT experiment provides a kind of concentrated drilling. After dozens and dozens of trials, subjects internalize patterns that they cannot fully describe—just like the Kingstree traders. Most important, this learning is not the kind of absorption of facts and figures that occurs in classrooms. Rather, it is motor learning—the connection between a perception and a response. Perhaps this is why so many highly successful traders are not distinguished by their book learning. When they say they have a "feel" for the market, they are speaking a literal truth.

Expertise is not what is known, but the connection between knowing and doing.

IMPLICIT AND EXPLICIT LEARNING IN PERFORMANCE

Ted Williams is considered by some to be the greatest hitter in the history of baseball. His book *The Science of Hitting* is a classic account of elite performance. Williams spent long hours, indoors and outdoors, perfecting his swing. He carefully placed his feet 27 inches apart and made sure his bat was a proper weight. He divided the strike zone into 77 regions—seven rows and eleven columns—and calculated his batting average in each region. Armed with such a spatial awareness, he developed a keen sensitivity to whether pitches were in or out of the strike zone. Perhaps even more impressive than his ability to hit over .400 in a season was the fact that he struck out only 709 times in 7,706 career at bats but walked over 2,000 times. His formula for hitting success was simple: "Get a good pitch to hit."

Notice, however, that getting a good pitch to hit is not something that can be accomplished by explicit thought alone, given that pitches are typically coming at the batter at speeds up to 100 miles per hour. Knowing what are good pitches and what are bad requires motor anticipation not unlike the skills displayed in the SRT experiments. From the motion of the pitcher's arm to the point of the ball's release to the spin of the ball, hitters like Williams rapidly assemble cues that alert them to the probable location of the ball. It is impossible to imagine such expertise developing without thousands of learning trials.

If you watch footage of Muhammad Ali's early fights, you cannot help but be impressed by his body control and foot speed. He would pull his upper body back when he anticipated his opponent throwing a punch. As a result, many jabs and punches thrown by opponents hit nothing but air. I have observed expert traders suddenly remove orders from the book in response to a single trade or large order being entered. Just a second or so later it became clear that they avoided being filled at a bad price. Is this so different from the skills of an Ali?

The advantage of the very short-term trader is that every trading day contains hundreds of learning trials. *It is as if the trader is in a continuous SRT experiment.* Implicit learning occurs rapidly under such conditions. This helps to explain a phenomenon that initially baffled me. The highly successful traders that I encountered at Kingstree were, for the most part, in their 20s or early 30s and had only been trading several years before reaching a point of making an excellent living from their craft. Recall Chapter 1, in which we encountered the 10-year rule, a durable finding from performance research. It generally takes 10 years of preparation and deliberative practice to attain expertise in a performance field. To my surprise, none of the highly successful traders I was observing had anything like 10 years of experience.

The solution to the puzzle, I believe, is that *it is not the number of years that is necessary to generate expertise, but the quantity and quality of the learning trials.* A short-term trader can place 100 or more trades a day, day after day, and observe thousands of trading patterns in the order book. A surgeon, however, would need months to complete a similar number of learning trials. A baseball hitter would become quite sore trying to swing at an equivalent number of pitches each day. Expertise, for them, takes longer because learning trials must be spaced out over a relatively extended period.

For this reason, I strongly suspect that the learning curves for longer-term traders and scalpers are quite different. (See Exhibit 5.2.) A trader who trades on an end-of-day basis might observe only a few hundred patterns in a year—the same number that a scalper might encounter in a matter of days. Nor is it entirely clear that implicit learning plays the same role in longer-term and shorter-term trading. The advice "plan the trade and trade the plan" makes sense to a position trader, but is irrelevant to a scalper. There is no explicit planning to scalping; it draws upon the motor anticipation we see in the SRT studies. Yogi Berra once responded to a questioner who asked what he thought about when he was at the plate by saying that he didn't think about anything when batting—he didn't have time for both activities. So it is with the very short-term trader.

The longer-time-frame trader, however, is more likely to rely upon explicit patterns for entries and exits. These might be chart patterns that unfold over minutes or hours, or they might be patterns from statistical analyses. These patterns form the basis for trading plans and systems. Such traders behave in rule-governed ways, and a large part of their

EXHIBIT 5.2 Differences in Expertise Development Between Longer and Shorter-Term Traders

	Shorter Time Frame Trader	Longer Time Frame Trader
Thought process	Implicit	Explicit
Learning process	Repeated trials	Market research
Trading style	Intuitive, by feel	Analytical, by rules
Source of trading edge	Experience	Knowledge
Duration of the learning curve	Accelerated	Extended

success consists of following their rules. Pitching great Nolan Ryan, for example, was rule-governed. He studied the tendencies of each of the hitters he was scheduled to face and knew whether they were fastball hitters or not, whether they preferred pitches high or low, inside or out. He mentally rehearsed this information before each time and used it to help him select pitches in particular situations. As Ryan describes in his *Pitcher's Bible*, he knew that the Yankees' Steve Sax was a high fastball hitter. This led Ryan to emphasize low breaking pitches to Sax. This is similar to a trader who calculates the odds of a market making a breakout move and then uses the information to either jump on board new highs or fade them.

When performance is largely dependent upon explicit reasoning and learning—as in the case of chess or the medical professions—we can expect a lengthy learning curve. Indeed, one advantage of systems trading is that it can test trading patterns over years of market data quickly, condensing lengthy experience into a brief period. It also can eliminate the learning curve associated with the development of execution skill by automating order entry. The longer-term discretionary trader faces the reality that, without simulation, it would take years to experience the full panoply of bull, bear, and rangebound markets. *The value of simulation for the longer-term trader is that it permits many more learning trials than could be achieved through live trading.*

In reality, most performance expertise is a blend of explicit and implicit knowing. Despite his rules, Ryan was quick to acknowledge that you could not predetermine how you'd pitch a game while you were in the dugout waiting for the first at-bat. A feel for the hitters and for your own pitching that day play an important role. Too, while Ryan used explicit information to guide his pitch selection, his actual pitching mechanics were honed through a process of drilling and implicit learning. In his book he explains that he came to the Major League with a dominating fastball but poor control. Concentrated work on his delivery and accuracy allowed him to slow his fastball as he got older and yet maintain his effectiveness. Similarly, a surgeon's expertise is the result of explicit knowing of the body and intimate, implicit feel for the instruments. A cyclist like Lance Armstrong begins with an explicit race plan and considerable knowledge about the course, but relies on an implicit feel for race conditions to know when to make a breakaway move.

Perhaps the greatest shortcoming in traditional trader education is that it is heavily skewed toward explicit learning. Seminars, web site articles, books, and magazines are explicit by their very nature. These produce a knowing *about* markets and trading, but cannot possibly generate the market feel that we observe among expert traders. *Drilling to the*

*point of implicit learning is the missing ingredient in most traders'
development.*

WHAT MAKES EXPERTS DIFFERENT: PERCEPTION

Exhibit 5.3 summarizes research on the development of elite performers
and the ways in which they change in response to deliberative practice and
implicit learning. What we see is that intensive learning changes the performer cognitively as well as behaviorally. This truly is real-time evolution.
Elite performers perceive differently, think differently, and act differently
from their less expert counterparts. In a very important sense, when
traders develop expertise, the markets they see are different from the markets everyone else sees.

Let's start with chess and the classic research of Chase and Simon. In
their studies, we have two groups of subjects: expert chess players and
nonexpert. We then briefly show each group chessboard positions taken
from the middle of a game. Our goal is to see whether one group has a better memory for the positions of the pieces than the other. Sure enough, as
you might predict, the chess masters recall many more board positions
accurately than the nonexperts. This, you might conclude, suggests that
experts have a superior memory for performance events than nonexperts.

Cleverly, though, Chase and Simon added a second condition to the
study. They briefly showed each group of subjects a random arrangement
of pieces on a chessboard and then tested for recall. In this situation, neither group performed very well. Indeed, the expert group did not outperform the nonexperts.

The researchers concluded that experts do not have better memories than nonexperts. *Rather, they have a superior ability to process
performance-related information than nonexperts.* For instance, let's
say that one portion of the board displayed a castled king. This implies a
certain structural relationship among the rook, king, and pawns. The

---

EXHIBIT 5.3 Ways in Which Experts Differ From Novices

How Experts Change During Their Development

- *Altered perception* Chunking information efficiently
- *Altered reasoning* Updating knowledge in a forward progression, flexibly
- *Altered knowledge* Generating elaborated mental maps
- *Altered behavior* Rapid decision making and response

expert processes this as a single chunk, or unit, of information. The non-expert does not group the pieces in such a meaningful way and instead tries to recall the position of each piece separately. The ability to process information in chunks based upon meaningful criteria allows the chess masters to recall more pieces than nonexperts when viewing actual chess positions. When a randomly arranged board was shown, there *were* no meaningful chunks and the experts displayed no memory advantage.

Note that this chunking of information—and the efficiency of perception and memory that it allows—is not a conscious process on the part of experts. The expert does not see a separate king, rook, and pawns. The expert sees a castled king. Similarly, when a client comes to me and complains of sleep loss, low mood, and poor concentration, I do not see three separate problems and begin multiple inquiries. Rather, I perceive potential symptoms of depression and ask questions to sort depression from other possible causes of those symptoms (substance abuse, grief, etc.). A quarterback dropping back into the pocket to throw the ball does not see separate linebackers, linemen, and safeties. He sees a zone defense and a seam in the zone where he can throw the ball. "Zone defense" and "depression" are for the quarterback and therapist what "castled king" is for the chess master: performance-related groupings of information.

Expert traders similarly chunk information into meaningful groups, aiding their recall and speeding their responses to market events. Let's say we have three consecutive bars on a chart. The first one is a decline on high volume. The second one descends slightly below the first on lower volume, but closes higher. The third bar shows lower volume still, and its low is above the lows of the preceding two bars. This configuration is not seen by an experienced trader as three separate bars. It is perceived as a single unit that might be called "selling drying up." If the lows of the bars correspond to lows made earlier in the day, the configuration might be processed as "selling drying up at support." This is seen as a single meaningful event, which allows it to be processed as a potential trade idea. If the bars were seen separately—and separately from the bars earlier in the day—they would convey no meaning. They would not form the basis for a trade.

Research suggests that elite performers do not have better "hardware" than average performers—their eyesight, memory, and reflexes are not necessarily outstanding. Rather, experts have accumulated so much implicit learning that they process events more efficiently and effectively than their counterparts. Their training has provided them with new ways of seeing the world based upon the grouping of their perceptions.

Deliberative practice and implicit learning yield new, more efficient perception, allowing for rapid and creative response.

WHAT MAKES EXPERTS DIFFERENT: REASONING

Experts not only see the world differently from nonexperts, they also *think* differently. This is a natural consequence of their perceptual differences.

A fascinating research look at physicians by Patel and Groen found that expert diagnosticians and nonexperts displayed similar amounts of knowledge. What distinguished their ability to make accurate diagnoses, the authors found, was expertise—not recall. The expert physicians made use of what the authors call *forward reasoning* to arrive at their diagnoses. The nonexperts employed backward reasoning. A look at these ways of thinking will illustrate how they apply to trading.

Imagine two people putting a jigsaw puzzle together. The first one looks at pieces that have flat edges and those that belong in the center and sorts them out. Then she separates out the pieces based on their colors. She starts to find connections between the flat pieces and the similarly colored pieces and, every so often, steps back to look at the picture and guess its meaning. Before too long, she figures out it is a nature scene and begins to assemble more pieces based upon her view of trees, sky, and mountains. This is a forward-reasoning process: It moves from meaningful groups of information to inferences about the whole, which in turn guide the further grouping of information.

The second person takes a very different approach to the puzzle. He guesses early on that the scene is one of a jungle. He then seeks pieces that look like parts of jungle animals, tropical plants, and jungle natives. Rather than grouping pieces into meaningful categories (flat pieces, pieces with similar colors), he reasons in a backward fashion that brown must be a tree and green must be a plant. When he sees that there is too much brown to be trees and too much sky blue to make for a jungle scene, his reasoning process has to return to step one. For this reason, it is inefficient.

An experienced physician collects information about a patient's pain and nausea and takes the patient's temperature as first steps in a differential diagnosis. Moving forward from the data collected, the physician will ask questions and gather further information to rule out competing diagnoses and formulate working hypotheses to guide data collection. After multiple questions and tests, the final diagnosis will be the one remaining.

A medical student, however, will not be able to see the pain, nausea, and temperature as part of a web of diagnostic possibilities requiring increasingly refined queries. Instead, the student might leap to the conclusion that the patient has influenza and will pursue this path exclusively. Reasoning backward from the conclusion, the student becomes tunnel-visioned in the search for information. When information emerges that contradicts a flu diagnosis, the student must return to the beginning to gather information and attempt a new assessment.

Novice traders reason in the backward fashion: They look for information to support their opinions rather than assemble their trade ideas from their readings of the market. Expert traders often talk about "letting the market come to me"—another way of saying that the right trades, like the right diagnoses, will emerge from gathering the right data. This is only possible, however, when traders, like physicians, have internalized a kind of decision tree that guides the circular process of collecting information and formulating tentative ideas.

Patel and Groen report results very similar to those of Chase and Simon. When the symptoms of a case were arranged in the way that they would normally be collected, expert physicians obtained accurate diagnoses significantly more often than nonexperts. When the symptoms were randomly arranged, however, the two groups performed equally poorly. *The order of the information collected did not affect the diagnoses of nonexperts, but was all-important to experts.* This is because skilled physicians collect information in an order that reflects a forward-reasoning process. This process facilitates perception-action links that allow expert surgeons and emergency room physicians to make informed life-and-death decisions in a matter of moments.

> Decisive action begins with efficient perception and organized information.

Zeitz presents a large body of findings that reveal how the ways that experts process information aid their reasoning, yielding superior performance. She refers to MACRs—moderately abstract conceptual representations—as a cornerstone of expertise We can think of MACRs as a kind of road map—like the physicians' decision trees—that organize the perceptions of experts. The chess expert encodes the positions of pieces in terms of strategies; the physician organizes symptoms into clusters based upon a system of diagnosis. As I am writing this, stock markets in Europe and Asia are down sharply in the wake of poor earnings news after the New York close and a panicky response by Japanese investors regarding alleged wrongdoings at a popular Internet firm. Bonds around the world are firm, oil is higher, and the S&P 500 futures are down sharply. An experienced trader possesses a MACR that links all of these markets, viewing different instruments across countries as part of a single pattern: Assets are being shifted from speculative sectors to relative safe havens. Novice traders, lacking internal road maps, focus only on their markets, misinterpreting strength or weakness.

Notice that these mental maps allow experts to be more flexible than nonexperts in their reasoning processes. For instance, a map that distinguishes financial panic days from normal days leads a trader to look for intermarket relationships that would not exist otherwise. Lacking this flexibility, the novice trader on a day like the current one cannot place the effective trades in which movements in one safe-haven market (German Bund) lead moves in a different, speculative one (U.S. stocks). A novice trader, fixed in a view that falling interest rates are good for stocks, cannot sell stocks when very weak economic news leads bonds to rally and stocks to tumble. *Where the novice thinks concretely, the expert reasons contextually.* Instead of thinking A always leads to B, the expert creates a web of possibilities in which A leads to B under conditions X and Y, but leads to C under other conditions.

Paul Feltovich and colleagues emphasize that *an important way of developing flexibility is to practice skills with as many variations as possible.* This allows performers to develop rich mental maps that can guide performance under almost any conditions. Recall McNab's observation that only 15 percent of troops in World War II combat actually fired their weapons. Because they had not encountered similar battle situations during practice, they lacked the mental maps needed to guide them under such dangerous conditions. This has significant implications for traders. Not infrequently, traders make money under one set of market conditions only to give it back when the market changes. As we shall see shortly, rehearsing trading with historical data enables traders to encounter multiple trading scenarios and conditions. This is a highly effective strategy for building the maps and flexibility needed to make rapid, accurate decisions under conditions of high risk and reward.

WHAT MAKES EXPERTS DIFFERENT: ACTION AND REACTION

Imagine a professional trader who makes a million dollars per year trading E-mini futures actively. Most of us would conclude that such a trader has a huge edge in the market. Consider, however, that the trader might place 50 trades per day at an average size of 200 contracts. Trading 10,000 contracts per day or approximately 2,500,000 contracts per year, the trader is making less than a tenth of a tick per contract per day to generate the large profits. Contrary to writings in the popular media, such an edge does not come from finding a foolproof chart pattern, a better momentum oscillator, or a superior numerology for calculating buy and sell points. *Rather, better execution— trade in and trade out—allows the professional trader to obtain better prices when entering and exiting trades.* Part of this execution advantage is having the right trading platform and speedy connections to the exchanges. The other part is superior reaction times. The expert trader, quick to recognize when buying or selling is waning, rapidly translates this perception into an action pattern, entering or exiting a market a tick ahead of slower colleagues. That extra tick of execution, compounded over the course of many trades and repeated daily, is more than enough to account for superior trading results.

Over the course of sustained deliberative practice, the expert trader gains the perceptual advantages that we noticed among chess players in the Chase and Simon research. Seeing the trading landscape in meaningful chunks of information, elite traders build mental maps that combine these chunks into patterns that can be readily acted upon. The emergency room physician looks at a set of injuries and vital signs and quickly makes triage decisions: This patient goes into surgery; this one receives CPR now; this one should receive painkillers and be admitted for observation. In the doctor's head is a scheme with the categories routine, urgent, and emergent. Quick evaluations, supported by many observations of different cases, determine whether a patient will be treated later, soon, or immediately.

A review of research with athletes conducted by Williams and Starkes found that, across a variety of sports, skilled performers utilize advance perceptual cues earlier than novices. Placed in a laboratory environment and shown brief film snippets from actual sporting events, skilled athletes can more quickly identify a player's next move than novice athletes. For example, elite tennis players more quickly detect the likely location of an opponent's shot based upon cues from the positioning of the opponent's shoulder and racket. This allows the skilled player to move into position more quickly than the novice, ensuring a greater number of successful returns. Similarly, elite baseball hitters more quickly pick up on the delivery of a pitch; skilled quarterbacks rapidly read shifts in the opposing team's defense. Each of these perceptions is tied to a response pattern, enabling the performer to rapidly exploit the situation.

Notice the overlap between the researcher's conclusions and the characteristics of implicit learning that we encountered earlier. Cleeremans and colleagues found that implicit learning is actually an acquisition of knowledge about the statistical structure of events. Williams and Starkes, writing in a completely different field, find that experts possess knowledge about situational probabilities that guide their actions. Thus, for instance, the tennis player can make reasonable probabilistic assessments of the location of a hit ball based upon the movements of the opponent. This accounts for an interesting finding from the research: Not only do expert players make more accurate assessments of ball location, they are also more confident in their assessments than nonexperts.

Let's take a look at how this applies to trading. One of the expert traders from Kingstree that I introduced earlier is Scott Pulcini. As a short-term trader of the S&P E-mini futures market, Scott rapidly enters and exits positions, making hundreds of trades and trading thousands of contracts daily. In recent years, it has not been unusual for him to personally account for several percent of the entire volume in that very liquid marketplace. To move in and out of trades in a matter of seconds, he needs to process large amounts of information quickly and accurately. His generosity in allowing me to observe his trading while he talks aloud about his thought processes has provided a valuable window on the mind of an expert.

Scott's talk-aloud processing of the market mirrors the findings of Williams and Starkes. He has a very detailed knowledge base specific to his market. He knows the major traders and trading patterns of the market and uses this information to make sense out of what others would find to be random ("Locals are the only ones in this market, and they keep selling"). Scott also can read orders and trades coming into the market and pick up subtle cues about their size and prices to provide an anticipatory sense of buying and selling likely to come. A very common occurrence when I'm following Scott on my risk screen is that he'll enter a position and I'll glance at my charts to see what's happening in the market at that moment. It looks like a bad entry to me, so I go back to the screen—only to find that Scott has already flipped his position and made a couple of ticks. In the time it took me to process his position, check it against my read of the market, and look back at his position, he had already peeled out of his trade and initiated a new one based on fresh market information.

A major factor behind his speed, noted by Williams and Starkes, is that many of his action patterns are automatic. He has learned that, when he sees X, he should do Y. The X-Y linkage, repeated many times across varying conditions, becomes part of his instincts. My explicit processing cannot hope to keep up with such automatic, implicit thinking.

Many expert traders, of course, are not moving in and out of markets with the rapidity of a Scott Pulcini. Nonetheless, they display the essential characteristics of Williams and Starkes's ballplayers. They exhibit specialized knowledge bases and rapidly process large amounts of information in real time to arrive at quick, accurate assessments. Their ability to respond to events is the result of highly refined perceptual and cognitive processes that evolve through varied and repeated exposure to different market conditions.

Practice makes permanent: Repeated, challenging experience creates fundamental changes in the way we perceive, think, and act.

THE ROLE OF MENTORING IN EXPERTISE

Recall the research of Bloom and colleagues, in which they found that expertise progresses through a series of stages. In the earliest stage, mentors play a supportive role, teaching basic skills and sustaining the student's motivation. As the student's talent becomes obvious, mentorship enters a second phase. Practice is more structured and regular, with an emphasis on the development of competence. For example, an early-stage mentor might be a Little League baseball coach; a mentor in the middle phase could be a high school coach.

During competence development, some performers stand out as unusually talented. They learn skills quickly and rapidly adapt these to a variety of situations. Frequently they are singled out by their coaches as being promising prospects for future development. At that point, a third phase of mentorship kicks in, devoted to the cultivation of expertise. This is when the performer begins working with a Dean Smith in basketball, a Nick Bollettieri in tennis, a Dan Gable in wrestling, or an Olympic trainer. Under the tutelage of an expert trainer, the student now faces new and higher levels of demand. Practice is for hours a day, working intensively on highly challenging drills. Mere competence is no longer the focus. World-class expectations are the norm.

This has been a common feature of every successful trader I've known: Success is followed by higher expectations. The really good traders are so competitive that they do not stay content for long. It is not at all unusual for traders I've worked with to make five or even six figures in a day and tell me that they traded poorly. This is not modesty or perfectionism. It is a reflection of expectations at elite levels of performance.

Lauren Sosniak, a researcher for Bloom's University of Chicago team, concludes that the most crucial step in the transition from competence to expertise is work with a master instructor. Such mentors are distinguished by their expectations for their performers, at times demanding all that was humanly possible of their students. Recall Ericsson's point that expert performers are always moving beyond the skill levels that become automatic in their repertoire—that is the only way they can develop further. This is why a Navy SEALs training program will not just ask recruits to assemble a weapon; they will insist that it be done underwater in a requisite time frame. Expert mentors are battleproofers: They place their students under levels of demand that elicit extraordinary adaptations. They are catalysts of personal evolution.

These adaptations, we've seen, include radical changes of perception, cognition, and behavior. Having been tested under the most extreme conditions, experts develop ways of automatically responding to situations that would freeze the majority of individuals. The magazine *Trader Monthly* recently published a story about activist hedge fund manager Bob Chapman. On an excursion to the Cambodian jungle, he was confronted with a pack of wild, aggressive apes. Seeing that the apes were baring their teeth and were ready to pounce, Chapman went into a sprint—right at the apes, growling loudly and showing his teeth. The apes, no doubt startled at the unaccustomed sight, fled. I suspect I was not the only reader with the reaction: Only a great trader would think to do that. As Chapman emphasizes later in the article, those reflexes were drilled into him by an aggressive mentor who routinely chewed his head off. "But because of that," Chapman explains, "I am a far better trader" (page 79).

At the level of expertise, mentors need to be familiar not only with the basic skills of the performance field, but also the nuances. As Bloom's research group found, this means working on performance at a high level of technical detail. Chris Carmichael, Lance Armstrong's cycling coach, helps Lance by breaking sprinting down into four elements: explosive acceleration, high top-end speed, high pedal cadence, and overspeed (riding at speeds greater than normal, such as downhill). Each of these facets of sprinting is accompanied by specific drills, with Carmichael and other coaches observing these carefully to make adjustments in technique.

Nick Bollettieri works with expert tennis players by following detailed statistics on their games. For instance, he may find that a player is returning a high percentage of first serves but losing a high percentage of points when the opponent is serving. This suggests to Bollettieri that the player is returning the serve to the center of the court, where the opponent can readily dominate play. He thus works with the player on specialized drills to rehearse the placement of returned serves.

By the time skilled performers begin work with a mentor to develop expertise, their motivation to excel has been established. As Bloom's group found, most elite coaches will not take on a student unless such motivation has been internalized. This is not merely the will to win, as Bob Knight emphasizes, but the will to prepare to win. And yet, as we've seen, it's not just about will. Elite performers draw upon extreme effort to generate the flow state, making normal hard work look like hardly working. *Once that internal drive is present, the mentor's role changes from that of motivator to that of performance tuner.* If you're coaching a wrestler like Dan Gable, you don't need to keep him focused or disciplined. You might, however, need to help him scout his upcoming opponent, recognize the opponent's lesser upper body strength, and develop a plan and set of tactics to exploit this advantage. Similarly, I don't need to encourage expert traders to make money. I do, however, have to help them recognize that trading conditions have changed due to developments in leading, correlated markets, such as oil, necessitating a tactical shift. Such shifts do not come easily or naturally;

it is difficult to change something that has been making you money. The mentor's role, however, is to help expert traders avoid the comfort of the automatic and sustain the far more rewarding gratification that comes from expanding mastery.

How do mentors help expert performers? One way is by serving as role models for high-level information processing and reasoning. Matt Ford, faculty member at Northern Kentucky University and dean of the University of Minyanville online education effort to train traders, observes, "Knowledge that is difficult to codify defies transfer by conventional classroom means. Instead, vicarious learning processes, where learners observe the behavior of expert models . . . have proven to be an effective way to transfer tacit knowledge." His goal with the university is to enable traders to "peer into the thought processes of experts in real time" to advance skill development.

If successful, the Minyanville effort will achieve what researcher Timothy Salthouse calls the "circumvention of human processing limitations." Contrary to the advertisements common in the popular media, trading expertise is not a function of possessing a superior indicator, mind-set, or chart pattern. Expert traders process market information differently from nonexperts, cultivating sophisticated mental maps that enable them to eliminate irrelevant information and implicitly process the patterns amid the market noise. Armed with such maps, expert traders respond more rapidly, confidently, and accurately to market events than do nonexperts. In the coming chapters, we will explore how traders can circumvent their own processing limitations by systematically observing and altering their trading and emotional patterns.

CHAPTER 6

Mechanics, Tactics, Strategies

Climbing the Performance Pyramid

People come out to see you perform and you've got to give them the best you have within you. The lives of most men are patchwork quilts. Or at best one matching outfit with a closet and laundry bag full of incongruous accumulations. A lifetime of training for just ten seconds.

—Jesse Owens

It was the Big Ten meet and it looked as though Ohio State University's star would not be able to perform. Having fallen down a flight of stairs during the week prior to the event, Jesse Owens received treatment but continued to experience back pain. He talked his coach into allowing him to run the 100-yard dash and, amazingly, tied the world record at the time: 9.4 seconds. Just 15 minutes later, he participated in the broad jump. With an audacity and confidence reminiscent of Babe Ruth, Owens placed a handkerchief at the world record distance and proceeded to beat the record by almost six inches. Shortly thereafter he participated in the 220-yard dash and the 220-yard low hurdles. He not only won both of those events, but set new world records as well. In all, Jesse Owens set three world records and tied a fourth one in the span of 45 minutes—while in pain. The following year he would participate in the 1936 Olympics and become the first American to win four gold medals in a single year.

Jesse Owens had raw talent and the lifetime of training that prepared him for the 10 seconds of a 100-yard dash. Yet he also had mental edges: a resilience that allowed him to play through the pain and an unshakable confidence in his own skill. He displayed an emotional toughness that was every bit as impressive as his physical conditioning. Instinctively, we recognize that the ferocious confidence and competitiveness of a Muhammad Ali, Michael Jordan, Lance Armstrong, or Dan Gable make these performers different from their competitors, who may have had bodies that were equal, but not the hearts. How do expert performers develop an elite psychology? Can such a mental framework be acquired? To those questions, we now turn.

SUCCESS AND THE MECHANICS OF PERFORMANCE

An expert performer is one who is mechanically sound. By that I mean that the performer executes the right actions, the right way, with consistency. A mechanically sound automotive manufacturing plant turns out the same highly reliable cars the same way every day. Variability is the enemy: The goal is consistent execution. The reason franchise restaurants such as McDonald's have training programs and manuals of operating procedures is that they strive for consistency across restaurants. This ensures that customers will receive the same Big Mac and dining experience in Missoula, Montana, as in Mobile, Alabama. The good surgeon is one who makes the same clean, accurate cuts the same way for all patients; the good parent is not just loving and caring, but consistently so.

Elite performers display remarkable mechanical soundness. When Wendy Whelan, the noted ballerina for the New York City Ballet, was photographed by her husband-to-be, he noticed something striking. Different photos of her performing the same leap looked identical. The turn of her head, the angle of her feet—all were precisely the same, time and again. Tiger Woods's biographer, Bill Gutman, reports that tests on Tiger's swing showed that he made contact at the dead center of the club with remarkable consistency. Each of his swings was at what scientists consider the ideal angle: nine degrees. Nolan Ryan reports that he studied videotapes of his delivery while he was pitching for Houston, poring over computer analyses to correct small errors that made a pitching difference, such as leaning forward while lifting his left leg and opening his hips too soon. His pitching motion was broken down into checkpoints: performance elements that he had to execute the same way with each pitch. One checkpoint, for instance, was bringing his leg up to shoulder level before starting any movement to the plate; a second check was not releasing the ball until his lift leg had reached the ground. The combination of these movements ensured that his body was closely tucked during his windup—concealing his pitch as long as possible—and his release would have maximum forward momentum.

Like Tiger and Nolan, Ted Williams dominated his sport by the consistent application of proper mechanics. He stood with his feet 27 inches apart, held his bat nearly perpendicular to the ground, and cocked his hips as he strode forward. His bat had to be a precise weight—not an ounce more or less. In his book *The Science of Hitting*, he tells the story that he was once given six bats by the Louisville Slugger company, one of which was half an ounce heavier than the others. Blindfolded, Williams picked out the heavier bat. He was tuned for precision.

The poor trader is one who, given a setup with a demonstrated edge, will trade it differently each time it occurs. Sometimes the trader will catch the setup, sometimes not. Occasionally the trade will be with large size, other times not. The entry will be late at times, early at others. With such variation in execution, ticks are lost. At $12.50 per tick on the ES contract, for example, this may not seem like a steep price to pay. Multiplied by the number of contracts traded each day and roughly 250 days in a year, you can see how inconsistency becomes expensive. Just one tick lost per trade for someone who trades two lots twice a day ends up costing $12,500 per year, or 8 percent of a $100,000 portfolio.

Some traders create consistency by generating rules, much as Nolan Ryan created his pitching checkpoints. The rules may be broad and simple—trade only in the direction of the day's price trend—or they might be more concrete: exit the position when the five-minute volume at your stop price exceeds the volume registered in the previous five minutes. The advantage of rules is that they allow you to review performance—much as Ryan examined videotape—to see where your trading might be less than mechanically sound. Rules, like the restaurant guidelines at McDonald's, create an ideal by which performance can be gauged.

When trading is discretionary and subjective, it is more difficult to evaluate the soundness of mechanics, but it's not impossible. When working with traders, I observe how they put on and take off positions, how often they trade, and where they tend to place their trades. I create a model in my mind of how each trader trades when he or she is making money. That model, for me, is like the set of rules: It provides a yardstick by which I can assess a trader's performance.

Recall Marc Greenspoon, the expert trader at Kingstree. Many of his best trades are breakout trades, in which a rangebound market will explode to higher or lower price levels. Marc's best entries are near this point of breakout—and often slightly after the break initially occurs. When he enters far from the point of breakout, predicting the move rather than identifying it, he is much less likely to be successful. Often, all I need to do to help Marc is simply hold the metaphorical mirror to his mechanics. The model I've built while observing him becomes a set of ideals that he can use to assess his own performance.

Scott Pulcini, however, possesses a very different kind of expertise. He rapidly enters and exits the marketplace and rarely has a directional bias. When he is trading soundly, he is quickly scaling out of both winning and losing trades. He is looking for steady, repetitive small gains rather than the explosive profits of breakout moves. When Scott does not scale out of losing trades as fast as winning ones, he can have more profitable trades than losers but still not make money. His mechanics, like Nolan Ryan's, then need an adjustment—perhaps one as simple as making tighter exit criteria explicit at the time trades are entered. Many times, the mechanical corrections that traders need are small shifts that, repeated over time, accumulate into large performance effects. Ted Williams demonstrated how the difference between his being an average .250 hitter and a hall-of-fame .400 hitter was the ability to lay off pitches low and away in the strike zone. Excellent traders also know when to lay off certain markets and actively participate in others, when to work orders and when to go at the market.

> Great results come from small improvements that are implemented with consistency.

When you are mentoring yourself as a trader, you are tasked with the responsibility of monitoring your own mechanics. This is not easy. It is difficult to see oneself from a neutral, objective vantage point. After writing segments of this book, I need to put the manuscript away for a while and then return to it as a reader. That allows me to identify sections that are unclear, poorly written, or insufficiently engaging. I cannot appreciate those deficiencies while I am writing, and if I tried to do so, I would wind up with a severe case of writer's block. *Similarly, traders cannot monitor their performance for mechanics while they are engaging in the very behaviors that need to be automatic.* Like me, they need to put their trading aside and examine it from a different, neutral perspective. Thankfully, there are specific tools that provide this perspective.

IMPROVING TRADING MECHANICS: THE TRADING GYMNASIUM

Videorecording, journaling, and the gathering of trading metrics are the strategies that I have found to be most helpful to the improvement of trader mechanics. In combination, and used with historical as well as live trading, they form what I call the trading gymnasium. A gym, of course, is a place where athletes can work on aspects of their conditioning. A weight room has various machines and stations, allowing users to work out very specific muscle groups. Similarly, running machines are highly flexible. They enable users to maintain an ideal sustained heart rate for maximum aerobic efficiency, but also allow runners to vary their routines and maintain their interest.

Every performance field has its gymnasium, allowing performers to work on their mechanics. The gym for a professional dancer is a practice room with a teacher, mirrors, bar, and partners. A chess champion might utilize a sophisticated computer program as a gym, testing out strategies, recording the results, and reviewing them for tweaking. The jazz musician gigs regularly not merely for enjoyment or revenue, but also to work on rhythm, timing, and improvisational skill.

Gyms build performance by honing mechanics. The racetrack is the gym for pit crews that work on the Winston Cup teams. These teams are models of consistent mechanics: Under the pressure of racing competition and amid the considerable dangers of the job, they change four tires and refuel a car in roughly 13 seconds. Each member of the team needs different skills. As Breon Klopp, Director of Development for the PIT Performance Program, notes, the tire carriers have excellent hand-eye coordination; the jack man is quick, with superior upper body strength to gain leverage. Teams practice with a stopwatch to improve their coordination and shave precious seconds from their times. Because pit work involves repair as well as maintenance, crew members must be ready to quickly assess and fix car problems as they occur. This means that, at any given time, you have many professionals swarming over the car once it pulls into the pit. The mechanics of good crew work involve not only performing one's own skills efficiently and accurately, but doing so in a way that causes minimal interference for other crew members. Simple elements, such as how a jack man positions his body and where a carrier sets his tires, become crucial in a field where every added second translates into car lengths of performance lost. Team rehearsals on the racetrack, under the watchful eye of a crew chief, provide the gymnasiums that enable crews to master the mechanics of performance, making the extraordinary automatic.

Novice traders tend to think of trading merely as the acts of buying and selling. They don't recognize the considerable role that mechanics play in success. Reducing trading to buying and selling is like describing NASCAR racing as stopping and going. Before we launch into the specifics of a trading gymnasium, take a look at just a few of the mechanics of trading and the difference they make toward profitability. Obviously, some of these mechanics will be more relevant for some traders than for others, given differences in trading niches. (See Exhibit 6.1.) Clearly, trading is not a skill, but rather a complex, coordinated set of skills not unlike athletics or medical practice.

An inexperienced trader will look at a chart and say, "I think we're going higher." He will then buy at the market with his maximum position size and see if the trade works out. Once it goes his way, he may or may not take profits. If it goes against him, he will get out when he is uncomfortable. The trades are neither planned nor systematic in their execution. The performance is not far different from that of a chess player who gets it in his head, "I think I'll move my queen right now."

Expert traders make a distinction between making money and trading well. That difference reflects an awareness of mechanics. When traders

---

EXHIBIT 6.1 Specific Skills that Comprise Trading Mechanics

Trading Mechanics

- *Idea development.* Translating observations about the market into specific trade ideas; gathering information the right way to produce useful conclusions.
- *Assessment of market conditions.* Evaluating whether the market is trending, rangebound, volatile, or slow; ensuring that the trade idea is appropriate for the present market.
- *Order placement.* Using the kinds of orders appropriate for market conditions to maximize the likelihood of getting filled at desired prices.
- *Order location.* Selecting prices for orders that correspond to turning points in supply and demand, thereby minimizing drawdowns and maximizing opportunity.
- *Order division.* Scaling into positions to reduce initial risk exposure and obtain superior average entry prices; scaling out of positions to secure profits and benefit from favorable movement.
- *Position sizing.* Risking enough on a trade to make a meaningful contribution to profitability while avoiding risk of ruin under adverse circumstances.
- *Position diversification.* Spreading risks among uncorrelated trades so as to benefit from market participation but limit risk exposure; selecting trading instruments most likely to benefit from the trade ideas.
- *Exit determination.* Defining clear criteria for when your trade ideas are wrong; implementing proper stops to manage the risk exposure of each trade.
- *Exit flexibility.* Moving stop-loss points to protect profits while retaining profit potential.
- *Speed of execution.* Making and implementing decisions rapidly.
- *Accuracy of execution.* Minimizing errors in order placement.
- *Efficiency of information processing.* Monitoring relevant variables in real time to properly manage trades.

like Scott and Marc say they traded well, they do not necessarily mean that they made a lot of money. They mean that they were fundamentally sound. Mechanics are rarely glamorous, but they account for a surprising degree of profitability. I have watched expert active traders sit patiently working an order in the book just to get a position filled at a desired price. The position was worth entering one tick below the market, not any higher. Similarly, I've seen excellent traders scale into trades as their confidence in the trade idea waxes, reducing their initial risk exposure at the same time that they exploit opportunity. On any given day, these mechanics may spare a trader one bad trade or add a few ticks to a good one. Over time, however, they can make the difference between profit and loss, just as the pit crew's seconds—over the course of a race—can determine the lead position and create a clear path for their driver. Mechanics are the building blocks of multiplier effects in performance.

WHERE THE GYMNASIUM BEGINS: OBSERVATION

You cannot work on your performance without having an eye for good mechanics and poor ones. Before you utilize the equipment in the gym, it's important to figure out what you're working on.

Carl was a trader who didn't know what to work on. Relatively new to the markets, he was trading one, two, and three lots following a period of simulated trading. I went into his office and watched him trading NASDAQ Index futures during an unusually slow midday period. The market, to my thinking, was going nowhere. It had been oscillating in a narrow range for quite a few minutes, with no discernable trend. The NQ contract ticked higher, and Carl suddenly purchased a three-lot at the market.

In my best neutral voice I asked, "What's your thought here?"

Carl looked up and said, with as much conviction as he could muster, "We can't seem to go lower."

The trade sat there for a few minutes before the market returned to its earlier level, leaving Carl two ticks in the red. Visibly uncomfortable, he sat in the trade. When it downticked one more time, he exited his three-lot. To my surprise, he expected me to applaud his discipline in quickly exiting a losing trade.

Carl was a study in poor mechanics. Let's play observer and review his shortcomings:

- *He had no real trade idea.* "We're not going lower" is not a firm foundation for a rational wagering of one's trading stake. The reality was that we weren't going anywhere, as long as the market was trading a few dozen contracts per minute on average. Without a valid trade idea, he had no edge in the marketplace.

- *He gave up the edge needlessly.* In a slow market, there was no urgency to getting in. If he had a valid reason to enter the market, he could have worked a bid and gained a tick simply by being patient. Instead, he took the offer after the market had already ticked higher, exposing him to those who had worked bids and now could take their scalping profits.
- *He wagered impulsively.* A good trending market will give multiple opportunities for entry, making it easy to scale into a trade even if you do have to go at the market as the trade picks up on a breakout. Entering with his maximum position exposed Carl to maximum risk before he had an opportunity to see if the position would move his way.
- *He exited emotionally.* Instead of exiting when the trade didn't go his way, he exited when it went against him. If his trade was truly predicated on a breakout move or surge of buying, it should have gone his way promptly. Instead, he waited until it reached his pain threshold before exiting.
- *He did not process information effectively.* At no time during Carl's trade was there evidence of bidders entering the order book or lifting offers in size. He failed to see bidders cancel their orders prior to the market moving against him, so he could not exit quickly.

Carl was a beginning trader, and problems with mechanics are certainly expectable among beginners. Interestingly, however, I've seen seasoned traders with some of the same problems of trading mechanics. Sometimes, as we will see later in the book, the flaws in mechanics are due to emotional factors. A trader, for example, might be pressing too hard to make money at the end of a difficult month and impulsively put on a trade without either clearly identifying an edge or waiting for a good price. Other times, the flawed mechanics represent bad habits learned over a trading career. Traders, for example, will place stops several ticks away from the market without looking at current volatility. In many markets with good movement, three ticks represent random movement: A single large order from an institutional participant can result in the hitting of a stop. This doesn't necessarily mean that the fundamental trade idea was incorrect.

My goal in working with traders such as Carl is to enable them to become keen observers of their own mechanics. This means emphasizing trade execution as much as overall profitability, and it means placing emphasis on the management of trades, from position sizing through exits. The majority of traders want to think about trades as things: events that are either profitable or not profitable. The mechanics approach to performance, however, views trades as *processes. It's not just what you do, but how you do it that matters to a mechanics-oriented mentor.*

Profitability is a function of good trading, not just good trades.

AN OBSERVATION CHECKLIST

What do you look for when observing your trading mechanics? Drawing upon the experience with Carl, here are a few considerations:

▶ *Did I have a well-formed trade idea?* Did my idea fit with market conditions during the time frame in which I was trading and one time frame above? Did it fit with what correlated markets were doing at that time? Did it fit with the supply and demand I was noticing in the marketplace? Was my idea consistent with my overall trading strategy and my strategy for that trading day?

▶ *Did I get into the trade at a good price?* How much heat did I take on the trade right away? If I entered at the market, did the position promptly go my way, or could I have gotten a better price by working an order? If I worked an order, did I get filled? If not, did I get into the trade near enough to my bailout level to maintain a good relationship between risk and reward on the trade? Did I enter at a price that enabled me to take maximum advantage of my trade idea?

▶ *Was my position sizing appropriate for my risk management?* Was I risking an amount on the trade that would not unduly damage my P/L for the day/week/month, or was I at risk of digging myself a hole if the trade went against me? Did I scale into the trade to minimize initial risk and see if the position would move my way, or did I expose myself to maximum risk before seeing how the market took my order?

▶ *Was I in the right instrument(s) to maximize my trade idea(s) and minimize my risk?* Was my risk diversified by trading multiple ideas, multiple instruments, and multiple time frames? Did I ensure that my trades were uncorrelated, or was I really betting the farm on a single idea or instrument? Did I assess and exploit the specific markets and instruments most likely to benefit from my trade ideas? Were my trade ideas independent of one another, or was I getting locked into an opinion about the market?

▶ *Did I clearly identify exit criteria that told me my trade idea was wrong?* Did I know in advance what would take me out of my trade, or did I exit when I had taken too much drawdown and the pain became too great? Did I identify that the trade was not going my way before I took a loss, or did I use the loss to tell me that the trade hadn't gone my way? Did I move my stop-loss point to protect profits in trades, or did I let winners become losers? Did I scale out of the trade to protect profits, or did I go for the home run and leave paper profits unduly exposed to risk?

► *Did I closely monitor the market during my trade to ensure that the supply/demand conditions that got me into the trade were still operative* Was I actively monitoring the market while the trade was on, or was I passively observing? Was I looking for opportunities to scale in or out based on market conditions, or was I not managing the trade? Did I actively reevaluate the risk/reward of the trade, or did I stay locked in my initial assessment?

These mechanics are to trading what footwork and stance are to boxing, what screening, boxing out, and passing are to basketball. They are different from tactics. Tactics tell you what to do and when to do it. Tactics are actions derived from a broader strategy. *Mechanics are the fundamentals that you execute regardless of your tactics.* Tactics dictate whether a basketball team plays a zone defense or man-to-man, whether it pushes the ball upcourt or sets up specific plays. Mechanics are the basics: staying in front of the ball when guarding the dribbler, moving without the ball, and so on. *Strategy and tactics ensure that we're doing the right thing; mechanics ensure that we do things the right way.*

The field is the gym for Army Rangers, as they conduct mock missions and drill basic skills until their mechanics are automatic. Following the simulated missions, there are after-action reviews, in which instructors go over what the teams—and their individuals—did right and wrong. The preceding checklist is a kind of after-action review for the trader: a set of criteria by which you can examine your own performance. *Your goal is to turn each of the checklist behaviors into a habit pattern by performing it again and again in the same way each time.* Good trading fundamentals are not a function of discipline but habit. You want to get to the point where you are entering and exiting trades the way you wash yourself and brush your teeth in the morning, not the way you try to make yourself include enough veggies in your diet.

THE MECHANICS OF RISK MANAGEMENT

Notice how many of the mechanics outlined here boil down to proper risk management. It amazes me that the majority of traders I come in contact with do not understand the risks they are incurring and how these line up with respect to potential reward. More traders blow up, I find, because they fail to hold the downside on a small number of occasions than because of consistent losing. It is not at all unusual to find traders who win more days than they lose, only to be down money at the end of a month or year. This can occur only if the average size of losing trades exceeds that of winners.

Academic studies tell us that returns from most trading instruments do not form a normal distribution. Rather, they possess "fat tails": more extreme occurrences than would be expected if returns followed the normal pattern. That means that extreme rises or declines of three, four, or five standard deviations are bound to occur, regardless of the time frame. In October 1987 and again in October 1997, we saw downside examples of such extreme returns. The start of the bull markets in August 1982 and March 2003 gave us examples of extreme upside returns. What makes these occasions dangerous is that they tend to cluster. This is known as *serial correlation*: Volatility tends to be followed by volatility. In a trending market, you can get several extreme upside or downside days in a row. Without proper risk management, these markets can blow out a trader.

In his book *Trading Risk*, Kenneth Grant recommends that traders limit their risk to a fixed percentage of their portfolios. Recall an earlier example: If you have a trading approach that is correct 60 percent of the time, you will encounter losers on 40 percent of trades, ignoring commissions and other costs. Your probability of encountering four straight losing trades is 40 percent to the fourth power or around 2.5 percent. If you trade frequently, this is bound to occur more than once a year. If you lose anything close to 10 percent on each of those occasions, you will severely dent your account, forcing you to make 67 percent on the remaining capital just to return to breakeven.

Another crucial aspect to the survival of market risk is the size of one's portfolio. One is better able to survive runs of losses on reasonable bets if those bets are a small fraction of one's total bankroll. Indeed, Victor Niederhoffer, in his book *The Education of a Speculator*, observes that a player who starts with $1.00 and tries to run it to $10.00 will face a 66.1 percent chance of ruin, even if the odds of winning each play are 60 percent. One needs more than a $4.00 bankroll to justify the pursuit of $10.00—even with favorable, 60/40 odds. It's not difficult to see how, without proper risk management and with a small bankroll, most beginning traders are doomed to failure.

Of course, this analysis does not take into account trader psychology. Faced with two or three consecutive large losers, many traders veer from proper mechanics. They second-guess their trading methods, add to their size to try to make their money back, or trade more frequently to recoup losses. The result is that what started as a 60–40 proposition with reasonable risk parameters is now a random coin toss with excessive risk. Under these conditions, I have seen traders lose months' worth of profits in a single day. It is difficult, financially and emotionally, to recover from such trauma.

If one follows the fundamentally sound advice of Grant and calculates one's maximum daily loss as a fixed fraction of portfolio size, it then follows that trading sizes will shrink as losses are incurred and expand during profitable times. This has the natural advantage of making traders trade smaller when they're losing and larger when they are trading well—a kind of trend following, in which trader performance provides the trend. The reality, however, is that risk remains constant. You are betting the same *proportion* of your portfolio on a 60–40 proposition during good times and bad.

> A surprising proportion of emotional problems in trading can be traced to improper risk management.

In my own trading I have made the rule that I want to survive, relatively intact, eight straight days of maximum drawdown. If I set that drawdown at 3 percent of portfolio value, at the end of my debacle I will still have over three-quarters of my capital intact. If I move the maximum daily drawdown to 5 percent, my account balance after those consecutive losses will now be cut by one-third. I will need a 50 percent gain simply to break even—not the less than 30 percent needed under the original scenario. For my own mental health, given my risk tolerance, I do not want a 50 percent drawdown. Ever. That means that my drop-dead level is going to be much closer to 3 percent than to 5 percent if I am not hedged. (Clearly, a hedged portfolio can sustain a greater degree of market exposure than one that is unhedged.)

Proper mechanics applied to risk management means knowing one's risk per trade, risk per day, and maximum allowable risk. These will dictate order placement, order size, and the setting of stop-loss points. There is a reason why so many institutional investors trade hedged portfolios. With proper hedges, you minimize event risks, from unforeseen market moves to unanticipated news events. Portfolio managers are also diversified, meaning that they spread their risk across uncorrelated trades. Most individual traders think in terms of market positions, not market portfolios. As a result, they are far more exposed to risk than their institutional counterparts. Very often, they attempt to control this exposure by limiting their holding times. This, however, can be deceptive. If you limit holding times to a matter of minutes, you are at the mercy of large traders who can push the market up or down in thin markets. Frequent trades with tighter stops can be as risky as holding positions without stops. One leads to death by a thousand random cuts; the other ends in sudden death with a single adverse market move.

Grant, who has managed risk for professional traders at hedge funds, concludes that 99.99 percent of traders, over the course of a career, will experience drawdowns of large magnitude. My personal strategy is to assume that I will get smoked at some point in time and trade in such a way that I will always stay in the game. This may not be as sexy as swinging large size, but it does wonders for the psyche and the account statement. As with the other mechanics, the key is making the elements of risk management—position sizing, stops, and so on—as automatic as possible. Like Tiger Woods or Ted Williams, you want your swing to be the same one, properly executed time and time again.

Advice from the shrink: Identify the level of loss (per trade, per day, per week, etc.) that would prove emotionally upsetting to you and set your risk parameters well within that level. You cannot have trading consistency if you do not have emotional consistency.

MECHANIZING THE SKILLS THAT SUPPORT TACTICAL DECISIONS

The best mechanics cannot make traders profitable if their tactics are flawed. Someone who is selling a strong market but placing and managing orders well, will lose less money than a selling trader who is fundamentally unsound, but he or she will lose money nonetheless. While poor mechanics can undermine good trade ideas, good mechanics in and of themselves do not provide opportunity. If a trade idea does not exploit supply/demand imbalances in a particular time frame, it will not pay out, no matter how well it is implemented.

Traders are increasingly finding that proper tactics require an investment in technology. When Jon Markman began his career in stock selection and financial journalism, one of his first steps was to spearhead the development of the MSN Money StockScouter, which screens the market for stocks that meet a variety of technical, fundamental, and institutional ownership criteria. Without sophisticated screening tools, it is unlikely that he could dig deeply enough into the market to find high-performance stocks that are off the beaten path. Similarly, David Aferiat, managing partner for the Trade Ideas screening software, recently emphasized to me that "good technology will help a trader level the playing field" against more experienced and better capitalized market participants. He likens the Trade Ideas program, which creates multitiered screens that update in real time, to a deep-sea voyager. If the sea life at a particular market depth is not interesting, the technology allows the trader to move to a different depth and uncover previously unseen life. Just as the military utilizes satellite photography and electronic intelligence gathering for decision support, traders can expand their cognitive capacities with the assistance of such screening tools.

The best performers also study their opponents and use their observations to shape their tactics. Dan Gable writes about videotaping opponents to learn about their strengths and weaknesses. He also advocates studying statistics to evaluate opponents. Nolan Ryan similarly studied the tendencies of batters, just as Ted Williams knew what to expect from pitchers. Chess grandmasters study the games of tournament opponents; basketball coaches spend considerable time watching their foes' game films to find weaknesses to exploit and strengths to prepare for. Just like Rangers conducting reconnaissance and using the information to guide an attack, expert traders adapt their tactics to current market conditions.

In *The Psychology of Trading*, I used the case of Muhammad Ali fighting George Foreman as an example of a rapid tactical shift. Ali, facing Foreman in the heat and humidity of the outdoor arena in Zaire, began the "Rumble in the Jungle" by taking the offensive, utilizing his greater hand and foot speed. By the end of the first round, however, he realized that he could not keep up this pace for the entire fight. Nor could he keep the stronger Foreman off him. Reversing tactics, he adopted a defensive posture later to be known as the "rope-a-dope" and allowed Foreman to take the offensive, periodically taunting his rival and showing that he couldn't be hurt. Eventually, Foreman wore himself down in the Zaire heat, creating the opportunity for Ali's dramatic knockout. Ali's rapid processing was not so different from the shifts that traders might make upon detecting a breakout move. Once they see that fading the edges of a range no longer is working and volume is entering the market to push it beyond those extremes, they switch tactics and jump aboard the developing move.

Here is a simple example from my own trading. One of my most important tactical decisions of the trading day is whether or not to trade and, if I do trade, whether to do so cautiously or aggressively. To make these decisions, I rely upon predictive models for anticipating the volatility of the coming trading day. Some of the inputs to these models include the volatility of the prior day, the volume and volatility of the overnight trading range, the market behavior of the European averages prior to the U.S. open, and the volume during the market's opening periods. If the models suggest a low-volatility day, I am unlikely to trade a trend-following mode— low-volatility markets tend to be rangebound ones—and I am unlikely to trade actively. My tactics will be to identify spots near the edges of the market range where buying or selling cannot sustain a breakout and then enter at a price that allows me to benefit from a movement back into the trading range. Should the models indicate the likelihood of a high-volatility day, I will operate in a short-term trending mode and exploit pullbacks in rising markets or bounces in weak ones.

Much of my market reconnaissance is conducted as historical studies of market behavior. These analyses follow a consistent pattern that I have drilled daily. (See Exhibit 6.2.) This pattern is to find several distinctive features in the present market and then investigate what has typically occurred in the past when those features have been present. Because I have learned which variables in my data set define the most meaningful distinctive pat-

---

EXHIBIT 6.2 Making Tactical Information Gathering Mechanical Through Analysis

---

Using Historical Market Information to Identify Edges in Trading

---

- *Identify what is distinctive about the present market.* Often these will be some kind of extremes, such as a large price movement within a period of time or a very high or low reading from an indicator. The extreme might be on a one-day basis, but often might cover several days.
- *Identify a historical lookback period that is similar to the present market.* If we're in a bull market, I will only include data from the bull market or data from this and recent, similar bull markets. If we're in a low volatility market, I will only include data from this market and ones of similar volatility. You want to see what the market has done historically under conditions similar to the ones faced at present.
- *Determine how the market has behaved when the distinctive events have occurred in the past.* I look for deviations from the sample average in two ways: (1) Does the market move, on average, significantly higher or lower after the distinctive events, and (2) is there a significant difference in the ratio of rising to falling occasions following those distinctive events? I also look to see whether one segment of the market (for instance, small-cap stocks) displays more of a directional bias than other segments following the selected market events. This helps guide my decisions about what to trade.
- *Break the lookback sample into halves based on time.* I want to see if the patterns I've noticed over the entire sample apply to both halves of the sample. If the most recent instances are different from the ones that occurred early in the sample, I need to entertain the possibility that the market is changing its behavior. In general, I will weight the most recent instances more heavily than the more distant ones.
- *Run fresh and independent tests.* I will return to the first step and identify other, independent, distinctive features of the present market, usually on different time frames, and run fresh sets of tests to see if the directional biases from these new models correspond to ones found previously. The best trades will emerge when nonoverlapping analyses point the same way.

terns, I can run these tests efficiently, with a minimum of dead ends. The entire process generally takes under an hour. Once I am finished, the results fit one of three profiles:

1. *There is no edge.* The tests are inconsistent or do not show a distinctive set of expectations going forward. I either will not trade or will trade small and cautiously, relying on patterns that I identify during the trading day.

2. *There is a modest edge.* The combination of tests shows a directional bias, but there is either enough discrepancy among the tests or the results are of sufficiently small magnitude that I will trade the pattern selectively, only if I can get very good prices and carefully manage the downside.

3. *There is a strong edge.* The combination of tests shows a distinct bias for the day, a clear advantage going into the session. This is where I want to be most aggressive and maximize opportunity.

The advantage to this procedure is that it provides me with a road map of expectations for the current day. This is both a psychological advantage and a logical one.

Notice that one of my most crucial tactical decisions is when to not play. If I do not see adequate volume and volatility in the market, I know that the odds of directional movement in my time frame are poor. Rather than widen my time frame and get out of my game, I choose to not play. This is very much like the poker player who begins with 2 and 7 unsuited and decides to muck the hand. Why play if the odds are not on your side? Many of the best traders I've worked with leave the premises around midday when the trade slows down. This serves several functions: (1) It allows them to clear their heads and recoup their concentration, (2) it keeps them away from pursuing trades during times of low opportunity, and (3) it saves their bullets for periods of highest opportunity.

The monitoring of volume and volatility is a way of keeping on top of the issue of how much movement is likely to be in the market. The historical tests are a means of identifying whether there is a directional bias to the expectable movement and which instruments are likely to best capitalize on this movement. Jeff Hirsch, publisher of *The Stock Trader's Almanac*, observes, "Those who study market history are bound to profit from it." The sweet spots for trading, like Ted Williams' sweet spots for hitting, are those where we can expect good movement with a demonstrated directional bias. The pitches to avoid taking are those periods in which little movement can be expected, with no discernable directional edge. *Much of profitability, I've found, is simply staying away from markets and market periods that do not offer a distinct edge.* After all, as *Almanac* founder Yale Hirsch emphasizes, "If you don't profit from your investment mistakes, someone else will."

> How to trade and what to trade are subordinate to when to trade.

When I recently asked Trevor Harnett, developer of the Market Delta program, what he felt was essential to trader performance, he pointed to one of the most important tactical considerations of all: an awareness of the trading environment. "An example of what I mean by 'environment,'" he said, "is simply trending or sideways markets. Many traders lose sight of what type of market they are trading in. . . . This happens so often because traders fail to step back and try to understand how the market is developing as the day progresses." He created Market Delta as a visual representation of the factors—the activity of buyers and sellers—that cause environments to shift, providing traders with a resource to develop their skills at reading changing markets. Such a tool, properly employed, is a device for learning tactics and when to employ them.

Your specific tactics may well differ from mine and Trevor's, requiring a different gathering of information. To the extent, however, that you can break your information gathering down into the kinds of checkpoints described by Nolan Ryan, you turn much of the process of selecting tactics into one of mechanics. The bottom line is that, for any style of trading, there are mechanically sound and unsound ways to gather information and make decisions from the data. When the information used for trading decisions flows from replicable procedures and focuses on essential dimensions of trading, the how to trade (long or short), what to trade (which stocks, sectors, or markets), and when to trade will follow naturally and—as for Ali—rapidly. One mark of a truly expert trader is the ability to rapidly adapt trading tactics to shifting market conditions. When you think about it, this is also a hallmark of expert emergency room physicians, battlefield commanders, and coaches.

WHEN STRATEGY FAILS: PROBLEMS AT THE TOP OF THE PYRAMID

Just as solid mechanics cannot produce profits in the face of improper tactics, the right tactics will not succeed if the overarching strategy is incorrect. Tactics win battles, but strategies win wars. Good tactics will sell a product to a customer, but the company will fail if it is the wrong product for the marketplace or a defective product. Strategy defines opportunity; it is not just about finding edges on given days, but establishing one's *overall* source of edge in the marketplace. Ideally, tactics implement strategy just as mechanics implement tactics. This can be conceptualized as a kind of pyramid. (See Exhibit 6.3.)

Trader problems can occur at any level of the pyramid. Rookies tend to make mechanical and tactical errors simply as a function of lack of experience: They can't find good prices, don't have defined exits, and expose themselves to undue risk. They fail to discern current market conditions and, hence, can't adapt to market changes. When experienced, successful traders make mechanical and tactical mistakes (i.e., trade like rookies), the problem is very often an emotional one and requires hands-on intervention to reestablish control. Those interventions will be covered in our final chapters.

There are times, however, when very successful traders—ones that might have made six or even seven figures for a considerable period—will suddenly go cold for an extended time. Almost always, these are times when strategies fail.

Marcus was a perfect example of such a trader. He made a substantial living trading individual equities and became a minor celebrity on the trading boards. He understood market technicals quite well and developed a style of trading that could be described, loosely, as trend following. What he did was screen for stocks each day that showed upside strength. He would then enter positions in these stocks during the first hour of trading when he saw firmness in the broad market. The strategy made sense, and his tactics—finding good relative strength issues to trade, trade during the most active time of day—were sound. Mechanically, he was careful to not chase stocks for purchase, and he used leverage wisely, spreading trades across different trade ideas. He also shorted weak stocks while buying the strong ones, creating further diversification. In short, he was a solid trader.

The only thing was, he stopped making money.

EXHIBIT 6.3   The Performance Pyramid

One by one, his trades failed to pay him out. He racked his brain to see what he was doing wrong, generating considerable frustration in the process. This only accelerated his decline. It also convinced him that he needed to talk with me.

One of the most difficult challenges facing a mentor is deciding whether a problem is primarily an emotional one interfering with performance or a performance problem generating emotional fallout. The two are closely connected, and there is a dynamic interplay between emotions and performance. Nonetheless, deciphering chicken and egg is crucial. Substantial time and effort can be wasted by working on psychological strategies when the problem is ultimately one of trading mechanics, tactics, or strategy.

I performed a little research on Marcus' strategy, and here is what I found. The universe of stocks from which he placed trades increased their average daily trading volume over time. Many were members of the Russell 2000 small stock universe; many were also high beta NASDAQ issues. Their increase in trading volume reflected, in part, the growing popularity of those sectors. I noticed that, as the volume in these sectors grew, their short-term price correlations to the large stock indices increased. Small and medium-sized stocks began trading more similarly to stocks in the Dow and S&P 500 averages. My best guess is that this was due partially to increased arbitrage trading that kept market indices and sectors in line with one another.

As volatility left the large-capitalization indices from 2003 to 2005, this loss of movement affected NASDAQ and smaller stock indices as well. It was clear that strength in the large stocks, in the near term, tended to reverse rather than continue, creating trading ranges across time frames. My research suggested that, as smaller stocks gained correlation with their larger counterparts, they also began trading in a countertrend style. Strength no longer begat strength.

Marcus's problem was not a psychological one. It was one of strategy. His perception was that the market had changed. It was as if a lightbulb had been turned off—what once worked no longer did. This was not an exaggerated perception. The strategy indeed did work at one time, and now, because of different participation in the marketplace, it no longer provided an edge. Working on improving his psychology would not help his P/L, but neither would sharpening his mechanics or tactics. Such adjustments, like the proverbial movement of deck chairs on the Titanic, would only forestall a grievous outcome.

There were only two solutions to Marcus's problem: Either he would have to shift strategies or he would need to find alternative trading instruments that fit his existing strategy. He could no longer count on following momentum patterns as his bread and butter in stocks that made up the major indices. When IBM realized the world was moving toward word processing, it did not stick forever with its strategy of marketing Selectric typewriters. It shifted its resources to the personal computer market. When that market became commoditized, the company shifted again to emphasize high-level services to computer users. Just as business markets change, prodding companies to evolve, financial markets undergo radical shifts, requiring traders to alter their strategies.

In short, Marcus displayed first-order competence at trading, but was struggling with second-order competence. He could successfully trade a market one way, but now had to learn to adapt to altered market conditions. Like a college basketball team that graduated its stars, his task was to remake himself. To find and trade a new strategy, he would have to reenter a learning curve.

> Expert traders most often lose when markets change, reducing their edge.

THE ONE THING THAT BEST PREDICTS THE ABILITY TO COME BACK

Marcus is well on his way to recovery. He tweaked his strategy to emphasize the shorting of issues that could not rise with the general market and the buying of stocks that held up well during market declines. This allowed him to benefit from the broad market's tendency to reverse short-term movements, while still drawing upon his stock-picking skills. He reduced his size while implementing the new strategy and defined new tactics for getting into trades. For instance, he is using some of his new market observations with issues that trade actively around the time of earnings news, tracking shifts in those issues' relative strength. This allows him to get into trades when the stocks move and benefit from investor and trader overreactions.

But Marcus is not on his way to recovery simply because he found a new strategy. Most experienced and successful traders, given enough time, could find a promising strategic variation to trade. *The problem is that they run out of time.*

The reason is simple. During the glory years—the times when their strategies were working well—they didn't save their money. They bought expensive houses, took lavish trips, and lived large. Having found success, they wanted to flaunt it, enjoy it. Never did they consider that the glory days, as in Springsteen's song, would soon be behind them.

Let me be plain about this. I have seen more successful traders derailed by personal financial mismanagement than for any other reason.

Once a trader becomes wrapped up in the need to live a life of conspicuous consumption and success, it is very difficult—emotionally—to return to square one of the learning curve. It is difficult to reduce one's size and learn new ropes, and it is difficult to find the humility to return to a simulator and test out new strategies. Caught up in their own hubris, traders keep trading long after their strategies have demonstrably failed. They go so far into debt that they never get the chance to retool.

Recently I was walking to the elevator at Kingstree with Pablo Melgarejo, the expert trader who had once shocked—and then enlightened—me by suggesting that new traders learn to trade by trading as often as possible on the simulator. We were discussing changes in the marketplace, and Pablo mentioned that the traders with long-term careers were the ones who kept their heads above water during the difficult times and then prospered when their strategies flourished. That meant accepting smaller trading size and lesser profits when edges were lean and pursuing opportunity aggressively in the good times. The traders who fail never get to the good times. By the time they can see the bulls-eye, it's too late: They're out of bullets.

Pablo has been with Kingstree since its inception in 2000 and has seen several changing markets. The shifts have taught him to seek success in multiple markets: U.S. and international stock indexes, Bunds, bonds and notes, and a range of commodity markets. "Some people get stuck in one market," Pablo explained. "Don't be scared to try something new. You need to be humble and approach it as a career, not a job." Indeed, Pablo attributes his success to a "strong value of the dollar. My risk/reward has been the best part of me. . . . Even if I get cold for a while, I'll be back."

The absence of that humility is what allows traders to dig holes for themselves that they cannot escape. They assume that the good times are just around the corner and that they will always be able to get the money back. With such overconfidence, traders lose their sense for the value of a dollar. "The worst part of this business," Pablo told me, "is that it changes people." Ironically, the changes wrought by success can be every bit as damaging as the changes resulting from failure. Once a trader becomes attached to the income of trading and the lifestyle it can bring, it becomes psychologically difficult to reenter learning curves.

Every dogma has its day, as the saying goes, and so it is with trading strategies. No strategy works for all time—a truth that becomes readily apparent when one develops mechanical trading systems and then trades them in real time. If you have been successful with a strategy, the chances are good that others will be attracted to the strategy, find ways to exploit it, and eventually reduce its edge. Trends come and go; volatility waxes and wanes. Second-order competence is the ability to keep one's head above water while defining new strategies or new applications of existing ones.

The best predictor of a trader's ability to adapt to new markets is that trader's liquidity. The nest egg from the good times provides the opportunity to survive the lean ones. Expertise development is more of a circular process than a linear one. The need to remake oneself is the norm, not the exception.

If you take away nothing more from this book, let this be it. The best attitude for traders, in good times and bad, is this simple wisdom: *This, too, shall pass.*

THE GREATEST OBSTACLE TO DEVELOPING SUCCESSFUL STRATEGIES

Successful trading begins with an edge in the marketplace and the proper mechanics and tactics to exploit that edge. Traders' strategies *are* their sources of edge, their ability to discern and act upon patterns of supply and demand in the market auction. Such strategies are cultivated over time, whether they are based on tape-reading skills from long hours of screen time or well-constructed trading systems born of exhaustive research. *Superior strategies lie at the intersection of talents, skills, and opportunities.*

Unfortunately, many traders do not allow themselves the opportunity to cultivate superior strategies. They flit from one trading approach to another, in search of rapid rewards. They become a jack of many trading techniques, but they master none.

This often occurs when we lose confidence in our abilities. Shaken by a series of losses, we will abandon what had been successful and begin trading in a style that fits neither our personalities nor our skill sets. System traders may begin overriding their systems with discretionary judgments; short-term traders will second-guess their signals and hold longer-term positions. It is one thing to adjust our trading methods to changing market conditions; it is quite another to abandon our niche entirely and lurch from one method to another.

John Carter, author of *Mastering the Trade* and developer of the Trade the Markets mentoring service, has seen more than his share of traders in search of holy grails. He recently emphasized to me, "Amateur traders turn into professional traders once they stop looking for the 'next great technical indicator' and start controlling their risk on each trade."

"The search for that fail-safe indicator that's going to work nearly every time takes a trader down a path littered with corpses, broken dreams, and stuttering fools," Carter explained. "Many traders stay on this search for the rest of their lives. The irony is that individuals in this phase think they are developing as traders, when in reality their development is dead in the water." Carter includes in this category traders who pursue curve-fitted trading systems, trend-following methods that fail on the 75 percent of occasions when markets trade sideways, options strategies that make money when underlying instruments don't move but give it back on break-out trends, and endlessly tweaked indicator settings.

Perfectionism clearly plays a role in preventing us from cultivating superior strategies. In a very important sense, perfectionistic traders are not seeking to make money. *They are trying to not lose money.* Their intolerance of loss keeps them moving from method to method in search of a certainty that markets cannot provide.

> Successful traders embrace risk and uncertainty; unsuccessful traders seek to repeal them.

"The bottom line is that professional traders are not searching for the next best thing," Carter stresses. "Professional traders focus on limiting risk and protecting capital. Amateur traders focus on how much money they can make on each trade. Professionals always take money away from amateurs."

Successful strategies maximize opportunity; they do not eliminate uncertainty.

SELF-OBSERVATION AND VIDEOTAPING

Nothing so interferes with a performance as thinking about the performance while engaging in it. Most of us are familiar with the performance anxiety that affects speakers and test takers: The worries about how one is doing take one out of the flow of doing. For this reason, your observation and evaluation of your mechanics, tactics, and strategies need to occur outside of trading. While you're trading, you're the trader. All other times, you're the mentor to that trader.

It is impossible for active traders to recall all the details of their trades. Even if they could recall prices where they entered and exited, they would not remember all of the mechanics that went into the trade— the reading of supply and demand, the scaling in and out. Nor would they necessarily recall the tactics that animated the trade: how the market was trading at that moment relative to its day's range and relative to other markets. Cognitive psychologists find that recall is a fickle phenomenon. We tend to remember what is most vivid, what occurs first in a sequence, and what occurs last. Recall is also affected by our moods and by experiences that occur between events and our eventual recollection.

For this reason, videotaping is a powerful piece of equipment in the trading gymnasium. It allows us to reexperience each trading day and review each and every trade as it was made. Videotaping is particularly helpful when following markets and learning market patterns. You can play and replay turning points in markets and setups for various trades to see how they evolved in real time. This is far more powerful than reviewing static charts. When working on trading mechanics, however, videotaping is used to show both how the market traded *and how you traded it*. It is a means of reviewing performance.

Two videotaping solutions are readily available to traders. The first is a simple camcorder setup that records the day's trade. Because videodiscs do not hold enough data for a full day of trading, it is convenient to have the camcorder record directly to a hard drive, where it can be compressed and stored as part of an archive. The second solution is a desktop program such as Camtasia (www.techsmith.com), which assembles frequent screen captures in a video. This is convenient in that it eliminates the need for separate equipment, but it also locks you into recording a single screen. Too, it can slow down the performance of your machine if you attempt to record large screen areas over an extended period. The ideal setup is one that allows you to recapture markets and trades as faithfully as possible, so that you can see what you did, when you did it, and recreate why you did it.

My favorite application of videotaping is talking trades aloud so that your tape captures the thought process behind the trade, as well as the trade execution. This adds many dimensions to the review. First, it allows you to determine where along the pyramid the trade might have faltered. The tape will reveal where the thinking behind the trade might have been flawed (improper tactics) and where the idea was good but the implementation poor (improper mechanics). The tape will also capture those occasions when all elements of the pyramid are aligned: The tactics follow naturally from the basic strategy, and the mechanics effectively implement the tactics. *It is every bit as important to review successful trades as unsuccessful ones*. As I emphasized in *The Psychology of Trading*, these reviews create models of success that we progressively internalize.

Videotapes are especially effective at capturing those occasions on which emotionality derails trades. When you see yourself on tape trading well and trading poorly, you become sensitive to the physical, emotional, and cognitive cues that differentiate the two. My best trades are accompanied by active risk management immediately following the entry: I am talking aloud the criteria that will have me exiting the trade and I continuously update the evidence that the trade idea is working or not working. Throughout the duration of the trade, I am actively involved, monitoring how much volume is trading, where the volume is trading, and how the volume is divided among buyers and sellers. Other times, the trade goes my way immediately and I sit back, convinced that I'm riding a winner. When this happened most recently, a trade that was a quick one-point winner did not engage my active involvement until it was underwater. A simple review revealed to me that I could have easily scratched the trade. Instead, over-confidence led me to take a modest—but needless—loss.

During my graduate school days, I taped my therapy sessions with clients (with their permission), so that my supervisor could review the tapes with me. I learned a great deal about strategy and tactics from such reviews. An unintended consequence of the taping, however, was that I knew that my performance would be reviewed by my mentor. This kept me on my toes. I was less likely to veer from my treatment plan if I knew that I would have to explain my actions to my supervisor. Similarly, videotaping of trading can keep us on the straight and narrow. This is especially true if you show your tapes to a mentor. Just knowing you're on tape introduces an element of self-observation to trading, making you more cognizant of your tactics and mechanics.

> During trading, you watch the market. Videotaping enables you to watch yourself.

VIDEOTAPING AND SELF-EVALUATION ALONG THE PERFORMANCE PYRAMID

I find the notion of a performance pyramid to be particularly helpful in reviewing tapes. (See Exhibit 6.4.) The idea is to conduct an efficient after-action review at the end of trading that highlights what you did right during the day and what you need to improve. In my reviews, I'm especially looking for themes: common elements that link the errors made by traders. Sometimes these are emotional, as when a trader is trying too hard to come back from a slump. On those occasions, the tape may show the trader entering with excessive size and staying in trades longer than normal. Frustration is evident in the trader's voice, especially as the trades do not work out. Other times, the tape reveals themes that are purely related to the reading of markets, as when traders fail to recognize that markets have slowed down and continue their previous trading. Like quarterbacks that

---
Does my trade exploit my basic
strategy (i.e., my edge in the market)?

Does my trade tactically exploit market conditions
existing at the time?

Did I implement my trade idea in a mechanically sound way to maximize
opportunity and manage risk?

EXHIBIT 6.4   The Performance Pyramid as an After-Action Review

fail to see the whole field, they become tunnel-visioned and miss what is in front of their faces.

When working on my own trading, my preference is to implement reviews in a top-down manner. I first ask myself if the trade is consistent with my strategy. In my case the strategy has two components: a structural edge and an informational one. The structural edge, to which I have alluded earlier, is based upon knowledge of the participants in the equity index marketplace. Many of these are day time frame participants, and many are highly leveraged. This creates situations in which traders behave as a herd, jumping aboard whatever movement they can detect in the market. It also creates situations in which these same traders have to exit positions quickly as part of risk management. Because of this, much of the day's trade in the ES consists of waves of buying and selling attributable to herd behavior and the mass exiting of positions that are going underwater. Identifying spots where the herd is loaded up in one direction and will need to unload their holdings if their anticipations prove incorrect provides a structural edge.

The informational edge comes from my historical studies, such as those posted to my TraderFeed site. As I am writing this, the previous day in the ES was a slow day with a narrow range—an inside day in technical parlance. Going back over three years in my database, I found that similar inside days tended to be followed by market weakness. This led me to expect a move today below yesterday's lows. My core strategy, then, is to combine the structural edge with the informational one: When I see buyers enter today's market and unable to push prices to new highs, I enter my short position with a price target below yesterday's lows. If I buy today's market, I am violating my strategy by trading against the informational edge. If I sell the market during a waterfall decline, I am equally violating my strategy by failing to exploit the structural edge. Combining the two keeps me trading selectively, limiting risk exposure to those occasions in the market in which I perceive odds to be genuinely in my favor.

If my trade fits my strategy, the next level down on the pyramid has me reviewing tactics. One of my tactics, for example, is to find the market that is best positioned to exploit my strategy and trade that market. I may notice, for example, that traders are caught long in the ES during a market that I have forecasted lower (with the historical studies), but also observe that the NQ is trading weaker than the ES. I may, therefore, try to take advantage of this relative weakness. Another tactic is that I will scale into trades that go my way, but only at certain times of day and when the volume attributable to large market participants is above particular threshold levels. My research tells me that moves are more likely to extend on those occasions. This means that, at slower times, my tactics have me looking to scale out of trades—not add to them.

Notice that a profitable trade is not necessarily one that is tactically sound. If I am trading around noontime and add to a position, making money on the initial position but giving some back on the added piece, my tactics were poor regardless of the P/L. A tactic that I favor is to stay in a trade as long as volume is expanding in the direction of my position. This affirms that either traders who had been caught leaning the wrong way are rushing for the exits or new market participants are joining the fray. Either way, the expanded volume is generally associated with expanded volatility, encouraging me to remain in a position and not take profits prematurely. If I take a one-point profit in a position that shows expanding volume and would soon thereafter have paid me two or three points, my tactics have been poor although I made money on the trade. If I do not institute corrective measures, it's only a matter of time before those tactical shortcomings will come back to haunt my account statement.

In short, there can be a world of difference between a profitable trade and a good trade, between an unprofitable trade and a bad trade. Good trades exhibit proper execution at all levels of the pyramid; bad trades do not. You have no control over whether an individual trade will go your way; all you can do is align yourself with the odds through good ideas and sound execution.

> Profits take care of themselves when you have a legitimate edge and execute properly.

Only after reviewing the strategic and tactical facets of a trade will I examine mechanics. One measure I like to follow is how much heat on average I take after putting on a trade—and how much a trade went further in my direction very shortly after an exit. These tell me if I'm getting in and out at reasonable prices. I also like to follow my holding time per trade. I have a defined time frame for most of my trades. This stops me out after a period of time in which the market fails to go my way. Because my strategy is predicated on the urgency of loaded-up traders getting out of their positions, my trades should pay me out relatively promptly. If time passes and I am not making money, it tells me that the urgency is not there. I want to exit the position well in advance of being stopped out at my maximum allowable loss.

Video recordings will usually reveal quickly whether a trader has veered from proper strategy and tactics. It's not at all unusual to watch a tape with dropped jaw, thinking, "How could I have been such an idiot?" This is because, for experienced and generally successful traders, most deviations from strategy and tactics have a psychological root. They reflect either emotional arousal that interferes with information processing—as in the case of frustration during a slump—or fatigue and loss of concentration.

Mechanics, however, can require substantial review. The tape allows you to refresh your memory of the trade and get a sense for how the market looked at the time, but often it takes a further drilling down to see where you might have managed risk better or placed stops more effectively. Replaying portions of the market day in simulation mode can be extremely helpful, as can a review of charts and indicators. This is far and away the most time-consuming facet of self-mentoring, I find, but also the one with the greatest yield. One of my tactics, for instance, is to adjust the timing of my trades to market conditions. There are certain markets—those with low volatility but adequate daily volume—that are quite choppy. They may or may not trend over a longer time frame, but will lurch and reverse short-term moves. My tactic in trading such a market is fade countertrend extremes in the NYSE TICK (and similar measures) and make quick hit-and-run trades in the direction dictated by my strategy. The mechanics that implement these tactics involve entering positions at the market, but working orders to exit. The proper placement of those exits is something I constantly have to review and refine. There is a delicate balance between maximizing the likelihood of getting filled on the exit and maximizing the trade's potential profit. A great deal of information goes into proper exit placement, including the market's trading volume and volatility at the time, the presence of obvious support and resistance levels, depth of market, and the market's recent willingness to do business at that price level. My cautious nature as a trader has me exiting trades where I'm sure I'll be filled, often leaving more on the table than I would ideally like. For that reason, I will spend considerable time reviewing such statistics as the percentage of times I'm filled on my exits to monitor my mechanics. I also assess the percentage of times I could have been filled at better prices.

Like refining a golf swing, I suspect the adjustment of my mechanics will always be a work in progress.

Perhaps most important of all, such review and adjustment force us to *see* market action. I have become far more sensitive to the impact of short-term market considerations on order placement as a result of daily review. That cannot help but fuel the implicit learning of markets. If you watch markets enough, you begin to internalize and anticipate their patterns. *If you watch yourself sufficiently, you begin to identify and anticipate your own patterns.* Observation is the first and most important step in self-mentoring. Fortunately, there are powerful tools in the trading gym that will help us translate observations into concrete plans for development. To those we now turn.

CHAPTER 7

Performance Dynamics

From Diagnostics to Enhancement

*Enthusiasm is everything. It must be taut and
vibrating like a guitar string.*
                    —Edson Arantes do Nascimento ("Pele")

No one can accuse soccer great Pele of lacking enthusiasm. From his professional debut at age 16, in which he scored a goal, to his stardom—during which he became a target for other teams' aggression—Pele retained a love for what he called "the beautiful sport." His performance was almost superhuman: Over the course of a career spanning 1,360 games, he scored 1,280 goals. Observers have likened this to a baseball player hitting an average of one home run every game of the major league season—162 in all—and then repeating the feat year after year. Such was the fascination with his performance that two warring countries—Nigeria and Biafra—declared a temporary truce in order to see Pele play. European teams bid large sums to lure Pele from his home team, but Brazil declared him a national treasure in an attempt to retain his talent. Hardly dominating physically—he was actually rather thin compared with other players—Pele blended speed, vision, and accuracy as no one had previously. His formula for success? "Practice is everything."

PERFORMANCE AND PREPARATION

Let's jump from the soccer field to the NASCAR pits. What we find is that performance is increasingly becoming science, as well as art. Recently, crews from semiconductor leader Intel donned crew suits and raced the clock in Pit Row, changing tires and performing routine maintenance on race cars. Despite the Intel crew members' experience with principles and practices of efficient operation, the best times they could muster were over half a minute. Professional pit crews generally achieve turnaround times closer to 13 seconds.

Breon Klopp, director of development at PIT Instruction and Training, explains that performance is not about speed, but rather about process. "Being fast comes with having lean processes. If you just focus on speed, you wind up with mistakes." This is why instructors at PIT advise aspiring crew members, "Go slow to go fast." The goal is smooth, lean operation—not hurried behavior.

Lean processes apply to trading as well. If I do not do all of my homework in advance of the open—if my tactics are not researched and thought through, complete with a variety of what-if scenarios—I can guarantee you that my early trading session will feel like a frenzied pit stop. *The subjective experience of time is highly dependent upon our perceptions of control and familiarity with events*. Time passes more slowly when we are prepared than when we are rushing from one thing to the next. So it is with markets. They seem to move more slowly when we're prepared, when we know what to look for. If I am frantically searching for trade ideas as markets are moving, the markets will feel fast regardless of how much business we're doing at the time.

Many a performance is won or lost in the preparation.

For this reason, pit trainers such as those at PIT Instruction and Training, emphasize working smart rather than fast. Crews consist of seven men, each with a clearly defined role. Nothing is left to chance. The team stakes out where the car will pull in, where each man will stand, and what each will carry. Tasks are performed in parallel, not series, so that a single slipup will not disrupt the entire team. They are also performed so repeatedly in practice that they are near-automatic, despite the dangerous and noisy racing conditions. The Intel workers, for all their experience, lack such specific training for race car maintenance. As they rush about, they bump into each other, drop tires, and fail to tighten lug nuts properly. Each small mistake costs the driver seconds—and car lengths.

It's relatively easy to watch videotapes and catch the bad trades you make. Less apparent are the good trades you never make because you're two steps behind the market. Missing a trade here, getting in or out at a worse price there: The costs of inefficiency add up. It's the difference between an Intel crew changing tires and gassing a car up in 33 seconds and a pit crew's performance of the same tasks in 14 seconds. Those are differences that win and lose races. Breon Klopp of PIT emphasized to me, "Practice makes permanent: Good and bad." His point was that how we perform day after day becomes our habitual performance—for better and for worse. *What we routinely do becomes our natural routine.*

PREPARING FOR MARKET AMBUSHES

When Richard Machowicz, author of *Unleash the Warrior Within,* left the Navy SEALs, he began a business teaching self-defense methods to interested students. He found that many of the students, despite skill and practice, froze during realistic simulated attacks. Not having a preprogrammed sense of what to do or where to strike, they suffered from what's commonly known as analysis paralysis. He found, however, that when they were focused on potential targets—eyes-throat-groin—they were much more able to select their weapon—a fist, knee, or heel, for instance—and execute needed movements.

Because fear disrupts normal thought processes, Machowicz trains his students with real throat grabs and other such attacks. The elements of any successful attack, he notes, are surprise, speed, and violence of action. All of these fall outside an opponent's norms, making usual judgment and planning impossible. If targets are preprogrammed through experience, someone who is attacked can rapidly respond and save their life. Without such programming, like the World War II soldiers who never fired their weapons, we are apt to freeze, as we cannot grasp events outside our norms.

What we do not envision, we cannot prepare for. NASCAR crews don't merely anticipate routine maintenance; they are also prepared for the unknown: mechanical failures and damage caused by accidents. When SWAT teams breach an entrance and move into a room, they are prepared for any form of resistance. Surprise is the great enemy. All training is for naught if we are taken by surprise and cannot make sense of our experience.

Traders will commonly review markets by looking at charts. These static images fail to depict the surprise, speed, and violence of action that lie behind many market moves. A five-minute bar chart may show a high-low range of five ticks on 8,000 contracts traded. This looks like very moderate market behavior. What the chart doesn't show is that four of the five ticks occurred in a matter of seconds, as the pulling and replacing of bids caused prices to suddenly drop—and then rise again. The short-term trader unprepared for such sweeps easily can be tricked into exiting a good position or entering a new one at an unfavorable price.

In any time frame, you will notice periods of market consolidation—usually slow—alternating with busier periods of sudden rises and declines. The vast majority of these moves are not responses to fundamental news or events. They are generated by those with the size and savvy to ambush market participants that act in a herd. *If your only market rehearsal and training is with static charts, you are like soldiers preparing for battle by reading battle plans.* In the heat of an ambush, the enemy is likely to disrupt all of that planning. Markets will move—or fail to move—just beyond the level of expectations of participants. That is the only way the ambusher can take money from the ambushed. Preparing for expectable market events is important, just as preparing for routine car maintenance is the bread and butter of any pit crew. It's the preparation for the unexpected, however, that, over time, wins the Winston Cup.

Fighter pilot Colonel John R. Boyd was known as "forty-second Boyd" because of his challenge that he could win any dogfight—ride the tail of any challenger—within 40 seconds. His ability was to operate from inside the mind-set of his adversary: what he called the OODA (observation, orientation, decision, action) loop. Actions, Boyd held, emerge from decisions, which in turn hinge upon orienting ourselves in accordance with our observations. When you become predictable in a dogfight, you are inside the OODA loop of the other pilot. The pilot who wins is the one who stays outside the opponent's loop. This is why the surprise, speed, and violence of action mentioned by Machowicz are so effective. A predictable attack, such as when British troops would line up in formation in their red coats, complete with flags flying and music playing, was within the OODA loop of savvy colonists. It is the swift, unexpected, violent attack of the guerilla force that can unnerve a much larger opponent.

What is well known and well publicized—from chart patterns to news stories—represents the OODA loop of the average market participant. If what you lean on for your edge is information that can be readily accessed by any trader possessing a decent real-time charting or market depth application, you are within the OODA loop of the pros, not outside it. When the John Boyds of the market challenge your positions, they won't announce their arrival with loud music and bright red coats. Nor will they provide you with 40 seconds of leeway. They will move the market sufficiently quickly to create surprise, and they will do so with violence. Their edge is the ability to create chaos in the minds of their counterparties. Our job is to treat trading like a Ranger treats patrols: watchful for the ambushes, focused on our mission, enemy, terrain, troops (resources) and equipment, and time. It is vitally important that you know the enemies who operate in your particular niche; they are the ones who can dislodge you from your sound ideas and interfere with your well-honed reflexes. Different markets feature different enemies: Forex is not like the stock market, which is not like sugar. Who is bigger than you, and who is faster than you? They are the ones who can hurt you. Risk management begins by knowing who is in the game and how they typically behave.

> The markets move more slowly when you operate outside their loops.

PERFORMANCE: FROM ART TO SCIENCE

When reviewing a variety of performance fields, one cannot help but be impressed by the degree to which the art of performance has given way to science. Athletes are now trained by specialists, utilizing sophisticated dietary, aerobic, and strength-building regimes. Lance Armstrong rides a bike specially fabricated to accommodate his ideal riding position, minimizing wind resistance. His workouts track his pedal speed, the force of his upward and downward leg movements, his oxygen consumption—all to maximize his edge. The NASCAR pits utilize tools and parts specifically manufactured to make each task smoother. Lug nuts are larger than normal to ease tightening; studs are tailored to the lug nuts. Gas cans are specially designed to empty as quickly as possible; jacks are tested and optimized for one-pump lift. To no small degree, human performance—that evolutionary thrust—is engineered, not just acquired.

Key to this engineering is the collection of data. Mere tracking of the profits and losses in an account statement is giving way to the broader collection of metrics that precisely measure facets of performance. With the computerization of trading, it is more possible than ever to evaluate one's strategy, tactics, and mechanics. This allows traders to hone performance much as a race car team shaves seconds off its times.

My first experiences with the collection of trader metrics came through the use of the Trade Analyzer module that is part of the Trading Technologies platform, then through the use of the TraderDNA program. Later, I learned that the simulation module for Ninja Trader was accompanied by the collection of trading metrics. I am confident that this functionality will become a staple of most trading platforms in the not-too-distant future. It is one of the single most powerful steps a trader can take toward performance improvement, supplementing the art of trading with science.

Let's take a simple example of metrics collection and how it might be utilized. Marisa is a short-term trader in the crude oil market. She enters and exits positions within a single session, looking for price trends that are generated by supply/demand shifts for crude and news from politically volatile oil-producing countries. Let's say that we track over time her profit and loss each day, but also break down her P/L into several categories. For instance, we might go back and code each day for the past three months as uptrend days, downtrend days, reversal days, and rangebound days. Uptrend days open near their lows and close near their highs; downtrend days do the reverse. Reversal days trade well off their opening prices only to close near them or at the opposite extreme. Rangebound days close near the middle of their ranges, close to their opening prices. We then map Marisa's P/L as a function of the type of day she encountered in the market. (See Exhibit 7.1.)

For the purposes of this initial illustration, I have greatly simplified the data grid. For instance, I would normally separate scratched trades from profitable ones, and I would also include data regarding the number of profitable versus unprofitable trading days (which we will discuss later) and some indication of profitability as a function of the number of contracts traded. It is also important to track performance after commissions and other expenses, which I have not done here. This is merely an initial snapshot of recent trading performance across varying market conditions.

Most traders who contact me for advice know only that figure in the lower right-hand corner of Exhibit 7.1. Many cannot even specify that

EXHIBIT 7.1   Tracking P/L As A Function of Type of Trading Day

	Number of Profitable or Scratched Trades	Number of Losing Trades	Total Profits	Total Losses	Overall P/L
Uptrend days	50	35	$55,000	$35,000	$20,000
Downtrend days	45	30	$75,000	$30,000	$45,000
Reversal days	35	30	$45,000	$30,000	$15,000
Rangebound days	30	45	$25,000	$65,000	($40,000)
TOTALS	160	140	$200,000	$160,000	$40,000

number. If we focused only on that number, we would say that Marisa is a modestly successful trader. She is taking something out of the market but probably is not making a lot of money after costs—especially given the commissions associated with the frequency of her trading and her size.

A close look at Exhibit 7.1 reveals why she is not more profitable. Her total profit across trending days is $65,000. Her gross profit on nontrending days is no profit at all: a loss of $25,000. Indeed, she has lost as much on rangebound days as she has made for the entire three-month period. This clearly is impairing her performance.

Is this the only factor interfering with her overall profitability? Examine the table closely and see if you can identify any other trading problems. If you're eagle-eyed, you'll notice that Marisa's profit and loss per trade—column three divided by column one and column four divided by column two—are out of whack. Let's create a new table to illustrate this finding. (See Exhibit 7.2.)

Aha! Now we're getting somewhere. Marisa's average profit per trade is not much larger than her average loss overall. This limits her profitability. When we drill down with metrics, we can see that her performance is uneven. Not only does she have more losing trades than winners in rangebound markets, but the size of her losers in those markets overwhelms the size of her winners. The combination of the two—more losers and larger losers—creates outsized losses.

What this suggests on the surface is that Marisa is not seeing rangebound markets very well, but she is also probably holding onto losing trades

EXHIBIT 7.2 Tracking P/L As A Function of Average Profit/Loss Per Trade

	Number of Profitable or Scratched Trades	Number of Losing Trades	Average Profit per Trade	Average Loss per Trade	Overall P/L
Uptrend days	50	35	$1,100	$1,000	$20,000
Downtrend days	45	30	$1,667	$667	$45,000
Reversal days	35	30	$1,286	$1,000	$15,000
Rangebound days	30	45	$833	$1,444	($40,000)
TOTALS	160	140	$1,250	$1,143	$40,000

longer than winners in those markets. If this were a general tendency on her part, we would see it occurring across all market conditions. The fact that it is occurring only during rangebound markets tells me that something about those markets is getting her out of her game. This may well be a situation where the problem is partly a trading issue—the need to identify range-bound markets—and partly a psychological one—preventing narrow markets from triggering frustration and interfering with risk management.

Notice, however, that the metrics highlight strengths as well as weaknesses. Marisa is highly successful during downtrend days. Not only does she ride her winners for larger gains, but the average size of her losers is much smaller. This is a very unusual finding. Why? Downtrend days normally are more volatile than other days, making it easy to have larger-sized winners but also larger losers. Something Marisa is doing during downtrend days is keeping losses small at the same time that it lets her ride winners. This is clearly her best trading. A solution-focused coach would want to study how she is entering trades and managing them during downtrends so that she might be able to apply these skills to other market conditions—especially the rangebound days.

> Metrics reveal trading solutions as well as problems.

Is there anything else we can diagnose from Marisa's performance data? Let's assume that, over the course of the three months studied, there were a relatively even number of days falling into the four categories. What that tells us is that Marisa is trading the four types of days equally actively. Her number of trades per day does not vary as a function of market condition. This is a problem because during some market periods, such as downtrends, she has a real edge. At other times, she not only lacks an edge but gives up money. Realistically, all other things being equal, she should trade most actively in trending markets and less so at other times.

Where this would take me as Marisa's mentor is training that would be specific to her needs. I would want to provide her with guidelines and tools for trying to assess whether markets were likely to be trending or range-bound. These tools would probably make use of volume and serial correlation relationships between recent and upcoming volatility to aid her in assessing market conditions. If she could identify when markets were likely to be rangebound, she could adjust her trading accordingly and—at the very least—follow the physician's motto of "Above all else do no harm." Simply trading rangebound markets less actively and instituting improved loss control would greatly aid her overall profitability.

Notice how readily we can move from performance diagnosis to performance plans when we collect systematic data regarding our trading. As

TraderDNA founder David Norman emphasizes, this enables us to become scientific in studying ourselves. It is sobering to think of how much information we could have about our trading that we never think to collect. I am greatly indebted to David and his vision of trader psychometrics.

A SIDE NOTE ON RISK MANAGEMENT

If I had to make a generalization about Marisa from the performance profiles presented thus far, I would say that she trades quite well in volatile market environments and poorly in nonvolatile conditions. When markets reverse and show reasonable movement, she holds her own. This would help to explain why she makes more money—and achieves more profit per trade—during downtrends than uptrends. It also explains why rangebound markets are her nemesis. Clearly I would need to gather more data to support this hypothesis and observe her over a longer period of time. If I were working at her firm, I would stand by her side under a variety of market conditions and observe her patterns of success and failure.

If, however, my hypothesis is correct, Marisa is in trouble. The management of her firm may not think she's in trouble and she may not feel that she's in trouble, but she is in danger nonetheless. Her profits are largely a function of what the market is doing at the time, not a function of her mastery of different markets. She is exhibiting first-order competence, not second-order. Alternatively, we could say that she is displaying competence, but not expertise.

What if the crude market goes into a prolonged rangebound period? What if peace reigns supreme in the Middle East, diplomacy wins the day, and prices enter a period of great stability? No longer will there be a relatively even number of trending and nontrending days. Suddenly, markets will trade more often in precisely the way that Marisa trades worst. She will begin to lose money and, eventually, lose confidence. Her already poor risk management in thin, narrow markets could deteriorate even further. In a matter of weeks, even a consistently profitable trader could become a trader in debt.

This is where the preventive aspect of capable mentorship is most evident. *Metrics reveal blowups in the making.* By helping Marisa learn to identify rangebound markets and trade them more effectively—and by helping her extend her skills in downtrends to other market conditions—a mentor can facilitate the transition from first-order competence to genuine expertise.

Data-based mentorship provides proactive risk management.

Too often we think of risk management only after a losing period or we think of it narrowly, in terms of stop losses on individual trades. Good risk management, however, also dictates that we identify situations in which trading profits are concentrated in a relative handful of trades or market conditions. The more limited the trader's edge, the greater the risk that the trader will lapse into obsolescence. Treating performance as a science means that we take a hard look at where a trader's edge is really coming from and use that information to extend strengths, address weaknesses, and adapt to a variety of market conditions.

THE PSYCHOLOGICAL PARADIGM
AND THE PERFORMANCE PARADIGM

The example of Marisa's trading provides us with a particularly good opportunity to contrast what I call the psychological paradigm of trader development with the performance paradigm. Let's say that Marisa comes to me in a frustrated state. She has been making a modest amount of money each month but recently has been losing money. Some of her daily losses have gotten out of hand, causing concern at her firm and setting her account statement back. She is frustrated with the market—which she says is moving less than usual—and she's frustrated with herself. To keep her losses from mounting, she recently cut her size, but this only added to her frustration when she could participate only modestly in a market downtrend following the release of crude inventory numbers.

If I am operating with the psychological paradigm, I make the assumption that Marisa's trading problem has a genesis in her handling of emotions. I would assess her attitudes and beliefs, observe her behavior, and show her some techniques for changing her thoughts, feelings, and actions. Alternatively, I might explore her past to see if conflicts she had first experienced outside of trading were now interfering with her decisions and actions. For instance, I might work with her to develop a trading plan that focused on avoiding trading during frustrated periods and, instead, writing in her journal to gain perspective on the situation.

If, however, I adopt the performance paradigm, I rely on trading metrics to diagnose Marisa's problem. These lead me to believe that she lacks a fundamental trading skill: the ability to recognize shifting market conditions, such as when trending markets become rangebound. The assistance I provide to her is one of information and skills building. Perhaps I will help her develop a spreadsheet application that monitors markets in real time and spits out green numbers when markets are gaining trendiness and red ones when they are becoming more rangebound. Alternatively, I might teach her how to hold positions differently in volatile versus nonvolatile markets by adjusting profit targets to current market movement. Instead of working on her head, I will work with her on improving her strategy, tactics, and mechanics.

The psychological paradigm stresses that profitability problems stem from emotional ones. The performance paradigm emphasizes that profits follow from the proper alignment of two sets of variables: (1) talents, skills, and markets and (2) strategies, tactics, and mechanics. If you're having trading problems, the performance paradigm asserts, you're either in the wrong market or you're trading the right market the wrong way.

Of course, reality is never as simple as our neat categories. *Most trading difficulties have* both *performance and emotional components.* Our behavioral and emotional patterns get in the way of our talents and skills, and our poor training generates emotional distress. There are times when I find that I need to operate primarily from the psychological paradigm, and there are times when the performance paradigm is essential. For me, as a psychologist, this is very much like knowing when a psychological problem, such as depression, can best be addressed by talk therapy and when it requires the use of medication. Often, the two in concert work best—which is how it often is with trading.

Marisa is an excellent case in point. Based on the early metrics we've collected, I would probably work with her in both performance and psychological modes. The performance mode would likely begin with my investigation of Marisa's market. I would investigate historical data to determine which pieces of data best anticipate near-term market conditions. For example, I might find that the volatility and opening range of crude oil is an accurate predictor of the day's behavior. I would share this with Marisa and illustrate ways of capturing and using the information early in the day's trade. I might also watch the market while she trades, updating her on information relevant to market conditions and illustrating how she could do this for herself. I would observe her efforts to gauge market conditions and provide her with feedback regarding the adjustments she made in her trading.

Because, however, the data suggest that Marisa's risk management is much worse in range markets than in others, I would also work with her in a psychological mode. I would observe her trade and become keenly attentive to signs of frustration or other emotional disruption. My particular focus would be on the triggers for this frustration: the market and trading events that precede her loss of control and deviations from sound mechanics. We would then work on specific brief therapy techniques for deprogramming these triggers and gaining cognitive and physical control over frustration (see Chapter 8). I would explain those techniques to Marisa, illustrate their use, and observe her attempts to employ them. For instance, I might come into her office during a particularly rangebound period, point out to her an indication of growing frustration, and encourage her to use behavioral self-control methods prior to entering any trades. This might lead her to take a small break from the screen, focus her attention and shift her thoughts with a session on the sound-and-light machine, and then return to trading after mentally rehearsing her trading plan for nonvolatile markets.

Notice that, whether I am working with Marisa in performance or psychological mode, I am generally assisting her while markets are trading and she is at her trade station. There is value in meeting and planning before markets open, and a review at the end of the day can be helpful. *Ultimately, however, people learn best when they are closest to the conditions of performance.* They learn to handle anxiety when they're anxious about a trade; they learn to place exits by being in trades and needing to get out. Observing a trader trade helps a mentor sort out the performance aspects of a problem from the psychological aspects, and it enables a mentor to detect patterns that might escape the metrics. Metrics wouldn't show, for example, that a trader is placing his largest trades when frustrated or is failing to act on valid trade ideas following losses. Live work with traders brings together the performance and the psychological paradigms, allowing teacher and trader to move seamlessly from mechanics to mind-sets and back again. Talking with traders about their trading is a far cry from working with them on their trading while they're trading. Successful mentorship—think John Wooden, Dan Gable, or Nick Bollettieri—is always hands-on and real time.

> The psychology and performance paradigms come together when mentorship occurs within the performance setting.

DAILY PERFORMANCE METRICS

Marisa's data were aggregated daily. We categorized days based on market action and reviewed her daily trading and P/L as a function of market conditions. Daily metrics provide a broad overview of performance, especially when they cover a period of weeks or months. Let's review a few basic measures and their meaning:

- *Number of trades and number of shares (contracts) traded per day.* Here we're looking to see how active the trader was, which should be a function of the opportunity identified in the marketplace. Ideally, we should see more trades and contracts traded when markets are busier and offering a greater number of trade setups. A relatively equal number of trades or contracts each day suggests a possible problem in spotting opportunity. When traders are active in low-opportunity markets, the first hypothesis that comes to mind is that they're pressing, trying to create opportunities.

- *The sequencing of winning and losing days.* This metric simply looks for patterns among winning and losing days: Are they relatively evenly distributed, or are there streaks of winning and losing days? If we see unusual hot and cold spells, it is worth drilling down and determining whether these might be due to market conditions or to shifts in a trader's frame of mind. In October 2005, for example, a number of traders contacted me by e-mail and told me that they had racked up strings of large losing days. While the World Series exploits of the White Sox might have been one distraction for local traders, the real reason for the cold streak was that the market gained volatility—and a downward trend—during that month. Traders accustomed to slower, rangebound markets were not prepared for the different trading conditions.

- *The number of winning, losing, and scratched trades and the number of shares/contracts traded for winners, losers, and scratches.* Most traders have a signature trading style. Some have a surprisingly large proportion of losing trades to winners but ride the winners for large gains. Other traders hit for a high batting average, winning far more often than they lose, but not necessarily holding trades for home runs. Keeping track of your winning, losing, and scratched trades helps you see if you are operating within your style and truly finding your edge. The number of scratched trades is very important for very short-term traders because it identifies occasions on which the trader has been quick to exit trades before they became losers. If the ratio of winning to losing trades is very different from the ratio of shares or contracts traded for winners versus losers, position sizing is generally the issue. A tendency to lose on one's largest trades may reveal difficulties handling the emotional pressures of size and risk.

- *The number of long and short trades and shares/contracts.* This indicates whether or not you traded with a bias during a trading session. If you had many more short positions than long, but the market was sideways or rising, your bias did not fit market conditions. If you were in a trending market, but had a relatively equal number of longs and shorts, you also might have been missing the big picture. Sometimes traders will notice a persistent leaning to the long or short side over a period of days, suggesting a longer-term bias at work. These biases are problematic if they are not firmly grounded in the trader's strategy and tactics. Once in a while, you will notice that the ratio of long and short trades is very different from the ratio of contracts or shares traded long or short. This is because of position sizing: Much larger positions might be taken on one side or another. Such disparities may point to psychological problems, such as plunging during periods of frustration or reducing size greatly under conditions of nervousness.

- *The number of profitable and unprofitable trades—and the ratio of shares/contracts traded—as a function of long versus short positions.* Now we're seeing whether you were more successful when trading from the long or the short side. Sometimes there will be a disparity simply as a function of market conditions: The market was rising, so long-side trades worked better than shorts. Other times, it's a performance issue: The trader is better at seeing evolving weakness or strength. When a trader is unbalanced in his or her development, it is like a bodybuilder who has developed his left side more than his right. The answer is to shore up weaknesses through systematic training. Simulator sessions with markets that are weak points for traders are especially useful. Once again, if we see that there are many winning long trades but not many contracts traded as winners from the long side, this suggests an issue with position sizing.

- *The average holding time for positions.* We're back to the issue of signature style: Most traders have a typical holding time for their trades. By examining average holding times, we're looking for consistency—if the trader is sticking with his or her usual style. Notice that longer holding times translate into increased assumption of risk—a potentially worrisome pattern if trading sizes remain the same or larger or if market volatility expands. Holding times are very sensitive to a trader's psychological state: Anxiety or stubbornness in the face of anger can alter holding times significantly, skewing performance.

- *Average holding times for positions broken down by winning, losing, and scratched trades.* This is perhaps the most basic discipline measure of all. It is exceedingly difficult to make money if you are holding onto losing trades longer than winners. Sometimes this measure is skewed by a few trades that were held for a long period of time, only to become large losers. This typically occurs when a trader rationalizes a short-term position as a longer-term hold when it goes underwater. Short holding times for winners are often the result of anxiety and lack of confidence, as traders become fearful of losing paper profits. While this may produce short-term profitability, it generally works to the trader's disadvantage over the long haul, as the larger losers overwhelm the winning trades.

The beauty of programs such as TraderDNA or Ninja Trader is that they calculate these statistics for you and neatly display the results in tables and charts. This makes review of performance quite easy, and it nicely highlights performance measures that are out of line. This is essential for self-mentoring. Even more helpful, the programs will allow active traders to review their performance within the trading day, so that they can make mid-course corrections. It's surprising how many traders, shown their statistics at midday, will say, "I didn't realize I was trading that much," or "I can't believe I was short more than I was long." For traders working at firms, mentors can follow TraderDNA measures in real time, tracking how traders are trading. This takes risk management to a new, proactive level.

Clearly, the measures you collect—and how you collect them—will depend upon your trading niche. A spread trader has to calculate profitability for each spread position as a single unit; a long-term trader will not collect performance data daily. For those who don't trade a large number of trades per day—and especially for those who don't place trades each day—a dedicated metrics program is less of a necessity. Such traders can create their own spreadsheets and enter the relevant data manually. The statistical and charting functions in Excel make this a workable alternative. For the trader making dozens of trades daily, such manual entry is burdensome and lacks the advantage of updating in real time for midday review. A dedicated metrics program is indispensable for active traders. I especially find it useful to collect metrics from trades placed in simulation mode. This allows new traders to track their learning curves, and it anchors the trading gymnasium for experienced traders who wish to try out new tactics.

The bottom line is that we cannot improve what we do not observe. Most traders haven't the slightest idea where they stand on these various metrics, nor are they aware of how their metrics are impacted by shifts in market conditions. We spend far more time studying markets than studying ourselves, and that is at our peril. The metrics will identify trading problems before they become financial problems. They will alert you to potential blowups before you incur devastating losses. Metrics complete learning loops, linking self-observation to self-improvement.

> Metrics focus on the process of trading. If you make steady performance improvements, the profits will come.

DRILLING DOWN EVEN FURTHER WITH METRICS

While most of the data you collect will be organized on a daily basis, it is possible for active traders to drill down yet further. Much of this drilling down will be an attempt to evaluate and correct specific trading mechanics. For example, the daily summary of performance statistics will not tell you if you're placing your stops appropriately or doing a good job of deciding when to enter trades at the market and when to work orders. This requires observations within the trading day, some of which may be possible only by reviewing videotape or by having a mentor observe you trade.

I generally like to observe the sequences of trades within a day for the same reason that I like to note sequences across days. Traders will have strings of winning and losing trades merely by random chance, but sometimes the strings are far more significant. A common occurrence is that a market that trends in the morning will become rangebound at midday. The trader will see the trend and hop aboard, making several successful trades. Then, however, the trader will continue to try to trade the trend throughout the rangebound period, getting chopped up in the process by being stopped out of one trade after another. *A series of losing trades means that either you're not seeing the market properly, your head is in the wrong place, or both.* Look at it this way: If your trades truly have an edge, a series of consecutive losers should be a statistical anomaly. If such strings occur with frequency, either your edge isn't what you thought it was or you are not properly exploiting that edge. At the very least, strings of losing trades can be an alert for a time-out, allowing you to reevaluate yourself and the market.

I also like to look for outlier trades when examining a trade-by-trade account of a day. Sometimes these will be those rogue losses when we fail to manage a trade's risk. Other times, the outliers will be distinguished by their large size or lengthy holding time. I knew one trader who would trade small and cautiously for 90 percent of the day, but then plunge on individual trades with positions 10 times the size of the previous maximum. Needless to say, he risked his entire day—and sometimes his whole week—on single trades. This created huge variability in his performance results. A most useful metric was to break out his P/L as a function of position size. What we found, unsurprisingly, is that he had no greater odds of winning with his huge trades than with his small ones. Indeed, on balance the large trades cost him money, because they often reflected frustration with his overall profitability. It is instructive to calculate the performance statistics without such outlier trades to determine your core effectiveness. If you are trading well and profitably the vast majority of the time, it may make sense to incrementally increase your size while, at the same time, working to eliminate the conditions creating the outliers.

When examining trades individually, accounting for profits and losses can become tricky. This is particularly the case when traders scale in and out of positions. What looks like two winning trades followed by a loser might actually be a single trade idea in which a trader twice added to the core position. I like to treat such trade ideas as single trades and then examine separately the size and P/L of the core position versus the added components. This will tell you whether the core idea was correct and also illuminate the degree to which scaling into the trade was successful. Many times, the core position—the basic trade idea—will be sound (suggesting favorable tactics), but the scaling in might be flawed (suggesting unfavorable mechanics). A true scalper may flow in and out of long and short positions as orders are filled, again complicating the accounting. In such instances, it may be necessary to define separate trades arbitrarily, by creating demarcations at each point where the scalper goes flat.

One of the most important drill-downs is P/L as a function of time of day. Because volatility can vary greatly during the day, it is not unusual for trader performance to reflect these changing market conditions. In general, I will look at morning versus midday versus afternoon P/L and compare these to the market conditions at those times to gain an idea of a trader's strengths and weaknesses. It is not unusual to find that trading performance will decline precipitously at a certain time of day, often one corresponding to a drop in volume and volatility. This can be highly useful information for traders, encouraging them to drop their size and trading frequency at those times. Indeed, those are great times to take breaks from trading altogether and regain concentration and market perspective. Viewed across days, differences in P/L as a function of time of day may reveal particular trader strengths as well as weaknesses. My own performance is much better in the morning than in the afternoon, as this time period seems to best exploit my historical analyses of market patterns. It is also the time I am most focused and alert. Interestingly, my overall profitability—and my mental state—improved tremendously when I limited my trading to morning hours and left the rest of the day for other personally rewarding pursuits.

Many, many further drill-downs are possible—some on wider time frames, others on narrower ones. Tracking P/L as a function of day of week—is there a difference in performance on Mondays versus Fridays, for example—and as a function of news events (scheduled economic report days) are examples. One measure I like to examine in a qualitative way is a trader's performance once he or she is down money. This is a rough measure of a trader's ability to operate in the red and dig out of a hole. Sometimes traders improve their trading when they are losing money, as this focuses them on the need for sound mechanics. Other times, the losses create emotional repercussions and become self-reinforcing. The ability to trade out of the red is one measure of resilience, and it is the mark of a good trader. A related measure—the flip side of the "trade out of a hole" coin—is the ability to retain or add to gains when a trader is up money. Once in a while, traders will change how they will trade when they are making money.

EXHIBIT 7.3 Strategies for Self-observation and Performance Enhancement

	Videotaping	Metrics Collection	Direct Observation by a Mentor
Strength of the method	Allows for replay and examination of one's mechanics and mind frame; ideal for tracking mechanics	Highlights trading patterns that may otherwise go undetected; tracks trader progress	Useful in sorting out psychological problems from trading issues; a neutral source of feedback
Limitations of the method	Cannot get the large picture of how trading is progressing over time	Does not necessarily capture details about mechanics that can only be observed on tape	Not always available; doesn't allow for replay; not quantifiable like metrics
Best use	To review and work on mechanics	To determine if strategy and tactics are effective	To diagnose performance problems

It is almost as if they now feel they are playing with house money and need not be as concerned with risk. Collecting information on P/L as a function of recent profitability is very helpful in determining how traders are handling the risk and rewards of trading.

> A useful measure of emotional mastery is consistency of results regardless of the profitability of the last several trades.

What we're finding is that there are many pieces of information you can gather about your trading and many ways to obtain that information. (See Exhibit 7.3.) Your performance plan—your way of creating your own learning loops and cultivating expertise—will reflect the combination that best fits your trading markets and style. The key is self-observation: constantly knowing—and wanting to know—what works and what doesn't. Do you really know your strengths as a trader? If not, how can you build upon them and extend them? Are you aware of the weaknesses of your strategy, tactics, or mechanics? If not, can you truly improve them? We as traders are every bit as patterned as the markets we trade. Exploiting our patterns is an essential part of profiting from those in the market.

PERFORMANCE JOURNALING: ANOTHER TOOL FOR SELF-OBSERVATION

Perhaps the most common tool that traders use for self-mentoring is the trading journal. Journals contain a variety of information, but usually consist of the following:

- *A trading plan.* How one intends to trade.
- *Goals.* Things to work on in trading.
- *Observations.* About oneself and the market.

Most journals are written in the form of diaries. They are verbal summaries of what has happened and what one plans for the future. Keeping such a journal is an excellent way to increase one's mindfulness. In the heat of market action, it can be difficult to keep specific plans and goals topmost in one's mind. Requiring ourselves to commit priorities to print increases the odds that we will remember them when we most need to be mindful.

When I asked John Forman, author of *The Essentials of Trading*, about what traders most need to do to improve their performance, he pointed to "the consistent application of one's well thought out and conscientiously designed trading plan."

As a recent content editor for the Trade2Win forum site, Forman has observed many of the problems most common to traders. The greatest challenge for most traders, he notes, "is doing what they know they are supposed to be doing—following their trading plan 100% of the way. The trading plan is the map which directs the trader to their goal, yet so often they toss it aside and end up lost in the wilderness that is trading the markets." In short, traders lose their mindfulness: In the heat of market action, they become less—not more—planful.

We can accomplish great things with journals if we think of them, not as written diaries, but as multimedia portfolios that encompass *all* your efforts to enhance your trading. Such performance portfolios would consist of your videotapes, printouts of metrics, summarized observations by mentors—and your diary based upon those. I like to think of the diary as a kind of report card: It captures what you are attempting to accomplish and how well you're doing each day. The diary distills the information from videotapes, metrics, and observations into actionable plans—and then evaluates your progress on those plans. Ideally, the diary would consist of longer-term performance plans as well as daily plans for improvement.

There is always a risk of becoming overwhelmed with information from tapes and metrics. Without integrating and prioritizing the data, we can wind up with reams of facts and figures, but nothing concrete to act upon. When coaches watch videos of opponents, as well as their own teams' performances, they integrate data on player and team performance into a game plan, with specific goals and priorities for each player. The trading diary serves a similar function. It takes all the information from a performance portfolio and creates a game plan for self-mentoring. *It translates observations into actions.*

Notice that the coaches' game plans cannot substitute for long hours of watching tapes and gathering data. The plan has to emerge from a detailed assessment of one's own strengths and weaknesses and those of the opponent. Relying solely on a diary for trading development is similarly flawed. It creates plans without data and, as a result, is usually so broad and nonspecific that it cannot guide meaningful, sustained improvement in tactics or mechanics. Physicians gather information and make a diagnosis before they treat a condition; traders can do the same with an integrated performance portfolio. Videotapes, metrics, and observations provide the data, just like blood tests and imaging. From those, we diagnose trading problems and develop concrete plans for tackling them.

It is an artificial distinction to think of simulated trading as practice and live trading as real performance. *All performance is practice if it occurs in the framework of concrete plans for self-development.* The evolving performer asks: What will I work on today? How will I work on it? How will I know if I'm successful? What have I learned from today that can be utilized tomorrow? The role of a diary is to structure responses to these questions and keep them in conscious awareness. This allows us to focus on achieving process goals rather than profits. In a very important sense, whether we make money or not—on any given trade or day—is not in our control. While we can tilt odds in our favor, there are always uncertainty and unforeseen market developments. *The day's trade controls whether we make money, but we determine whether and how much we lose.* If the strategy is sound, the edge is present. Over time, trading well will translate into trading profitably.

> Focused on trading well, expert traders compete with themselves, not with the market.

USING THE TRADING DIARY FOR TRADER DEVELOPMENT

As I described in *The Psychology of Trading*, a written diary can be very helpful in working on the emotional challenges of trading. The diary is especially powerful if it records processes as they are occurring, not just in hindsight. This is especially true if you are not employing videotaping. While there are many sources of emotional interference in processing information and making decisions, the common source of difficulty is our tendency to become immersed in whatever state we happen to be in at the time. No longer observing ourselves, it is as if we view the world through prism lenses and forget that the lenses are there. We take our subjective experience to be reality.

Our states of mind and body truly function as lenses through which we perceive the world. Aaron Beck, one of the pioneers of cognitive therapy, referred to the negative triad: Depressed people process information about themselves, others, and the future with a pessimistic bias. Similarly, anxious individuals perceive only the threat in situations, not the promise. When we take our lenses for reality, we no longer are fully in control of our thoughts and behavior. We act upon our distortions, not our best judgment.

The value of the real-time diary is that it pushes us to stand outside ourselves and remove the prisms. To simply ask the questions "What is my state right now?" and "How is my state affecting my perceptions and behaviors?" requires that we stand apart from our frames of mind. The diary cultivates the self-observer in all of us, building our capacity to shift our own states intentionally. Indeed, an entire approach to therapy, which we will explore in Chapter 8, is grounded in just such a use of journaling.

Charles Kirk, editor of *The Kirk Report*, a comprehensive digest of market information and trading ideas, recently shared his thoughts with me about the value of diaries to trader development. "The difference I have found between the good and the great traders is that great traders are always acutely aware of areas where they need to improve and they work very hard to eliminate those weak links. . . . There is no greater tool in my opinion than a good trading diary of things you've learned. When I read my trading diary from several years ago, I'm always amazed how many things I've actually forgotten." Kirk's valuable point is that journals are not just educational devices; they are also mechanisms for continuing education. *Many of the most important lessons in markets—as in life—need to be learned and relearned.* Journals support both.

Remember Marc Greenspoon, the expert trader whom we met in Chapter 5? Despite making millions of dollars last year, he continues to religiously keep a journal of his performance. He frequently refers to it during our conversations and uses it to track what he did right and wrong in the past. Insights from journal entries months prior helped Marc make an important change in his trading. That is using a diary as continuing education—and why Marc is likely to sustain success as a professional.

Maintaining a diary does not substitute for deliberative practice or the feedback from videotapes and metrics, but it does allow us to crystallize feedback into action plans and keep those plans separate from the blinding effects of state shifts. When we write about ourselves, we necessarily stand outside ourselves. At those times, we are identifying with the mentor within us, not with the trader having difficulties.

> The trading diary is a means of communication from us as mentors to us as traders.

GOAL SETTING: TRANSLATING SELF-OBSERVATION INTO PERFORMANCE PLANS

When you examine the field of performance coaching, whether in trading, athletics, or other fields, two interventions stand out: goal setting and visualization. Indeed, some writers would have you believe that there is little more to performance enhancement than formulating goals, believing in them, and visualizing their attainment. This is silly, of course. Setting goals and imagining reaching them cannot possibly substitute for talents, skills, and the building of those through systematic practice and feedback. Visualizing reaching a goal in the absence of a planful pursuit of that goal is self-deception, not positive thinking.

Nevertheless, there is evidence that goal setting can contribute to performance. In the business world, Locke and Latham reviewed hundreds of studies of the effects of goal setting and found consistent evidence that setting goals improves performance across a variety of activities. The authors suggest that goals enhance performance in several ways:

- Focusing the attention of performers
- Channeling the efforts of performers
- Encouraging persistence
- Facilitating new problem-solving approaches

A comprehensive review by Burton's research group also finds support for the role of goal setting in improving athletic performance. Interestingly, however, the evidence suggests that the effects of goal setting are not as strong in sports as in the business world. Studies also find that athletes rate goal setting as only moderately effective.

A careful look at this research suggests that *how* goals are implemented is an important determinant of their effectiveness. Unfortunately, many mentors and traders are not aware of this research and therefore cannot benefit from its results.

Summarizing findings, Lavallee's research group notes the difference between "result goals" and "performance goals," and observes that the latter have been found to be more effective than the former. A result goal, for example, might be a trader's intention to make $2,500 per day. A performance goal would reference actions directly in the trader's control, such as ensuring that one's largest losing trade is not greater than one's largest winner. The reason that result goals may not be as effective is that they can create divisions in the minds of performers, encouraging them to evaluate their performances even as they try to remain immersed in them. Writers experience blocks when they critique their prose as they write. The same division of attention creates performance anxiety for public speakers and athletes in big games. Much of performance relies upon implicit processes that are derailed when outcomes are the object of explicit attention.

Performance (or process) goals, alternatively, keep performers focused on the specific actions they need to take to perform well. A performance goal for a NASCAR crew in training would be to stand in exactly the assigned positions so as to minimize mutual interference during a pit stop. The short-term trader's performance goal might be to raise stops to breakeven whenever trades are a full point in the green. Performance goals such as these reflect mechanics: concrete actions that, performed well, contribute to results. They keep traders in a state of flow rather than compete for trader attention and concentration.

Despite the seeming advantage of process goals, Burton and colleagues found in their review that a combination of process and outcome goals was more effective than either by itself. They suggest that performers who are developing skills benefit most from process goals that keep them focused on proper mechanics, while experienced performers derive greater benefit from outcome goals that keep them motivated. *This raises the possibility that goals may serve very different purposes at various phases of expertise development.* Whether goals work or don't depends upon how well they meet the needs of performers at their particular stages of development.

The implications for trading are important. Beginning traders are likely to benefit most by setting goals that reflect proper mechanics and tactics, such as risk management goals. Their focus during videotaping and metrics collection should be on trading fundamentals and the achievement of their goals. Expert traders, however, might gain an advantage from outcome goals that are motivating. As I am writing this, one of the traders I am working with lost money early in the morning due to an error in order placement. I suggested that we just concentrate on getting green for the day. He knew what he needed to do to reach that goal, and my screen shows that he has achieved that goal. The outcome goal helped him focus on doing the right things in trading.

Research finds that not all goals are created equal. Lavallee and colleagues note the acronym SMART to capture the common features of effective performance goals. Such goals are Specific, Measurable, Action-Oriented, Realistic, and Timely.

Goals that are SMART set priorities for the trader. They translate performance diagnoses that emerge from observations on videotape and metrics into real-time behaviors that improve outcomes.

When goal setting is not effective, it is often because the goals are not SMART. Common deficiencies of goals include:

- *Not specific.* The goals are framed in general terms, such as "I will trade with more discipline" or "I will let my winners ride," so that they cannot guide specific actions and facilitate the development of positive habit patterns.
- *Not measurable.* The goal is framed as a state of mind—"I will trade with greater confidence"—or as an outcome that cannot be tracked with metrics, as in "I will trade well," preventing any assessment of progress.
- *Not action-oriented.* Goals are stated as end points rather than as activities to perform, such as "I will make money today."
- *Not realistic.* Goals are pie-in-the-sky, as in "I want to be green every day this month," or are so numerous that they cannot be addressed effectively at one time.
- *Not timely.* Goals are so far into the future that they cannot guide current performance, as in "I want this to be my best year trading."

The ideal situation is one in which traders clearly prioritize tactics and mechanics for improvement based upon feedback from mentors, observations on videotape, and the results of metrics. Each of these priorities can then be translated into concrete goals for the coming day and week, with progress being tracked in a performance journal. Structured in this way, goals orient the trader, focus efforts, and enhance motivation.

WHEN GOALS HURT PERFORMANCE

The thorough review conducted by Burton and colleagues came to several interesting conclusions. One of these, based on the work of Locke's research team, was that the specificity of goals and their difficulty greatly impact how effective they will be in improving performance. The first of the SMART criteria suggests that specific goals will help traders more than non-specific ones. This is true, but there are limits to the benefits of specificity in many performance fields. Specific goals are useful when the performer is attempting to maintain highly consistent levels of performance. Examples would be Wendy Whelan, the ballerina, who has learned to execute jumps the same way each time in a ballet, or Tiger Woods, who has achieved remarkable consistency in his swing. While traders need consistency, theirs are not skills that are repeated the same way across performance situations. Because markets and market conditions vary, it is rare for traders to take positions the same way day after day. Highly specific goals may therefore be of less help to a developing trader than to, say, a professional bowler. Goals would need to be sufficiently broad as to allow traders to adapt to changing situations. Placing stop-loss points based upon market volatility and recent support/resistance is a broader and more flexible goal than placing stops a fixed distance from one's entries.

What appears to be more important than the specificity of goals is their difficulty. In the business arena, difficult goals tend to be more effective than easy ones because they are more motivating and elicit greater efforts. This isn't necessarily the case in the sports world, however. Olympic athletes report a preference for goals of moderate, rather than high, difficulty— and for good reason: These have been found to be more effective than very difficult goals. The relationship between the difficulty of goals and athletic performance is an inverted U. Very easy goals do not motivate performers or energize their efforts, but very difficult ones also seem to have dampening effects. Goals of moderate difficulty allow performers to marshal their efforts while maintaining optimism over goal attainment. This is consistent with the research that we encountered earlier on the flow state, which found that matching tasks to ability level was essential to the maintenance of flow.

The importance of this research is that goals can actually hurt performance if they are pitched at the wrong level of difficulty. Perfectionistic traders will chronically set goals that are unreachable, creating experiences of frustration and failure. Equally important, insufficiently stringent goals appear to have a suppressive effect upon motivation, reducing the rage to master. One of the most valuable facets of performance portfolios is that they track the skill levels of traders over time. *This permits the setting of relative, rather than absolute, goals.* A relative goal is an improvement upon a prior performance, not an absolute level of achievement. If a trader, for instance, is working on entering trades at good prices, I might calculate the average drawdown during trades for a week and encourage the trader to set a goal to improve upon this figure. Relative goals avoid perfectionism and are more likely to be matched to traders' abilities than absolute targets.

Relative goals ensure that learning is challenging without being overwhelming.

Goals can also hurt performance if they are not implemented as part of an ongoing process. A goal that is not tied to immediate plans and feedback leaves a trader with no clearly perceived path toward goal attainment. Burton and colleagues make the excellent point that performers with lower levels of confidence and efficacy will especially benefit from goals that create experiences of success and control. When traders are given vague goals that are not concretely linked to planning, evaluation, feedback, and corrective efforts, there is no way for them to extend their sense of competence. Such goals neither focus nor motivate developing traders. Goals are effective to the extent that they are part of broad learning loops that build skills and cultivate the sense of competence. It is important for traders and their mentors to think of goals as components of learning processes, not as static targets to be hit and then forgotten.

IMAGERY: MAKING GOALS REAL

As we will see in Chapter 8, imagery is a staple of cognitive-behavioral therapies and is also a mainstay of sport psychologists and mentors in other performance fields. While most imagery work emphasizes visualization, it is possible to invoke other senses. The primary uses of imagery are twofold:

1. *Invoking particular emotional states.* People respond to images as real events. Imagining frightening situations can elevate our stress levels; imagining sexual scenarios can produce arousal. This ability of imagery to duplicate reality is particularly useful in generating desirable states. For instance, we might use soothing imagery to relax ourselves during a stressful episode, or we might imagine attaining a goal to heighten motivation.

2. *Rehearsing behaviors.* Here imagery is used as a mechanism for practice. For example, a trader might visualize a variety of what-if scenarios surrounding the release of minutes from a Federal Reserve meeting and how she will trade each of those scenarios. The purpose of the imagery exercise is to make a desired behavior more likely to occur in real-time performance.

Like goal setting, imagery can be a valuable performance tool, but how it is used makes a world of difference in its effectiveness. Once again, research proves most enlightening.

Research reviewed by Hall indicates that imagery is indeed effective as a stand-in for real experience. Imaging studies of the brain, for example, find that we respond similarly to events that are imagined versus experienced. Behavioral therapies that make use of imagery, such as the exposure techniques and cognitive restructuring methods that we will cover in the next chapters, are among the most effective in outcome research. Athletes report using imagery extensively across practice and competitive situations. Because imagery is functionally equivalent to actual experience, performers can benefit from skill building via imagery as a supplement to deliberative practice.

This is not to say that imagery can wholly substitute for real-world experience. Most studies find weaker performance benefits for imagery alone versus actual practice. In addition, imagery does not work equally well for all performers. Lavallee and colleagues summarize five major conclusions about imagery from the research literature:

1. *Mental practice improves performance.*
2. *Mental practice added to physical practice improves performance beyond the level of either by itself.*
3. *Mental practice improves cognitive skills more than motor ones.*
4. *Mental practice benefits expert performers more than novices.*
5. *The benefits of mental practice decrease quickly with time.*

An additional, interesting finding is that imagery-based practice is most effective when it is vivid and when it is positive. People differ in their abilities to produce vivid imagery, and it appears that highly vivid images best serve as rehearsals for live performance. One of the reasons mental practice may be less effective than actual deliberative practice is that it is difficult to achieve high degrees of realism when visualizing performance situations. Several studies, moreover, find that positive imagery—imagining successful performances—is much more effective than imagining unsuccessful performances. Although it may seem perverse for a performer to utilize imagery negatively, this, in fact, happens rather often as a function of worry and performance anxiety. Experienced traders know the difference between trading for opportunity and trading to avoid losing.

These findings may help to explain why imagery works best for experienced performers. They have an intimate knowledge of mechanics and tactics and thus can imagine far more vivid and realistic scenarios than can novices. Experienced performers have also had greater numbers of successful experiences and thus find it easier to tap into positive imagery. It is difficult for beginners to vividly imagine winning scenarios when they have not experienced many of these.

Employed properly, imagery enhances goal setting by making goals real. Imagery can engage motivation and enthusiasm, and it can augment physical practice to accelerate learning curves. It is unfortunate that most mentors in the trading world are not familiar with the large bodies of research on human performance, learning, goal setting, and imagery. This lack of information leads to situations in which the methods are applied crudely and indiscriminately—more in the mode of pop psychology than performance science. A more thoughtful approach to learning relies on systematic observation via videotapes, metrics, and mentorship and a translation of observations into performance plans pertaining to strategy, tactics, and mechanics. Performance journals, goal setting, and imagery are but a few of the mechanics of mentorship that can make the difference between good intentions and steady progress. How these are tailored to the learner's needs and learning styles, however, will determine their effectiveness.

> Trades are most likely to be works of art if they are guided by hard science.

A FINAL WORD ON THE SCIENCE OF PERFORMANCE

The message of this chapter is that there is a science as well as an art to expertise development. From the collection of data on trading patterns to self-observation to the use of tailored performance enhancement strategies, traders can accelerate their learning curves by drawing upon what we know about performance in other fields. It is not enough to read books and articles, attend workshops, and review charts. Performance development is planful, systematic work on oneself. We see it among NASCAR teams, Olympic athletes, and performing artists: The lessons of performance research are being put to good use. The trading world has been slow to pick up on the simple fact that trading is a performance activity. The principles and processes that guide elite performers in other fields can cultivate expertise among traders. This, perhaps, is the greatest—and least exploited—source of edge in the markets today.

What of those situations, however, in which our states of mind prevent us from immersing ourselves in proper training? That is a task for psychology and the trader's role as his or her own therapist. Can traders truly become their own therapists? Let's take a look.

CHAPTER 8

Cognitive Techniques for Enhancing Performance

It is the greatest mistake to think that man is always one and the same. A man is never the same for long. He is continually changing. He seldom remains the same even for half an hour.
—G.I. Gurdjieff

For the past seven chapters, I have emphasized that work on trading psychology is of limited benefit if one has not first found a market niche and entered into a learning process to cultivate competence and expertise. Now, however, we will look at the reverse side of this coin: All the training and skill development in the world will be for naught if your psychological patterns undermine your performance. In the next two chapters, I am going to attempt something unique: I will outline the major emotional problems that afflict skilled traders, summarize two brief therapy approaches that research has found to be most effective for those problems, and then illustrate how you can implement these change techniques for yourself. If you are truly to become your own performance mentor, you will also, at times, become your own therapist.

THE ROOT OF TRADING PROBLEMS

The Psychology of Trading made the case that the problems that most affect traders are variations of problems that impact all of us. This is important because it suggests that the same brief therapy methods that have been found successful in controlled outcome studies can benefit traders emotionally and financially. Unlike traditional psychotherapeutic methods, which rely on weekly talk sessions to explore the roots of psychological problems, brief therapies provide sets of hands-on tools and techniques for altering present patterns of thinking, feeling, and doing. Gurdjieff's fundamental insight—now finding validation in cognitive neuroscience—is that human beings are not "always one and the same." We experience different emotional, physical, and cognitive states in response to environmental events, leading us to think and behave one way in a given situation and quite differently in others.

An objective observer of the human race would conclude that people lack self-control. They are not always one and the same. This allows normally responsible individuals to forget about risk management when they are trading large size. It enables us to develop elaborate trading plans, only to see them fly out the window when markets move violently. We are not fully intentional beings: Too often our best intentions are derailed by momentary events and experiences.

How we think, feel, and behave are relative to our states of mind and body. We are not one and the same, because we continually shift states, processing the world very differently from one mode to another.

Popular psychology does not take this into account. It tells us that we can change if we just adopt more favorable attitudes, images, and self-talk. There would be no need for therapists if this were the case. Everyone would simply read self-help books and thenceforth live lives of fulfillment. For the vast majority of us, however, change does not follow from simple acts of will. Soon after I will something to happen, other selves inevitably take over and exert wills of their own. Why else would a chronic dieter suddenly binge eat—and then purge? Why would a trader who has written one rule after another in a journal lurch into a large position—and then hold it as it goes against him? It almost seems like self-sabotage, but in fact it is much worse than that.

It is the result of an absence *of a unified self.* Brief therapies are effective to the extent that they integrate our selves and help us become more intentional. Cognitive therapies accomplish this by training us to process the world differently. Behavioral therapies unify us by creating novel response patterns to challenging life events. *To think and act as we choose: This is the reward of becoming our own therapists.*

THE FRAGMENTED SELF

What is the self? It is what provides us with continuity from state to state. I experience myself as me regardless of the state I'm in. Similarly, others perceive us to be who we are despite our continual mood and behavior shifts. When I say, "I love you," it is understood that this is an expression of the self: something basic, fundamental, and unchanging. It does not mean "In the state I'm currently in, I feel love for you."

The fact that we experience continuity in the self and yet can be so fragmented is the source of many of our emotional difficulties—and most of the problems we encounter in trading. *Because of our sense of continuity, we identify with the states that we are in; each, we think, is a reflection of reality.* Gurdjieff's famous exercise is to ask people to sit quietly and remain fully self-aware for a period of time. Inevitably, we cannot do it. Our minds wander; we identify with the thoughts, images, or feelings of the moment and forget to remain self-aware. If we cannot sustain unity of purpose in such a simple, unemotional exercise, how can we possibly hope to remain consistent and in control during periods of risk and uncertainty?

Quite simply, the "me" in us—our sense of who we are—is stronger than our "I"—our ability to intentionally guide our actions. To the extent we are divided, we do not have a fully free will. We are at the mercy of environments and events and what those trigger in us.

Talk therapy, pioneered by Freud almost a century ago, is unfortunately inefficient in producing change. Too often therapy is long term, not because the problems are so severe and intractable *but because therapy is occurring while the client is in one state of mind and problems occur in quite another*. This is a limitation of most coaching of traders as well. Discussions of trading goals, plans, and methods occur outside the context of actual trading, when emotional shifts make it difficult to access those good intentions. Brief therapy yields changes in short periods of time because it operates in real time: It works with people in the settings—and in the states—in which problems typically occur.

A useful way to think of this is that *you cannot achieve unity of self unless you work on it while you are fragmented*. This is the essence of real-time self-therapy.

> Brief therapies exploit fragmentation in real time to create opportunities for mastery.

When I enter traders' offices as they are trading, I am doing so at times when they usually perform their worst trading. I might say to the trader,

"Look! You've just lost money in the market and now you've just started trading more actively. That's what lost you money last week. You were frustrated and tried to make something happen. Now you're frustrated again. We have a perfect opportunity to lose money just like before. Or—we could do something different."

Gurdjieff referred to my role as an alarm clock; Freud called it the "observing ego." What I'm doing is—metaphorically—shaking traders by the shoulders, holding up a mirror, and saying, "Look at yourself! You're worked up! Do you really want to be putting on trades now?" The goal is to help people stand outside themselves as observers, even as they are experiencing moment-to-moment state shifts. *That observing capacity is the glue holding the self together, allowing us to act with intention.* "You're frustrated; don't go there" is the message from the therapist in us to our trader self.

With self-observation, we become less fragmented. There is now a part of us that stands apart from events and asks the question "What do I want to do here?" With repetition, effortful self-remembering yields positive habit patterns. *If traders repeatedly rehearse stepping aside from markets and reviewing their tactics when they're frustrated, eventually the recognition of the state shift and trading review occur automatically, as a new part of the trader's behavioral repertoire.*

THE FAMILY MAN WHO LOST HIS ABILITY TO TRADE

A competent trader of notes and bonds, James had two years of profitability behind him and had gradually increased his size and success. Then he got the news: His wife, Victoria, was pregnant. At first James was excited. He was only too pleased to begin life as a family man. Victoria had always dreamed of being a mom and couldn't have been happier. The couple began shopping for houses, focusing on neighborhoods with the best schools. Housing prices were steep, but James knew that Victoria wanted to leave the city. For his part, he didn't mind a commute and felt that his trading career could sustain the new expenses of home and baby.

When the yield curve tightened—and then inverted—James struggled with his trading. Accustomed to playing off the spread among bills, notes, and bonds, James could no longer rely on old relationships. He experienced one of the worst trading weeks of his career, giving back a meaningful percentage of profits from the past two months. Normally this would not have been a problem; he had gone through losing periods before. Typically he would cut his size, observe new market relationships, and retool his trading.

Once before, when the government announced the reemergence of the long bond, he was hurt badly on several trades and took a break from watching the spreads. Trading outright positions with reduced size, he regained his equilibrium and quickly returned to his winning ways.

This time was different, however. The first thing James thought about after he lost his money was how much he needed to make back to meet his earlier financial projections. He was determined to not live life "house poor" like many of his trading colleagues. For that reason, he felt he couldn't afford to trade smaller. Indeed, he became more aggressive in his trading, determined to make the money back.

The strategy backfired badly. Also afraid of taking further losses, he stopped out his supersized positions quickly—much more quickly than usual. Unable to take even normal heat on positions, he found himself exiting potentially profitable trades. This generated added frustration, which in turn led him to trade more actively. By the time I started working with James, his formerly solid trading had deteriorated into a cycle of frustration, aggressive trading, anxiety, fearful trading, and further frustration. Normally sociable with the other traders, he now seemed withdrawn and disengaged.

It was as if he were a different person, a different trader. And he didn't like either one.

Let's figure out what happened to James, and then investigate the role of cognitive therapy in turning his trading around.

WHY COPING FAILS: THE ROLE OF COGNITION

The important thing to keep in mind is that, while the relationships among the fixed-income instruments changed as a result of the yield curve inversion, James's bread-and-butter trades did not change. Trends in the 10-year T-note, for example, did not change suddenly, nor was there a large shift of volatility. True, he could not lean on the old spread relationships, but he had dealt with that problem before and emerged even stronger as a result. There was no objective reason that James could not come back from his recent losses.

James, however, was no longer responding to objective market conditions. This is why his coping failed. *The threat was no longer the risk of a particular trade, but the threat of someday being unable to comfortably make house payments and support a family.* Trading was no longer about making good trades. It was about making a certain amount of money to support a lifestyle. Normal losses, as a result, now felt threatening. Although a normal loss on a normal position could not realistically damage his future prospects, he *interpreted* those losses as threats. His interpretations of events—not the events themselves—were generating the sense of danger that altered his trading.

This is how cognitive therapy works: It enables us to change our interpretation of events, so that we can reduce threats and rely upon our effective coping mechanisms.

Clearly James was exiting positions and altering his trading to manage his anxieties—not to properly manage trades. He was coping with internal threat, not market risk. This shifted his trading patterns, creating further distress and entirely new and different secondary coping efforts to manage this distress. Before long, a sociable and disciplined young man was behaving in a withdrawn and haphazard manner.

One of Freud's enduring contributions to psychology was his recognition that *when coping fails, people tend to revert to coping styles and strategies that had worked during an earlier period of life.* He called this *regression.* State shifts and personality changes, from Freud's perspective, are movements back in time to ways of handling threat that we had used in childhood. Often, these early coping strategies—though they worked in the past—are not suited to present-day realities. Instead of solving problems, they introduce new ones. By the time traders such as James seek counseling, it is because of problems created by their altered coping—not just because of the concerns that led to the initial state shifts.

Regression results in a shift of both state and personality that expresses itself in radically different coping. When we return to old coping methods again and again, the result is a problem pattern: a repetitive and self-defeating sequence of behavior that is actually the only kind of coping we know at the time. James did not want to be exiting trades prematurely and losing money, but found himself doing so nonetheless.

If you can grasp this concept, you are well along the way toward becoming your own therapist: When we overreact to situations, we are usually responding with past coping. Like James, we are reacting to our extreme interpretations of situations, not to the situations themselves.

> Psychological interferences with trading performance are the result, not just of problems, but of outdated coping with those problems.

Cognitive therapy is effective because it changes our interpretations of events and provides opportunities for an updating of coping skills. Interestingly, it does this through the same process that we found generates competence and expertise in performance: the progressive practice and immediate feedback of deliberative practice.

WHAT YOU SHOULD KNOW BEFORE STARTING COGNITIVE WORK

Before we launch into the how-to aspects of cognitive work, let's take a look at when self-help is appropriate and when outside assistance might be needed. When a person comes to me for help with trading-related concerns, one or more of the following is usually present:

- *Situational problems.* The trader is going through emotional interference with trading due to factors that have appeared recently: a trading slump, relationship stresses that are posing distractions, changes in health or finances, and so on.
- *Lack of training.* The trader is experiencing distress because of inadequate strategy, tactics, and/or mechanics, resulting in losses and frustration.
- *Changing markets.* The trader has good trading skills and a history of success, but his/her markets have undergone significant changes and now there is a need to adapt.
- *Chronic problems.* The trader is experiencing emotional interference with trading that is due to wider personality problems that have been present through much of the life span and interferes with multiple aspects of life, not just trading.

When I first meet with a trader, those four items are part of a checklist in my head to help me evaluate the trading problem. If the issue is one of lack of training or changing markets, brief therapy techniques may be helpful in gaining control over distress, but the ultimate answer, as we've seen, is to enter into a (re)training process. The trader who lacks training needs to work on trading skills through simulation and structured feedback. The skilled trader whose market has changed needs to use simulation and smaller size to explore new strategies and tactics—and sometimes new markets.

I cannot emphasize this enough: *Before beginning psychological work, it is necessary to figure out whether the problem is primarily a trading problem affecting emotions (lack of training, changing market) or an emotional problem affecting trading (situational or chronic distress).* The answer to this question will help determine the kind of mentor you seek and the specific type of assistance you'll require.

When the problem is a situational one, usually you'll know that because there has been a major life change corresponding to the time in which the trading problems have occurred. Situational difficulties may be trading ones—slumps and performance anxieties are common, as is overconfidence following success—or they may be traced to life outside of trading. It is not at all unusual for relationship and financial problems, for example, to carry over into trading, as we've seen with James. Interpersonal losses, either through divorce/breakup or death, are particular distractions from trading. These situational concerns are ideal for short-term therapy methods. The problem is coping with a situation; it is not a fundamental personality pattern.

Other times, traders do have chronic patterns that generate distress. This may be due to long-standing problems with depression, anxiety, attention deficits, or addictive behaviors. The key to identifying these is that the problems have existed before the trading career began and exist in areas of life separate from trading. Self-administered short-term therapy techniques can be helpful for managing distress from chronic problems, but consultation with experienced, licensed professionals is recommended. This may very well include medical consultation for careful diagnosis. What looks like a psychological problem sometimes has a purely medical cause, such as an endocrine imbalance. Ongoing emotional problems that interfere with work and relationships also may benefit from medications, the majority of which are non-habit-forming and mild in their side effects. Before pursuing self-help strategies for chronic emotional or behavioral problems, it makes sense to consult with an experienced professional.

So when is it appropriate to become your own short-term therapist? Exhibit 8.1 provides a short checklist that guides my own work with traders. If you fit into one or more of the categories of the checklist, the odds are good that you can significantly benefit from the brief therapy techniques I'll be teaching you.

EXHIBIT 8.1 Checklist of Trading Problems that Benefit from Brief Therapies

Trading Problem Checklist

- *Performance stresses.* Becoming more concerned about P/L than making good trades.
- *Performance anxiety.* Freezing up during trading; failing to make good trades.
- *Impulsive trading.* Overtrading (trading excessive size and/or trading too frequently) due to boredom, distraction, or loss of concentration.
- *Revenge trading.* Departing from trading plans because of frustration/anger due to previous losing trades.
- *Loss of self confidence.* Self-doubt and negative thinking due to trading slumps and/or recent problems in life outside of trading.
- *Attitudes that interfere with good trading decisions.* Perfectionism, negative expectations, overconfidence, basing self-esteem on P/L.

JAMES BEGINS COGNITIVE THERAPY

James was an ideal candidate for cognitive therapy. He possessed strong trading skills, so it was clear that rookie errors were not responsible for his frustration. He also was not someone hampered by lifelong psychological deficits. His problem, while exacerbated by market changes, was largely situational: A change in life—Victoria's pregnancy—had changed his views of risk and reward, and this undermined his trading. Let's see how cognitive therapy helped James turn his situation around, and then detail how you can implement these methods for yourself.

When James first met with me, he viewed the problem as the pregnancy and the financial pressures having a child placed on his trading. He felt guilty blaming the pregnancy, but could see no other reason for his trading woes. This was his construal of the problem: He believed that events were directly causing his distress.

"Let's try a little thought experiment," I suggested. "Suppose Victoria was pregnant, but neither of you knew it. Maybe you hadn't yet done any pregnancy test. Would her pregnancy hurt your trading?"

"Of course not," James responded.

"Or let's say that you knew she was pregnant, but you had $10,000,000 stashed in the bank. How would having a child affect your trading?"

James smiled, seeing my point. "If I had ten million," he joked, "I probably wouldn't bother with trading."

"If the pregnancy could possibly ruin your trading," I suggested, "it would ruin your trading whether you knew about it or not, no matter how much money you had. It would be like poisoning you. Poison would hurt you whether or not you knew you had been poisoned. It would hurt you no matter how much you had in the bank. Is pregnancy poison?"

James and I were engaging in what cognitive therapists call a Socratic dialogue. What I'm trying to do is encourage James to view his problem from a different angle—or, more properly, to see that his problem is a function of the angle from which he's viewing his life situation.

"What are you telling yourself about having this child?" I asked James. "What goes through your head when you're trading?"

"I want to be a good father; I want to provide for my boy," James explained. "I don't want his mother to have to worry about money."

"I see. A *good dad* provides for his son, right?" I asked James, stressing those two words. I paused ever so slightly and looked squarely into James's eyes. "So what does that make you if you lose money?"

James flinched. His cognitive therapy was under way.

THE FIRST CHANGE IN COGNITIVE WORK: JAMES MAKES THE TRANSLATION

My Socratic dialogue with James—of which the preceding was only a small portion—was designed to undermine his definition of the problem. "Events are making me feel and behave this way" is his definition. By playing devil's advocate, I am helping him see that the events in themselves do not have the power to interfere with his trading. Rather, he is pressured by his *interpretation* of events, by their meaning to him. James grew up in a poor family. He knew what it was like to live with parents who could not provide for him. The last thing he wanted was to inflict that on his own child. James wasn't pressured by Victoria's pregnancy; he was pressured by his fear that he would be like his own father, unable to take care of his family. Trading losses were merely the trigger for this fear. Unable to allay the fear with his usual coping mechanisms, he felt overwhelmed. He then tried to reduce his distress with other, earlier coping—escape/avoidance—that had helped him as a child.

Unlike a psychoanalytic therapy, cognitive work does not focus on those earlier events, although understanding them can be very helpful in appreciating our personality shifts. Rather, cognitive therapy helps people see that their reactions to events are a function of their self-talk about those events. James's trading problems, in a sense, have nothing to do with having a child. He is overtrading and then skittishly exiting good trades because he is telling himself that he needs to make money—and can't afford to lose money—in order to be a good father.

> If our ways of viewing the world are like glasses that we wear, cognitive therapy is like a change of prescription.

"How would you feel if I stood over you while you were trading," I asked James, "and I held a gun to your head and said, 'You have to make money, or I'll pull the trigger?' How do you think that would affect your trades?"

"I wouldn't be able to concentrate," James replied, "I'd be too scared."

"Scared, as in, 'You have to make money, or you'll be a failure as a husband and father?' " I asked. "Do you think it's possible you're putting an emotional gun to your own head?"

The first step of progress in cognitive work is seeing that we have more control over our reactions than we thought we had: It's our way of looking at things—and not things themselves—that maintain our problem patterns. James made that translation when he finally saw that he was, indeed, holding a kind of gun to his own head—not because he was self-defeating, but because he desperately wished to avoid his own past.

THE NEXT CHANGE: JAMES HOLSTERS HIS GUN

Once James came to the realization that it was his thinking about money and markets that was creating his distress, it wasn't too great a leap to entertain the notion that maybe his thinking was distorted—a remnant from his past. This is a critical phase in cognitive therapy, as traders make the transition from being aware of their negative thought patterns to actually questioning and challenging them. In the beginning, I was the one doing the Socratic questioning. Over time, James assumed that role.

The technique that most helped James make the transition was what cognitive practitioners call "collaborative empiricism." We decided to treat James's thoughts about being a good provider and making money in the markets as hypotheses. Like any good scientists, we agreed to conduct some tests of those hypotheses. One test, for example, was a simple thought experiment. I asked James to think about another married trader in the office who had recently lost money. "Would you call him a bad husband?" I asked James. Of course, James said no. He clearly could see that being a good or bad husband had far more to do with the quality of the trader's relationship with his wife than with his day-to-day, week-to-week trading results.

Another simple test occurred when I watched James trade and waited for him to have a run of winning trades. "Are you a better parent now than earlier today?" I asked him. James just smiled.

The best test of James's assumptions came when we brought Victoria into the sessions. To James' surprise, Victoria was not worried about money. She was thinking about returning to school on a part-time basis to finish her degree so that she could eventually teach and develop her career. Ironically, she had been hesitant to raise this idea with James, because she thought it would make her look like a bad mother to James if she were to return to work. She also didn't want James to think she was concerned about their finances, because that might place more pressure on him. She insisted that she was prepared to go through some lean times financially and just wanted them to be there for the baby. James was relieved to see that Victoria could accept his occasional cold streaks; Victoria was equally gratified to see that James supported her eventual return to work.

> Cognitive therapy is most powerful when it provides us with direct experiences that undermine our most negative beliefs.

I subsequently suggested to James that his pressuring himself to make money not only didn't make him a better father and husband, it actually compromised his effectiveness at home. I encouraged him to conduct his own tests at home and see if his pressured, worried periods were also his occasions of best parenting. When he saw that he was actually avoiding parenting when he was upset, I pointed out his increasing isolation and withdrawn, sullen mood during his losing streak. This, I rather pointedly suggested, is the essence of not being there for your family.

We then applied these new perspectives in real time as James traded. When he went through a losing period, we talked out loud about how he used to pressure himself, how this would only hurt his trading and home life, and how he could respond differently. A solution-focused approach was especially helpful at this juncture, as I asked James to replay how he had talked with himself the last time he successfully emerged from a losing period. He explained that he had reduced his size and took the P/L out of trading for a while, so that he could regain his rhythm. This became a core strategy whenever he lost money during the trading day.

We also made effective use of the gun metaphor. After James had lost money repeatedly in the morning, I asked him where his gun was and whether he was ready to point it to his head and pressure himself for the afternoon. He agreed to holster the gun and take some pressure off by calling home and taking a short break. Hearing Victoria's support reminded him to support himself and chip away at his losses. I knew that James was making real progress when I came into his office and, before I could say a word, he said, "No gun today." I congratulated him and promptly left the room. James was well on his way to becoming his own therapist.

WHAT COGNITIVE THERAPY ACCOMPLISHES

Cognitive therapy is one of the most extensively studied approaches in all of psychology. It has been found to be effective for such problems as anxiety, depression, anger, and impulse control. My own experience is that cognitive work is especially effective in situations like James's, in which loss of confidence, worry, and negative thinking are major elements. By framing these as part of our self-talk—our conversations with ourselves—traders can make rapid progress in distancing themselves from old patterns and beginning new ones. The value of this is that, without the negative self-talk, traders no longer experience the high levels of distress that trigger old coping patterns and generate further problems. Once James stopped putting the gun of self-pressure to his head, for example, he no longer lurched into trades with excessive size or pulled himself out of winning trades prematurely. He was able to cope with the market, rather than coping with his own internal demons.

Cognitive therapy is considered a short-term modality, but that doesn't mean that it works overnight. All the methods we will cover require ongoing rehearsal and application. How long it will take to see progress will depend upon the problems you're tackling, how entrenched they are, and how vigorously you work on them. In general, I encourage people to anticipate progress measured in weeks—not just a few days and not after months or years. *Research tells us that involvement in the therapy—practicing techniques on a daily basis, engaging in them emotionally, and applying them to actual life situations—accelerates change and improves the likelihood of success.* In therapy, as in performance, practice makes permanent.

As we've seen with James, cognitive therapy is based on a simple recognition: How we feel about life events is a function of our thoughts and beliefs regarding those events.

The goal of cognitive therapy is to help you become expert at thinking about your thinking: to become aware of your automatic thought patterns so that you can critically evaluate and change them. In a sense, cognitive therapy is an unlearning process. Learning makes a skill automatic; unlearning takes what is automatic and brings it into conscious control. By unlearning automatic thoughts, we regain control over our interpretations of events—and our reactions to them. The result is expanded free will.

STEP ONE OF COGNITIVE THERAPY: IDENTIFYING AUTOMATIC THOUGHTS

It's impossible to change our cognitive distortions if we remain unaware of them. The first step of cognitive therapy is to observe our thought processes in real time so that we can catch ourselves in the act of distorting events. At first this self-observation will take time and effort. With practice, it becomes an automatic skill in its own right.

Keeping a cognitive journal is an excellent first step that aids self-awareness. The idea of the cognitive journal is to interrupt ourselves when we're experiencing one of our characteristic problems—negative thinking or impulsive behavior—and identify the thoughts and beliefs that are associated with these problems. The journal forces us to become observers of ourselves rather than getting wrapped up in the problems of the moment.

Albert Ellis suggested a useful format for journals that he described as an A-B-C sequence:

- *Activating event.* The situation that is occurring at the time we are experiencing our problem pattern.
- *Beliefs.* The thoughts and perceptions that are triggered by the event.
- *Consequences.* What we are feeling and how we are behaving as a result of the triggered beliefs.

These can be written as columns in the journal, with entries at different points in the day, as illustrated in Exhibit 8.2.

The goal of the A-B-C columns is not to change how people think, but to make them aware of the connections between their thinking and their emotions and actions. Many times the B column will help traders become aware of core beliefs that cut across much of their negative self-talk. For instance, the belief from the second entry ("I need to get my money back") has an even deeper belief at its root, which we can identify by asking, "Or else?" *The trader believes he needs to get the money back or he'll feel like a loser.* His core belief is that he's only as good as his trading results for the day. This leads him to experience himself as a failure whenever his trades fail.

The other advantage of the A-B-C journal format is that it keeps traders focused on the consequences of their core beliefs. As I emphasized in *The Psychology of Trading*, the best way to change a pattern is to become emotionally connected to the negative consequences associated with that pattern. Time and again I have seen people make remarkable changes, including ending long-term addictions, when they start viewing their problem patterns as personal enemies. The cognitive journal keeps the trader focused on the message "I am not a loser; it's my negative way of thinking that's making me feel like a loser." By reinforcing this message again and again, the journal helps traders sustain the momentum of their change efforts.

How long should traders stick with the A-B-C journal format? There are two answers for that. First, the journaling should be conducted every day until traders can clearly identify the one or two core beliefs or distortions that are most interfering with their performance. It is important for traders to recognize their own patterns and appreciate the degree to which their thinking is patterned. Second, the journal is just a learning tool. The ultimate goal is to recognize our cognitive patterns as they are occurring. Once traders can catch themselves in the act of distorting events and falling into old, automatic thoughts, it is time to move to the next phase of cognitive work. In general, I have found that at least two weeks of daily work with the journal are necessary before patterns become clear and people are able to catch those patterns in real time.

STEP TWO OF COGNITIVE THERAPY: INTERRUPTING AND CHALLENGING NEGATIVE THOUGHTS

There is a very simple technique in cognitive-behavioral work called *thought stopping*. When people catch themselves falling into an automatic thought pattern, they purposely interrupt the negative thinking process by saying (out loud or to themselves): Stop! The purpose of this technique is to become more mindful: to not only recognize negative thoughts as they occur, but to actively interrupt them and decide to not run with them. In Gurdjieff's terms, thought stopping prevents the person from identifying with the "me" that feels negative and instead identify with the "I" that wants to process the world more constructively. Indeed, Gurdjieff used to use "Stop!" techniques with his own pupils, in which they had to cease all activity and simply observe themselves from an outside perspective. The idea was to build mindfulness.

The opposite of mindfulness is mindlessness. When we fall prey to automatic thoughts, we are mindless—we no longer exercise full control of our thinking and our experience. The next phase of cognitive work extends the journal to encourage mindfulness. We do this by not only noting the automatic, negative thoughts but by actively questioning them. This creates a fourth column in our journal, a D to accompany the A-B-C. The D stands for Disputation, because we will be using the journal to dispute and undermine distorting, self-limiting beliefs. (See Exhibit 8.2.)

The idea of the fourth column is to question the negative assumptions and beliefs, rather than automatically identify with them. By playing devil's advocate with your automatic thoughts, you reinforce the mindful part of you that does not want to fall into the old traps. The interesting part is that, as you repeat this devil's advocacy day after day through the journal, *the disputation process itself starts to become automatic*: You are much more likely to catch negative thought patterns as they occur and reject them.

Research suggests that disputations are most effective when they are performed with emotional force. Cognitive therapists refer to these as "hot cognitions": new thought patterns that possess emotional force. Imagery can be especially effective in turning routine journal entries into powerful emotional experiences. One technique mentioned in *The Psychology of Trading* is imagining a specific other person (usually someone you don't like) repeating your negative, automatic thoughts to you. In other words, you look at your core negative beliefs as a conversation that you routinely hold with yourself. Instead of continuing the self-conversation, you imagine someone else initiating the negative talk with you. It is truly interesting that most of us will not accept from others the kind of talk we engage in

EXHIBIT 8.2 Fragment of Cognitive Journal with A-B-C-D-E Columns

	Activating Event	Beliefs	Consequences	Disputation	Efforts at Change
9:30 A.M.	Missed an excellent setup when I waited for everything to line up exactly.	I can't afford to lose money because I've been in a slump.	Frustration, desire to chase the market higher.	Would I want someone else pressuring me to not lose money? Am I really going to trade better if I'm focused on not losing?	I don't need to be right all the time; I just need to make sure the odds are in my favor.
12 Noon	Placed several trades that went nowhere in a slow market.	I need to get my money back.	Chopped up and lost a little, feeling discouraged.	Beating myself up is not going to help me make good trades. It's what's making me lose money in the first place.	There's no getting that money back; all I can do is learn from the losing trades and do things better next time.
2:15 P.M.	Lost my data connection; equipment failure when the market was moving.	I have the worst luck; I can't win.	Feeling depressed, thinking about giving up trading.	Would I judge another trader to be a bad trader simply because of an equipment problem? Just because something goes wrong doesn't mean there's something wrong with me.	Trading isn't depressing me; it's my way of thinking. Luck has nothing to do with it; I need better backup systems.

internally. We can tell ourselves, "I can't do anything right; what's wrong with me?" but we don't like to hear someone else say to us, "You can't do anything right; what's wrong with you!" By translating self-talk into a conversation and vividly imaging the talk coming from another person, we become an observer of the distorted thoughts—much more able to view them critically and reject them.

Sometimes the easiest way to dispute our automatic, negative thoughts is simply to speak them aloud, so that we can hear them and listen to them critically. For instance, if my self-talk is telling me that I have to get my money back because of a recent loss, I might speak aloud, "I am telling myself that I have to get my money back right now because I lost money. Is that a trading idea that is going to make me money, or is that my frustration talking?" Speaking our thoughts aloud gives them objectivity, allowing us to adopt the role of listener as well as speaker. It is not at all unusual for traders to reject their negative thoughts before they've even finished verbalizing them—that's how silly they sound when they are given voice. I often think that my greatest value to traders as a therapist is simply to give them an opportunity to verbalize and scrutinize what is implicit in their minds—and that they therefore identify with.

> If how you're talking to yourself is not how you would want others to talk with you, that is your best indication that automatic thoughts are taking over.

The simple question "Who is talking right now?" is helpful in initiating entries in the D column of the cognitive journal. I will often ask the question "Is this the good trader within you talking, or is this your frustrated self venting?" The question is designed to mobilize the inner observer that stands apart from patterns of automatic, negative thoughts. If the trader acknowledges that this is, indeed, frustration talking, the next thing I will say is, "Okay, we have an opportunity right here, right now. You can choose to follow your frustration and continue the pattern that brought us together, or you can choose to do something different. Let's start beating the pattern right here."

STEP THREE OF COGNITIVE THERAPY: EFFORTS AT CHANGE

Ideally, cognitive therapy does not only challenge negative thought patterns, but also instills positive, enhancing ones. Each disputation is an opportunity to initiate and rehearse more constructive thought processes, until these become second nature. "What would you say to a good friend of yours who was in your exact situation?" is one question I often pose. Almost always, traders can recruit nondistorted ways of viewing situations if they imagine themselves talking to someone else going through their situation. Once again, imagery can be invaluable in bringing such constructive thought processes to life. I will ask traders to close their eyes and vividly imagine that the part of them that is acting as a trading mentor is talking to that other part of them that is a trader-in-training. "You are the trading mentor," I will say to traders. "What do you want to say to your student? What is going to help your student perform better next time?" The key is imagining the dialogue in vivid detail, and even talking about it out loud.

If you have experienced positive mentoring from a person in your life, such as a parent, teacher, or coach, it can be quite powerful to vividly imagine that mentor and what he or she would say to you in your current situation. By tapping into the emotional force of your previous mentorship experience, you interrupt the distress of the moment and shift gears toward a more constructive mind-set. Indeed, any role model can be recruited for this exercise. I've known Objectivists (traders who are steeped in the philosophy of the late Ayn Rand) who, in moments of emotional difficulty, will ask themselves, "What would John Galt or Howard Roark do in this situation?" Alternatively, a Christian might ask, "What would Jesus do?" Our belief systems derive their spiritual strength in part because they speak to our ideals. By consulting—and experiencing—our beliefs at times when we are talking to ourselves in our least ideal ways, we can go beyond interrupting automatic thoughts and reinforce positive cognitive patterns.

Perhaps my favorite strategy of all in initiating efforts at cognitive change is to encourage traders to mentor themselves by reexperiencing occasions in which they have successfully tackled their distortions. Readers of *The Psychology of Trading* will recognize this as the solution-focused approach to change. The solution-focused method has us looking at *exceptions to problem patterns*, rather than the problems themselves. These form the basis of solutions. For instance, if a trader has been experiencing automatic, self-critical thoughts triggered by losses, the solution-focused strategy would be to look at those times when the trader experienced losses and *did not* become self-critical. "What did you do instead?" is my typical question. "What did you do differently to not beat yourself up?" Often, by recreating the exception incidents, we can identify positive thinking patterns that traders have, but don't necessarily know they have. These then become models that we can use in our efforts at change by reenacting what we did right. To make this work, it is necessary to recall in detail specific incidents in which you faced a stressful situation and the specific things you did so that you did not fall into negative ways of thinking, feeling, and behaving.

Once you have those specifics, you can rehearse these as your own coping strategies and create solution patterns out of exceptions to the problems.

The common element in all of these approaches is that you are telling yourself, "The situation is not what's making me feel this way; it's how I'm processing the situation." Once you realize this, it gives you room to stand apart from your processing and try to look at things from different perspectives. Adding a Column E, Efforts at Change, to your cognitive journal (see Exhibit 8.2) is one way to structure efforts to change cognitive patterns. After you have identified the consequences of negative beliefs and challenged those, the last column allows you to take the time to formulate how you would *like* to process the activating events. Writing these down, as well as invoking them through the imagery methods mentioned here, is a further step in the direction of separating you from your automatic thoughts.

To repeat: The key to the success of cognitive therapy is repetition. One of the reasons it is a brief therapy is that it provides us with ways of working on problems every single day. Indeed, you make it a goal each day to find activating events that trigger your negative patterns and then challenge and reprocess those. Much of traditional therapy occurs weekly, with few structured activities for change between meetings. By structuring the activities yourself, you can become your own therapist and gain the ability to intercept and reprocess events in real time. In *The Psychology of Trading*, I referred to this ability as "trading from the couch." You become both the observer of the markets and your own observer. The cognitive journal, utilized daily, is a tool that builds the observer within you so that you experience emotions but do not become lost in them.

Where I have found cognitive methods to be most helpful is in normalizing the process of losing for developing traders. Chris Terry, professional trader and online trading mentor with Linda Raschke, stresses, "The one problem we as traders have is 'ego.' We cannot accept losing as normal. Losing means failing, and we are taught to not be losers. . . . There is a saying, '*Most people lose money trying to avoid losses.*' The most important step to winning is learning that losses are part of the game. Every successful person has failed many times before succeeding." Cognitive techniques reframe our perceptions of winning and losing, focusing us on *learning* and *improving*. By normalizing expectable losses attributable to market uncertainty, these methods help provide us with the resilience to sustain our learning curves.

WHEN COGNITIVE METHODS DON'T WORK

As Exhibit 8.3 indicates, many of the most common emotional disruptions affecting traders can be addressed successfully by cognitive methods. Still,

EXHIBIT 8.3 The Most Common Cognitive Problem Patterns among Traders And How These Can Be Recognized

Common Cognitive Problem Pattern	Core Negative Belief and Self-Talk	Common Manifestation in Trading
Perfectionism	You're only as good as your last trade or trading day; your worth is dependent upon your trading results; what you did isn't good enough; you should have done better.	Fear over making mistakes and resulting paralysis in decision making; frustration over not meeting lofty expectations.
Negative expectations	Whatever you do will go wrong; the market has it in for you; you're not good enough; you're a failure.	Trading to not lose, instead of finding opportunity; shifting between taking on too much risk (overtrading to feel success) and taking too little (missing opportunities).
Overconfidence	You've got the market figured out; you deserve to get paid out on your trades; if you just do this (make money) every day, you wind up with a huge income.	Overtrading, frustration when not paid out, impulsive trades made out of frustration or cockiness.
Money-focused	Constant watching of P/L during trades; frequent calculation of how much you need to make to stay afloat; goals and expectations stated in P/L terms rather than trading terms.	Overly aggressive trading to meet P/L needs or overly conservative money management to conserve capital; second-guessing of trades because of fear of losing money.

nothing is 100 percent. If you approach change in a stepwise fashion as outlined here and target specific patterns for your efforts, you are most likely to succeed. Should you find that you are not benefiting from the cognitive work, one of several factors may be the problem:

- *Lack of focus.* Sometimes people try to change too much all at once and bog down. It is usually not effective to work on multiple patterns at once. More promising is prioritizing patterns and tackling one at a time.
- *Lack of repetition.* Many times, you will be trying to unlearn patterns that have been present—and reinforced—over a period of years. This does not occur overnight. A daily focus over a sustained period provides an opportunity to internalize learning.
- *Lack of emotional intensity.* This is perhaps the most common mistake people make in cognitive therapy. Keeping a journal can become a routine, unemotional affair that never challenges old thinking patterns with passion and immediacy. Active methods such as talking about patterns aloud and utilizing imagery can yield greater emotional involvement.
- *Incorrect diagnosis.* Perhaps the problem is not what you think. If your negative thinking is grounded in a biologically based depression, cognitive work might help, but it should be guided by a professional. It may also need to be supplemented with pharmacotherapy. Alternatively, emotional patterns of frustration may result from trading problems, such as changing markets that have greatly reduced the edge of a particular strategy.

Most important, if the cognitive methods are not working and you continue to lose money, you want to either stop trading or trade very small size while you figure out what is going on and how you'll address it. The cost of a consultation with a mental health professional and/or a trading mentor is small relative to the losses you could incur by continuing to do what isn't working. Self-help is great, but if problems are significantly interfering with your relationships, work, trading, and leisure, do the right thing. You would take your car to a professional if it were ailing; you should do no less for yourself.

"How you think affects how you feel and act" is the motto of the cognitive approach. What happens, however, when feelings overwhelm us before cognition can even kick in? Is there a way of directly modifying our emotional experience? There is, and it's the cutting edge of an old therapeutic approach: behavior therapy.

CHAPTER 9

Behavioral Techniques for Enhancing Performance

. . . [C]rises or difficulties can often produce a sense of meaning when more pleasant stimuli have failed . . . danger can make you feel free when peace and serenity fail to arouse any response. It does this by forcing you to concentrate.
—Colin Wilson, *New Pathways in Psychology*
(pages 26–27)

In the last chapter, we saw how cognitive techniques can be powerful in changing the ways we view and respond to situations. Sometimes, however, it seems as though we react to events without thinking at all. It's not that trading outcomes trigger negative thinking, which in turn creates worse trading. Rather, our responses to trading situations seem to come out of nowhere, leaving us confused over our actions. Behavioral psychologists call these automatic action patterns *conditioned responses*. They occur when we so overlearn a response to a situation that it occurs without our conscious involvement. Often this overlearned response interferes with trading plans and good decision making, leaving us vulnerable. A host of brief techniques known collectively as behavior therapy have emerged to deal with conditioned responses. Like cognitive methods, they have been extensively studied and validated for effectiveness. Also like cognitive approaches, they can be utilized by traders willing and able to devote efforts toward becoming their own therapists. As we shall see, crises and danger are the source of many troublesome conditioned responses, but—as Colin Wilson realized—they also can be catalysts for positive change.

UNDERSTANDING CONDITIONED RESPONSES

Conditioning generally occurs in one of two ways. The first is through repeated association. This is the classic Pavlovian scenario. Let's say you hear the same song played over the speakers every time you enter a McDonald's restaurant. Later, when you're on the road and enter a different McDonald's unit, the song pops into your head and you find yourself humming it. That is a conditioned response.

The second way conditioned responses occur is through a limited number of events with high emotional impact. The best example of this is emotional trauma. For instance, I was commuting to work in Syracuse on a rainy day and stopped at a light. Shortly thereafter, the car behind me rammed very hard into the backside of my vehicle. It turned out that the driver behind that car never saw the stoplight and went full-force into the vehicle, pushing it into my tail. My head whipped back hard and my car shuddered from the impact. Although the collision was not sufficient to deploy my airbag, it was powerful enough to trigger an instantaneous memory of an earlier accident. I had no problem returning to driving after my car was repaired, but thereafter I found myself anxiously checking my rearview mirror every time I came to a stoplight. The fear response had been conditioned by the highly threatening episode.

My driving incident highlights an important facet of conditioned responses. They can either be highly adaptive or maladaptive. If my accident led me to be more careful at intersections during inclement weather, that could be quite useful. It might, for instance, lead me to be more cognizant of other vehicles and make doubly certain to secure my seat belt. Conversely, if my accident led me to experience debilitating anxiety each time I approached an intersection, it wouldn't be long before I avoided driving altogether. Many of the "instincts" displayed by great athletes—moves on a football field, sudden maneuvers by race car drivers—are sophisticated conditioned responses. Unfortunately, so are many of the anxiety episodes that plague thousands of people.

And nowhere do we see this more than in psychological trauma.

TRAUMA: UNDERSTANDING EXTREME CONDITIONING

If you are going to be your own therapist, it will be important for you to understand how conditioning occurs during trauma. This will help you appreciate how many of our emotional and behavioral reactions occur without our conscious thought, and it will point the way to innovative behavioral change approaches that make positive use of conditioning.

Consider a more complex example of a young woman who is the victim of an attempted rape in a park. Held at knifepoint, she feared for her life and felt completely out of control in the situation. Only her initial screaming and the response of a nearby jogger saved her from probable murder, as the assailant panicked and fled. Now, however, she reexperiences her terror at the oddest moments. The park setting, of course, is associated with the event, as is evening time. She also reacts sharply to any kind of surprise or unexpected physical contact. Each of these cues understandably triggers her anxiety. What troubles her is that the assault comes to her mind even in the absence of those cues. She will be calmly sitting at home or walking in public and suddenly experience severe panic. What is going on, she wonders; am I going insane?

Our young woman is finding that even seemingly remote cues are powerfully associated with the rape attempt. Consider her walk in public: A careful analysis shows that she noticed a large man who reminded her of the assailant. When she was sitting at home calmly? It was a television scene that she was watching that set her off. One time in a store, she experienced panic when she smelled a scent that reminded her of the man who held her down. Many different sensory cues became associated with the event, triggering her anxiety. As a result, a variety of seemingly innocuous situations were setting her off, leaving her feeling out of control.

It is only natural that a person in this situation would avoid the cues that trigger such fear. Gradually, however, this means avoiding an increasing number of settings that become associated with subtle traumatic cues. Eventually, trauma sufferers can become so preoccupied with self-protection that they become agoraphobic. They become fearful of their anxiety and frantically adjust their lives to avoid the restimulation of their fears. Because of this radically altered coping, traumatized people seem to have changed their entire personalities—all as the result of a single episode.

This *secondary anxiety*—fear of freshly experiencing the original traumatic feelings—is often what creates the most immediate problems for the trauma victim. It causes us to regress to older—and often less appropriate—forms of coping in order to manage our emotions. A trader who has experienced very large financial losses during emotional episodes with excessive positions has created the trading equivalent of trauma. Even normal losses may be sufficient to retrigger the anger, frustration, and fear from the initial episode, flooding the trader with distress. Unable to rely on his normal coping to handle this onslaught of emotion, the trader resorts to whatever had worked during earlier life periods, such as withdrawal and denial, impulsive confrontive coping, and self-blaming. At that point the trader is no longer objectively managing positions in the market. He or she is desperately attempting to manage these roiling emotions.

> What we do to avoid emotional pain is usually not what we need to do to best manage a trade.

If you have ever traded calmly, rationally, and in control for hours, only to have a single trade set you off and cause you to completely abandon all discipline, this is why: What looks like lack of discipline from a trader perspective is actually early coping rearing its head in the face of traumatic cues. Quite literally at those times, you become a different person.

TRAUMA AND THE BRAIN: HOW WE BECOME DIFFERENT PEOPLE

Cognitive neuroscience is helping us understand the brain pathways that distinguish traumatic stress from the normal stresses we commonly face. Most of our experience is processed consciously, allowing us to critically evaluate what we take in and what we don't. Let's say I am long a 10-lot and the market ticks a full point against me. If I'm a very short time frame trader, my entry was not particularly good. I may be a bit disappointed and frustrated, but I can shake off the loss, go back to my charts and my videotape, and figure out what I did wrong and how I can correct it. The loss poses a stress, but hardly a traumatic one.

Now let's imagine that my position was a 10,000-lot and not a 10-lot. In the S&P 500 E-mini contract, that would translate into half a million dollars per point. Those same four ticks that were an annoyance when I held a 10-lot now pose a potential threat to my livelihood. I am apt to respond to each tick with a heightened flight-or-fight response and an extreme perception of danger. It's conceivable that I could freeze entirely, dissociating from the entire situation, or instinctively react with panic, fleeing the position and the psychic pain associated with it. Most likely, I would not be able to sit in the position the way I would a 10-lot and coolly assess whether the market was likely to pay me out. My processing of the event is no longer conscious; it elicits automatic, conditioned responses, not carefully chosen ones.

The work of cognitive neuroscientists such as Joseph LeDoux suggests that conscious processing of events defuses their emotional and sensory properties. The analogy I like to use for this is the repetition of a joke. When we hear a joke several times, it loses its humor. That is true for all emotional stimuli: Repetition makes them routine, no longer capable of eliciting intense feeling. When we process emotional events cognitively, it is like hearing the joke. We digest those events and, in so doing, divest them of much of their impact. *Events that bypass consciousness—that are mediated by the brain's amygdala—appear to be encoded with their emotional components intact.* That is why post-traumatic stress disorder (PTSD) sufferers can experience vivid flashbacks to their original traumas years after those events. It is also why cues associated with the traumatic memories elicit such strong reactions. Traumatic events, unlike normal emotional ones, frequently go undigested, bypassing consciousness. It is as if we were Alzheimer's patients hearing a joke: Each telling would be as funny as the first, because we had not processed the experience in memory.

Behavior therapy works by reversing this process. It consists of a variety of techniques that allow us to process undigested events consciously, in essence reprogramming memory. It unconditions certain responses and helps us condition others.

MODERATE TRAUMA: A NEW AND POWERFUL CONCEPT

You may wonder what all of this has to do with trading. Yes, market losses can be emotionally upsetting, but few of us would place them in the category of such traumatic stresses as wartime and assault.

That's where we're wrong.

I believe that our failure to see trauma as a continuum—as a matter of degree—rather than as an all-or-none phenomenon is responsible for much of our inability to resolve problems with standard self-help methods.

The key to my realization was that a significant proportion of traders I have worked—and struggled—with have shown signs of moderate, but sustained, levels of traumatic stress. I realize that the notion of "moderate trauma" sounds oxymoronic, but bear with me here. A moderate trauma is one in which parts of the experience are processed normally and consciously, but other portions—associated with strong and usually painful emotions—are not. These experiences form the basis for conditioned responses that are triggered by environmental cues, even as the individual seems to suffer from no classic trauma. The result is a mixture, in which traders spend most of their time in normal states but experience sudden and seemingly inexplicable episodes of moderate traumatic stress. (See Exhibit 9.1.)

What is perhaps most fascinating is that moderate trauma—the conditioning of response patterns during highly emotional episodes—can occur during extremely positive experiences as well as negative ones. The addictive disorders that are difficult to treat are the ones involving substances that produce a powerful high. Like typical traumas that create intense experiences of fear and loss of control, substances such as crack cocaine produce intense experiences of euphoria. These experiences, like their traumatic counterparts, overwhelm conscious processing and remain undigested. They also become associated with a variety of contextual cues, which subsequently become further associated with cravings. Talk therapy aimed at curbing those cravings and reducing substance abuse is notoriously ineffective. Once the cues are triggered, the reasoning part of the brain that had been active in therapy is no longer in control.

This is a most important concept for those who seek to become their own therapists: *Trauma is a function of the intensity of emotional experiences, positive as well as negative.* Any emotional experience of sufficient force has the potential to overwhelm conscious processing and serve as a stimulus for conditioning.

I recall working with a young woman I will call LeeAnn. She was raised in an alcoholic family and experienced considerable neglect as well as

EXHIBIT 9.1   Traumatic and Normal Stresses

	Traumatic Stress	**Normal Stress**
How processed	Nonconsciously	Consciously
Emotions and sensation	Reexperienced over time	Defused over time
Coping	Regression to earlier modes	Usual coping methods
Consciousness	Dissociated	Intact
Subsequent reactions	Exaggerated, triggered by environmental cues	Appropriate to the situation, not associated with cues
Impact upon trading	Disruption of trading plans and intentions	Handled as expectable part of trading

physical abuse. Later in life, events in which she felt used or neglected left her with enormous reservoirs of anger that she could not handle. Then, one day, she became so angry that she took the feelings out on herself and cut her own arm. Apropos of Colin Wilson's observation, the shock of her action mobilized a sense of danger and concentration, temporarily freeing her from her rage. Indeed, her relief was so great that it became a conditioned response itself, associated with experiences of anger. By the time she came to me, she was as addicted to cutting herself as any drug user becomes dependent upon their fix.

Not surprisingly, LeeAnn entered a dissociated state during her cutting episodes. She later felt tremendous guilt over engaging in such obviously self-mutilating behaviors. In that sense, she was no different from a bulimic patient who feels guilty over eating a quart of ice cream after feeling depressed about her weight, a gambler who is filled with remorse after losing money in an attempt to dispel boredom and emptiness, or a junkie who shoots up just after vowing to go clean. Each of the addictive behaviors has become associated with either an intense positive stimulation or the removal of an intense negative stimulation. *This creates an imprinting every bit as deep as the traumas encountered in wartime.* LeeAnn was a successful student and had many friends. Her moderate level of trauma, however, led to significant losses of control at particular junctures in her life.

We tend to think of people as either sane or insane, in control or out of control of their lives. Those who have undergone moderate traumas, however—who are more numerous than is commonly acknowledged—possess *mixed control.* When their conditioned reactions are not triggered—when they are not exposed to cues associated with emotionally impactful events—they function quite normally. When they are triggered, however, their reactions become erratic and distorted, as if another person has taken over.

But why do so many traders display signs of moderate trauma?

HOW TRADING TRAUMATIZES TRADERS

The overwhelming majority of traders who seek me out for emotional assistance share a single characteristic: *They are overtrading.* When I say they are overtrading, I mean this in two ways: (1) They are placing more trades than they can reasonably justify, and (2) they are trading with size that is excessive relative to their account size and their emotional ability to tolerate loss. The combination of the two means that these traders have an unusually high financial and psychological risk exposure.

The traditional view among trading psychologists is that overtrading is the result of emotional problems, usually lumped under the category of "lack of discipline." I'm proposing here that the exact opposite is the case. *Overtrading—and the repeated exposure of traders to excessive risk and reward—creates moderate traumatic stresses that, over time, disrupt the ability to follow trading plans.* This explains why these emotional disruptions are so puzzling to traders and refractory to normal helping efforts.

The irony of this is that emotional interferences in trading are just as apt to be preceded by trading success as failure. It usually is not the beginning or unsuccessful trader who will ramp up trading frequency and size. Rather, the trader who experiences initial success will become (over) confident and begin exceeding reasonable risk parameters. A great number of traders I have worked with began their careers as rather composed, disciplined professionals. Only subsequently did they encounter problems with emotions, departures from trading plans, and erratic performance. One would think that, if the lack of discipline was based in personality traits, it would have been present throughout the trader's history. That, however, is not usually the case. Careful history taking generally reveals that the problems surfaced only *after* trading size and/or frequency increased substantially.

> Extreme trading success places traders in as much emotional jeopardy as extreme losses.

Moreover, I find that it is not just outsized trading losses that are the culprit. Traders are equally unprepared psychologically to handle very large trading gains. This is extremely important. Market participants who bet a large proportion of their portfolios (or a sizable portion of their maximum daily loss limits) on single trades—and who do that frequently—may initially profit from their imprudence. The result is a huge gain: a profit that is outside the trader's normal experience. The high of such a win is not unlike the high of a gambler's payout or a substance abuser's buzz. The intensity of the experience ensures that it will not be processed through normal, conscious channels. Such emotional imprinting is the basis for all addictive behaviors—even ones as destructive as cutting oneself or repeatedly betting one's livelihood on market outcomes.

What this means is that traders who overtrade are damned if they win and damned if they lose. If they make money, it will be a large amount of money and can cause a traumatic imprinting that leads to repetitive risk taking and eventual exposure to risk of ruin. If they lose money, it will also be a large amount of money, creating traumatic losses that cannot be processed normally and handled through usual coping mechanisms. In short, excessive risk and reward create excessive emotional experience, which yield traumatic impacts.

Because traders with emotional disruptions of trading experience moderate levels of trauma, they do not look like traumatic stress victims. They function normally and, under normal trading conditions, may perform quite acceptably. All it takes, however, is a single traumatic cue—an unexpected (and usually large) gain or loss—to set them off by triggering earlier modes of coping. Interestingly, many trading mentors seem to recognize this intuitively and will counsel troubled traders to reduce their size, become more selective in trade selection, and regain their composure. What the mentors frequently fail to recognize, however, is that size and lack of selectivity are the actual *sources* of the emotional disruption and need to be addressed on an ongoing basis.

Many independent, retail traders have implicit or explicit business plans that enshrine overtrading. Numerous traders with small account sizes have told me that they are trading large size in order to have a chance of making a living from their trading. Excessive risk assumption is embedded into their very trading plans. *The result is that they almost surely traumatize themselves over time—whether they win or lose.*

Training, we might say, is a preventive measure against moderate trauma. It ensures that high-risk/high-reward activities can be processed as normal stresses, not as abnormal, traumatic ones.

THE BEST PIECE OF ADVICE YOU'LL EVER GET FROM DR. BRETT

If you are developing your trading expertise, do it in a steady, progressive manner that creates neither excessive emotional highs nor extreme emotional lows. Do not traumatize yourself: *The best treatment of all is prevention.*

If pursuing trading success in such a moderate fashion seems boring to you and takes away the thrills and excitement of trading, find another source of livelihood. The traumatic impacts you will encounter will eventually come to hurt you, your trading, and those who depend upon you.

> The best way to incorporate psychology into your trading plans is to ensure, through risk management, that you never expose yourself to outsized market outcomes.

You've probably heard the saying about how there are old traders and bold traders but no old, bold traders. The overly bold trader, like the junkie in Neil Young's song "Needle and the Damage Done," is like a setting sun. I speak as an ever-so moderately traumatized psychologist who has seen the damage done. I've seen traders work for weeks to recoup losses, only to lose even more in a single large trade. I've watched traders run through family savings—and then borrow money—in pursuit of profits. Heroin addicts, when they can't acquire a fix, will "milk" their own blood—withdraw it, save it, and reinject it—to achieve a mild high.

The damage done.

Take it slow. Take it steady. Become competent, then expert. Don't become a casualty.

THE FIRST STEP OF BEHAVIOR THERAPY: RELAXATION TRAINING

As we've seen, traditional helping approaches are likely to enjoy limited success in changing behavior patterns conditioned by highly emotionally charged events. Sitting down with a traumatized trader to discuss trading plans, goals, the business of trading, discipline, or positive attitudes is like coaching a rape victim to find the right romantic partner. *If the problem is that highly emotionally charged events have been processed nonconsciously, the treatment must be capable of working at that nonconscious level to reprocess those experiences.*

Behavior therapy works in two basic ways:

1. *It deconditions established response patterns* Some behavior therapies reverse the trauma process by creating repeated neutral emotional experiences and allowing people the opportunity to process highly charged events in a conscious manner.

2. *It conditions desired response patterns.* Behavior therapies can create what I call "positive traumas" by generating highly impactful emotional experiences that become cues for constructive action patterns.

What we typically call behavior therapy is really a collection of techniques for unlearning harmful conditioned responses and instilling new, positive ones. In becoming your own behavior therapist, it will be necessary for you to learn and implement the more basic techniques before progressing to more advanced ones.

Let's start with the very most basic behavioral intervention: relaxation training. This is a method that is quite effective in dampening anxiety and frustration.

The first step in relaxation training is learning how to breathe diaphragmatically. Deep, slow, controlled breathing is one of the simplest but also most effective ways of checking your physical and cognitive arousal. To breathe diaphragmatically, you begin by seating yourself in a comfortable position and closing your eyes to remove distractions. You then take deep, slow breaths from your abdomen. In the beginning, it is helpful to place your hand on your stomach as you breathe, making sure that your belly expands as you inhale and contracts as you exhale. Breaths should be deep, smooth, and slow; you want to avoid hyperventilating. As you breathe in, count your number of breaths aloud. As you breathe out, say the word "Relax." As much as possible, just focus your mind on the counting of breaths and the word "Relax." In the beginning, you may be distracted and find the breathing from the abdomen difficult. With practice, it becomes quite easy and natural. After 10 to 15 minutes, one can typically achieve a highly relaxed state.

As a variation of the exercise, some people will listen to relaxing music and/or imagine relaxing scenes while they are performing the diaphragmatic breathing. The idea is to engage one's mind in a manner consistent with relaxation, whether it is by counting, imagery, or some other means. After doing the exercise with consistency, it is not at all unusual for people to reach the point where they can calm themselves with just a few diaphragmatic breaths.

The breathing exercise becomes relaxation training when it is paired with stressful situations. This can be accomplished in several ways:

- *Preventive intervention.* Traders can proactively relax themselves if they know they are about to enter a stressful market situation.
- *Early intervention.* Traders can take deep abdominal breaths while they are trading as stressful situations emerge.
- *Trading breaks.* After triggers for trading problems have already occurred, traders can remove themselves from their screens temporarily, conduct the breathing exercise, and return to trading in a more neutral state.

Clearly this method works by reversing the physical, emotional, and cognitive arousal triggered by traumatic cues. *By slowing breathing and focusing the mind on relatively neutral or positive stimuli, we shift our state from one that is associated with poorer coping to one in which we possess greater conscious control over our behavior.* Note that this, in itself, is not a treatment for trauma; it does not prevent cues from being triggered in the first place, nor does it reprogram those cues. It does, however, allow us to undo the effects of conditioning quite quickly, providing rapid relief. This is very helpful to traders who find themselves getting worked up while a position is on, when there is no opportunity to talk out the problem, write in a journal, or otherwise seek relief. With practice, relaxation becomes quite portable and rapid.

THE SECOND STEP OF BEHAVIOR THERAPY: IDENTIFYING TRIGGERS

In some ways, this is the most challenging facet of behavior therapy. As mentioned earlier, the cues that trigger altered coping and disrupt trading may be quite obvious, but many times they are so subtle that they go unrecognized. The second step in your behavior therapy is to conduct a cataloging. We want to find out everything that is happening leading up to a disruption of trading. This means cataloging emotional reactions, events surrounding these reactions, and all thoughts and sensations occurring at those times. The more complete your catalog is, the more likely it will be that you will discover your specific triggers. (See Exhibit 9.2.)

If you're having trouble identifying triggers, ask yourself after an emotional trading episode, "What set me off?" Usually you will be able to identify a period in which you were feeling and trading fine, and then something triggered your reactions. *It is this trigger that we wish to target.* It is not necessary that you deeply analyze why this is triggering you. It is only crucial for you to know that "When X happened, it set me off." Very often, the trigger will be an event or perception that had a strong emotional impact. You'll know it's an important trigger when you see it reappearing in your catalog.

EXHIBIT 9.2   A Catalog of Cues for Trading Disruptions

Common Triggers

- *Euphoria.* Highly excited, positive feelings trigger overconfidence and overtrading.
- *Anxiety.* Intense fear triggers impulsive actions to relieve the state.
- *Boredom.* Lack of activity and feelings of emptiness trigger stimulation seeking activity to relieve the state.
- *Sudden market movements.* These become associated with particular emotional states and trigger fear, greed, overconfidence, or frustration.
- *Large and/or sudden losses.* These trigger feelings of loss/depression, frustration/anger, or fear, which, in turn, trigger coping responses to dampen these.
- *Strings of wins or losses.* These also trigger overconfidence and frustration and result in overtrading and distorted trade management.

THE THIRD STEP OF BEHAVIOR THERAPY: CONSCIOUSLY PROCESSING OUR TRIGGERS

Perhaps the simplest exercise for reprocessing our triggers is the stress inoculation method originally introduced by psychologist Donald Meichenbaum. The idea of stress inoculation is that you can expose a person to low levels of an anticipated stressor in controlled circumstances, arousing appropriate coping. This makes it more likely that this coping will manifest itself when the stressors are experienced in real time. Meichenbaum likened this process to the inoculation that occurs when we receive a vaccine for an illness such as influenza. Exposing the body to weak levels of a virus arouses the body's defenses, which then are prepared for full viral contact.

One way to conduct stress inoculation is to pair the relaxation training described here with the triggers that you've cataloged. Imagery is quite useful for this purpose. If, for instance, a fast-moving market is a trigger for anxiety and the trader knows that with the release of a report, the market is likely to become much faster moving, she can prepare for this event by vividly imagining the release, the market's reaction, and her own effective coping *while conducting the relaxation exercise*. The idea is that you use the power of imagery to create a mild form of the traumatic trigger, keep yourself under control with the abdominal breathing, and then rehearse the coping behaviors you would like to utilize in the situation. Ideally, this is repeated with a variety of imagined scenarios, each reinforcing desired coping responses. For instance, if you wanted to ensure that you honor your stop-loss points during adverse market movement, you could vividly imagine markets moving against you while you sustain your slow, deep breathing. You would then envision yourself exiting your position at your chosen point, even as you focus on the adverse market movement.

This basic exercise accomplishes the two ends of behavior therapy. First, it allows you to face a threatening situation while you are rehearsing self-control. With repetition, you loosen the associative link between the trigger event (adverse market movement) and your conditioned response. A major reason for this is that *you are requiring yourself to process the trigger event consciously, with full awareness*. In an important sense, you are building your capacity to remain self-aware during events that, in the past, had overwhelmed consciousness. The second end of the behavior therapy is the creation of new associative links between relaxed self-control and the trigger situation. With repeated enactment, you are literally crafting a new conditioned response, in which you face emergency with a calm focus. As you might imagine, repetition is crucial to the success of such reprocessing. Vivid imagery, emotional involvement in the scenario, and frequent repetition increase the likelihood of altering existing conditioned responses and creating new ones.

Related to the stress inoculation exercise is the behavior therapy known as systematic desensitization. In systematic desensitization we not only identify individual triggers for unwanted behaviors, but arrange them in hierarchies based upon their association with subjective distress. Exhibit 9.3 illustrates a condensed hierarchy for a trader whose performance anxiety leads to an inability to act upon valid trade ideas. Observe that the hierarchy, at its beginning, lowest, level, includes mild triggers and gradually builds to highly charged ones. Psychologists sometimes ask clients to rate their triggers on a 0-to-100 scale of SUDs (subjective units of distress). The lowest items on the hierarchy thus might be rated from 0 to 25 and the highest items would range from 75 to 100.

Notice that the hierarchy contains triggers that are imagined, as well as ones encountered in simulation and in real-time trading (in vivo). Many of the lower-hierarchy items will be trigger scenarios that are imagined. These same scenarios can then be made more realistic by facing them in simulated and actual trading sessions. The simulation programs that we discussed as learning tools for trading play a valuable role in behavior therapy, enabling traders to face their triggers in a realistic but safe context. Mastering anxiety and impulsivity in simulation provides confidence-building experience for tackling emotionally charged situations when money is on the line.

Before working on the hierarchy, it is necessary to develop basic competence in the breathing exercise (or a similar relaxation skill) mentioned

EXHIBIT 9.3   Condensed Hierarchy of Triggers for Systematic Desensitization

Hierarchy Level	Trigger	Modality	SUDs
High	Seeing the market move violently while I am in a position	In vivo	90
	Seeing the market move violently while I am in a position	Simulation	75
Middle	Seeing the market move against my position	Simulation	60
	Thinking that the market will move against my position	Imagery	40
Low	Looking at my account statement before I trade	In vivo	30
	Looking at my account statement before I trade	Imagery	10

earlier. Generally I will not begin targeted work on the hierarchy until traders can relax themselves on demand through diaphragmatic breathing. Once the relaxation skill is acquired, you create a detailed hierarchy—one with at least 10 levels—making sure that there are several items at low, medium, and high levels. It is important that the hierarchy take you through increasingly realistic encounters with your triggers, culminating in in vivo work for the highest items.

Once you create the hierarchy, you work from the bottom up, pairing the relaxation exercise with the trigger defined at the first level. You experience the trigger situation as vividly as possible while performing the diaphragmatic breathing. Each time you encounter the situation—in imagery, simulation, or in vivo—you rate your subjective distress on the 0-to-100 scale. *The key to the technique is that you keep repeating the trigger situation during the behavior therapy session until the subjective distress is a zero.* That means repeating imagined or simulated scenes many times while performing the relaxation work. Eventually, with repetition, the triggers defined on the hierarchy begin to lose their impact.

A cornerstone of systematic desensitization is that you do not move to higher levels of the hierarchy until you have completely eliminated distress at the lower levels. If distress is not desensitized at the level of imagery, for example, jumping to simulated and in vivo encounters would simply retrigger old patterns. Systematic desensitization is effective, in part, because it creates progressive experiences of mastery and efficacy. By creating large hierarchies that progress smoothly from one level to the next, you can ensure that encounters with triggers will be processed consciously, with a minimum of cognitive, emotional, and behavioral disruption. Once again, the key to success is repetition: Repeated, conscious exposure to traumatic cues is particularly effective in unlearning conditioned responses to those cues.

> Successful behavior therapy creates experiences of being in control of situations that had formerly been out of control.

EXPOSURE THERAPY: ENHANCING THE ROLE OF CONSCIOUSNESS

Research from Edna Foa and colleagues at the University of Pennsylvania finds that it is the exposure to traumatic cues that provides the bulk of therapeutic benefit in behavior therapy—more so than such techniques as diaphragmatic breathing. She also finds that many people do not need the gradual approach of a hierarchy. Indeed, prolonged sessions of exposure, sometimes referred to as "flooding," can be highly effective in reprogramming traumatic events.

Exposure therapy may utilize breathing and other relaxation techniques during the period of exposure to traumatic cues, but typically employs other coping methods as well. Some of these are cognitive, such as rehearsing particular ways of thinking about the situation. Others are purely behavioral, such as talking aloud through situations as they are occurring to ensure conscious processing. One coping technique I have found particularly effective is actively talking to oneself during periods of exposure, as if you are your own therapist. For instance, in the aforementioned situation in which the trader was afraid of entering the market due to a fear of loss at times of volatility, the trader would talk herself through a simulated market exposure, providing reassurances, encouragement, and perspective. The idea is to activate effective coping in the face of potent emotional triggers.

Exposure therapy is effective because it engages attention, concentration, and directed effort during exposure to traumatic stimuli. In essence, exposure work activates the brain's frontal regions—its executive center— at those times when consciousness is most likely to be bypassed. If this is the case, exposure therapy should be effective precisely to the extent that it successfully engages the reasoning mind during vivid, impactful exposures. My reading of case transcripts with clients who have undergone exposure treatment for problems ranging from panic disorder to post-traumatic stress supports this notion. Their therapies consist of a reexperiencing of their fears at times of heightened conscious processing. *The key to the success of this approach is activating this enhanced processing precisely at those times when we are most likely to respond automatically, forcing us to process consciously that which had bypassed consciousness.*

STEP ONE OF EXPOSURE THERAPY: CREATING THE YODA STATE

The initial step of exposure work is to create a reliable procedure for entering into a state of enhanced conscious processing. This means that you will need two things: (1) a process by which you can reduce stimulation and enhance concentration and (2) distinctive cues associated with the process that become associated with the state of enhanced focus. Both of these elements allow for a great deal of room for creativity to see what works best for you.

The first method I use is a variant of meditation. By seating myself in a very still position, closing my eyes, and focusing on a repetitive stimulus for a lengthy time, I can reach a highly focused and calm state. As I described in *The Psychology of Trading*, I have found the early music of Philip Glass particularly helpful as a focus. The prolonged reduction of sensory stimuli—some traders I've worked with have used noise-canceling headphones while closing their eyes and focusing on a repeated phrase to fix their attention—and heightened focus facilitates enhanced conscious processing. The key to the success of this method is sticking with it long enough to adapt to the altered sensory conditions. If you find yourself bored with the exercise, you haven't stuck with it long enough for the adaptation to take hold. Over time, given sufficient practice, the enhanced state can be reached rapidly—usually within seconds.

A second method uses forehead skin temperature biofeedback to track frontal activation. I have found that prolonged playing of the popular game Sudoku—while I am seated very still and in an extremely quiet setting—will reliably sustain heightened temperature readings, suggesting that blood flow has shifted to the brain's frontal regions. This method of assessing frontal activity through monitoring shifts in blood flow (and resulting temperature changes), known as *hemoencephalography*, has gained recognition since I wrote about it in *The Psychology of Trading*; it has been the subject of a special issue of *The Journal of Neurotherapy*, recently issued as a book edited by Tim Tinius. During periods of emotional and physiological arousal, skin forehead readings are lower; during periods of concentration, they are higher. Interestingly, relaxation does not raise the temperature readings, nor does effortful straining. There has to be an element of quiet focus. Dr. Jeffrey Carmen, one of the pioneers of hemoencephalography along with Dr. Herschel Toomim, points to the *Star Wars* character Yoda as an embodiment of the proper attitude: letting the force of concentration work through you.

Unfortunately, we are not yet at the point at which hemoencephalography units are widely available. Fortunately, other forms of biofeedback appear promising for this application. For instance, the Journey to Wild Divine program links computer-based games to heart rate and skin conductance feedback, facilitating the Yoda state. While traditional biofeedback does not measure blood flow and frontal activation per se, the on-screen programs for controlling galvanic skin response and heart rate do require sustained concentration and thus are useful for our purpose. For example, in Journey to Wild Divine, the user has to move a balloon across the screen by lowering his or her arousal level. A different program, called CalmLink, actually conducts a kind of exposure therapy by placing users in a "stress" environment (a Pac-Man-like video game) while they perform the relaxation exercises and receive feedback about galvanic skin response.

The combination of on-screen activities with the biofeedback makes such programs quite useful for traders who have difficulty structuring their own immersions into the Yoda state through such means as meditation. The immediate feedback is also helpful for people who are motivated to continue to work on their skills by seeing their scores improve over time. My experience with Journey to Wild Divine is that the same calm focus that increases my forehead temperature on the hemoencephalography unit also successfully completes the games of the program. While I find some of the audio features of the program distracting, the basic tasks require both calm and concentration. With repetition, you begin to literally get a feel—a sense in your mind and body—for what you need to do to successfully complete the games. This feel incorporates some of the positive conditioned cues you will be bringing to real-time trading.

> Achieving the Yoda state is itself a performance skill that develops with practice.

Sophisticated biofeedback units for mental health professionals—particularly EEG units—require training and often lack user-friendly interfaces. I generally do not recommend these for traders. As of this writing, a slew of "brain development" electronic games are scheduled to come to market, following the success of these in Japan. Combining these games with simple heart rate or skin conductance feedback provides a potential gymnasium for cultivating frontal activation.

Whether you employ meditation or biofeedback to achieve increased frontal activation, it is vitally important that you perform the routines the same way each time. This will create positive conditioned cues for your Yoda state. For example, the Glass music and still sitting position are two of my cues. Alternatively, performing the biofeedback games while burning incense or under altered lighting conditions would create vivid cues that, over time, become associated with the calm focus. Those are the cues we will bring into our trading.

STEP TWO OF EXPOSURE THERAPY: GRADED EXPOSURE DURING THE YODA STATE

Research by such leading clinicians as Edna Foa and David Barlow suggests that exposure therapy is effective because it produces a cognitive restructuring. People learn, through their exposure, that they can, indeed, handle their worst fears and control their responses and coping. It is the direct experience of success that is critical. That is why exposure work is most powerful when it is in vivo: applied to real-life stresses.

It is worth noting that Foa's work with exposure typically involves two-hour sessions, not the standard 50-minute therapeutic hour. This suggests that the intensity and duration of the exposure are critical elements in the behavioral therapy's success. Many of the conditioned responses we acquire as the result of traumatic stresses are ones that involve an avoidance of the distress associated with the traumas. For instance, we might respond to the fear of market loss by impulsively exiting positions before our profit targets or stop-loss points are hit. Exposure work prevents such avoidant responses and, indeed, immerses us in the very stresses that we tend to avoid.

The pairing of triggers with the heightened conscious state can be accomplished with live trading, creating an immersion throughout the trading session. The way to do this is through *graded exposure*. Instead of manipulating whether the trigger situations are mildly or highly stressful, as in systematic desensitization, you deal with all of the trigger situations that present themselves all trading session long—*but start with highly reduced trading size*. You then increase your exposure by *very gradually* increasing your trading size. Because the risk of a trade is a function of its size, manipulating the size of trades during exposure work creates a more finely graded exposure than any constructed hierarchy. The use of size to grade exposure also means that it is not necessary to stop trading to work on exposure. *Indeed, the advantage of this method is that it creates an immersive experience in safe trading.*

> The most rapid way to reprogram traumatic cues is to evoke them persistently in a safe context.

The key to the success of this graded exposure technique is replicating the actions that kept you in a state of heightened processing while you are trading. Thus, for instance, if you conditioned your state of focus and concentration to repetitive music, you would play the music while you are trading. If your entry into the flow state was associated with sitting very still and reducing sensory exposure, you would remain perfectly motionless as you follow the market, wearing noise-canceling headphones. Because of the repetition of your efforts to enter the Yoda state, you have learned to associate particular cues with that state. Evoking those cues allows you to summon the state in real time and access the coping associated with focused concentration, just as traumatic cues elicit distress and result in regressive coping. This is an example of creating a "positive trauma": a powerful experience that evokes a desired set of responses.

Your training to achieve the flow state has become a kind of classical conditioning.

To repeat: It is important to master the entry into the focused mode prior to conducting the actual exposure in trading. *I am convinced that several highly extended sessions to enter and sustain the focused mode are much more effective in helping you master the Yoda state than a greater number of brief sessions.* When I first trained myself, it was with $3\frac{1}{2}$-hour sessions conducted to Glass's *Music in Twelve Parts* in the dead of night, with no distractions. It was the smartest thing I could have done. Over the course of more than 200 minutes straight, you encounter one internal distraction after another and learn what you need to do to tune it out and sustain your focus. That same tuning out and focusing is what you bring to the graded exposure of trading.

The beauty of working in vivo with very small size is that every trigger will eventually occur, *but now in a way that does not threaten your account statement.* This makes it much easier to practice retaining focus and concentration when those triggers occur. Only once you succeed in avoiding your negative trading patterns at the smallest size do you increase your size very gradually. The idea is to create success and repeated experiences of mastery.

> When you perform the exposure work, you are not trading to make money. You are trading to reinstill a sense of control and safety so that you can later trade profitably.

Thanks to the creation of biofeedback tools that provide graphical feedback on your screen, it is possible to integrate biofeedback into your graded exposure while you are trading. Heart rate and galvanic skin response (GSR) feedback are fine for this purpose. While trading, you certainly won't have the biofeedback games playing; all you need is a reading of your levels—preferably one that charts your levels over time. *That way, your own readings can alert you to the presence of triggers before you necessarily identify them consciously.* High readings become opportunities—while you are still following the market—to dampen your arousal and increase your focus. You don't engage in actual trades until you have succeeded in reducing your readings through the trigger events. At times this may mean closing out positions, leaving the trading screen, and performing the Yoda exercises to regain focus. If that becomes necessary, you know that you need more time trading under control at that size—and you may even want to return to the next smallest size to reinforce gains at that level before stepping up.

PROPER TRAINING: THE BEST TREATMENT OF ALL

Since writing *The Psychology of Trading*, I have worked with many traders, quite a few in real time. My experiences have led me to an inescapable conclusion: *A majority of emotional trading problems are the result of partial traumatization.*

This means that many psychological disruptions of trading are iatrogenic. They are caused by trading itself, not by factors separate from trading. We create emotional disruption when we trade without proper training, when we trade with size that neither our accounts nor our minds can properly accommodate, and when we trade so frequently with that size that we invite risk of ruin.

It should never be necessary to conduct exposure therapy to treat trading-related traumas. If you train yourself properly and operate with prudent risk management, you will experience trading losses, not traumas. The best therapy for trauma is not behavioral or cognitive; it is prevention through structured training. My goal in writing this book is not to encourage you to perform your own therapy for trauma. *My goal is to make such treatment unnecessary in the first place*

Trading, ideally structured, is a vehicle for expanding consciousness, not damaging it.

The Making and Remaking of an Expert Trader

> . . . *When men live by trade—with reason, not force, as their final arbiter—it is the best product that wins, the best performance, the man of best judgment and highest ability—and the degree of a man's productiveness is the degree of his reward.*
> —Ayn Rand, *Atlas Shrugged*

What we know about expert traders has come mostly from interviews, not from direct observation. Interviews are informative, but they are distant from firsthand experience. For the past year, thanks to Kingstree Trading, LLC, owner Chuck McElveen and expert trader Scott Pulcini, I have been granted daily access to Scott and his trading. I have sat in his office and watched him trade, I have followed his development as a trader, and I have interviewed him—and his friends and family—at length.

What emerges is a portrait of an expert trader that will put flesh on the bones of the ideas we have encountered thus far. This is not a pretty, sanitized portrait. I have observed Scott at his best and at his worst. I have seen him make significant money every day for a month, pulling more than a million dollars from the market in a matter of days. I've also witnessed his struggles as markets have changed, his frustration during slump periods, and his ongoing efforts to adapt to shifting market conditions. Here is a person of incredible loyalty to family and friends, whose greatest virtue, in his words, is being a "dreamer." Here, too, is someone with a temper so volatile that, by his own admission, he can trade "like a jerk."

In short, here is a real human being, who just happens to have a phenomenal gift for reading short-term patterns in markets. How else do you explain someone who violates the well-known 10-year rule of expertise by making over $2 million in his first full year of trading—and then multiplying that fourfold his next year? No, this was not accomplished by hitting on a few leveraged and lucky trades. Instead, Scott beat the market by trading thousands of S&P E-mini contracts every single day, incurring all the slippage and commissions that entails. Having watched Scott's trading as he put up some of those numbers, I find it difficult to entertain the notion of random, efficient markets. His achievements are possible only in a performance field in which talent and training make the difference between success and failure. His struggles are possible only in a field in which long-term success is a function of constant adaptation to market conditions.

What goes into the making of such a trader? It's not exactly like Oz: When we pull back the curtain, we see that the wizard is just a man, but also that the man is a wizard.

PORTRAIT OF THE TRADER AS A YOUNG MAN

Scott Pulcini was born on March 1, 1972, in Chicago Heights, Illinois. He dealt with loss long before he made his first trade. His biological father died from a heroin overdose when Scott was only two years old. To this day, Scott remembers seeing his father dead on the floor, recalls the blanket he lay on. Early in his college years, he witnessed a friend and football teammate stabbed to death outside a restaurant—an event that haunted him long afterward and derailed his education. At the age of 21, he watched his adoptive father waste away from liver cancer. Researcher Dean Keith Simonton observes that many gifted individuals have a history of early family loss. Such events either make you or break you; force you to become self-reliant or leave you rudderless.

Scott learned self-reliance.

It is difficult for a boy to internalize an identity of manhood in the absence of a male role model. Early in life, Scott experienced himself as vulnerable—and he was picked on as a result. He points to an incident from his first-grade year as a personal turning point. A bully chased him home every day, terrorizing him. Scott's adoptive father taught him to hit a Darth Vader punching bag, and, lessons in hand, Scott stood his ground against the boy, who was four years older. He hit him in the mouth, bloodying him. To this day, Scott laughs aloud at the consequence: The boy's mother came to Scott's home and complained bitterly that Scott was beating up her son! With that incident, however, Scott felt that he "went from being a weakling to standing up for myself."

Each of us reworks a set of themes throughout our lives, and this was one of Scott's, shaped by the early loss of a role model. Little did he know that this theme—the weakling versus the man—would emerge years later during the challenges of his trading career.

Where Scott missed a role model most was the absence of a father figure to guide him athletically. An active child, Scott experienced his time in the classroom as difficult, despite the motivation provided by his family. "I hated sitting in one spot in a boring classroom; it felt like jail just sitting there," he told me. "But if I found a subject that interested me, I enjoyed school." After his mother remarried when Scott was four, he was adopted by his new father. His father was not athletic, however, and the Little League in which Scott starred was not well organized. "I never had anyone to teach me," he explained, so he devoured books and taught himself. "I used to get up at 5 A.M. to practice with a batting tee," he described to me. "I would throw balls against walls to field grounders—all on my own." This self-reliance, so unusual in a youngster, would become an important facet of Scott's trading development years later, as he spent long early morning hours teaching himself to trade by breaking all the rules in the trading books.

Resilience and perseverance are traits we observe among highly successful individuals, and Scott displayed those from an early age. Speaking of his early athletic determination, he explained, "That's how much I loved baseball. If I want something, I'll pour myself into it. I'll master it."

> Most achievers display the rage to master from an early age.

An incident from seventh grade turned out to be one of those crystallizing experiences for young Pulcini. He was shooting baskets in the rain late at night, trying to develop his skills so that he could make the cut at the upcoming team tryouts. A car pulled up, and the driver called out to him, "You're going to be a winner, kid!" Scott never forgot the man—or the message. Indeed, recognizing that his friends were falling into drugs, Scott chose to enter Marian Catholic High School, where he would have a better peer group and stronger academics. He sees the choice as one that quite likely saved his life.

Armed with his determination, Scott built solid baseball skills. He started for his high school team all four years and was an all-star third baseman. At six feet tall and 205 pounds, he was also his high school football team's starting center. "Football made a man of me," Scott recalls. "You go there and bust your behind blocking and driving the sleds." His dream, however, was to play baseball for Stanford. Sports was the outlet for the young man's competitive drive, and already he was a dreamer, imagining himself as a college and pro star. Soon, however, that dream would be shattered and young Scott would lose his way.

PORTRAIT OF THE TRADER AS A COLLEGE STUDENT

Scott's first exposure to the stock market was through his grandfather. He recalls looking up stocks and becoming fascinated with their movement. "I like the unknown—not knowing what's going to happen the next day," he explains. In high school he entered the ATT Investment Challenge and finished in the top 100 in the country. He was proud of that effort, and from that time forward he knew he wanted to be involved in the market.

He majored in finance in college, struggling in his freshman year at Illinois State after his friend and football teammate was stabbed to death in an altercation outside a restaurant. This was extremely upsetting for Scott—the emotion in his voice is evident even now as he describes the circumstances. He lost his academic focus and left Illinois State with poor grades. He attempted to transfer to St. Ambrose University in Davenport, Iowa, but was rejected. Only after writing two letters displaying unusual motivation to enter school did they accept him on a trial basis. He did not let them down, graduating with a GPA higher than 3.0. Still, he had not found his niche. His career in baseball fell by the wayside when Scott assumed he could make the team with skills alone. He wasn't in shape and didn't make the team. "It was one of my real life letdowns," Scott recalls. "I was devastated."

Scott's love of the unknown—his sense of thrill over not knowing what's going to happen next—found an outlet in gambling during his college years. He gravitated toward horse racing because of the intellectual challenge of handicapping. He spent hours poring over racing forms in hopes of hitting it big. "I'm a dreamer," Scott observes. "I always think anything's possible. If other people can do it, why can't I?" Still, without the dream of athletics, Scott lost his rudder. "I went out a lot, drinking and gambling," Scott recalls. In spite of this, he retained his drive to succeed. He taught himself golf and developed a single-digit handicap.

Let's freeze the frame and take an objective look at young Scott. He grew up in modest circumstances and faced early loss and negative peer influences. Still, he displayed determination to succeed at sports and had the courage to dream big. By the end of college, however, no one would have tapped Scott to be a highly successful professional. His baseball demise revealed confidence to the point of overconfidence, as he stopped the hard work and training that developed him in the first place. His drinking and gambling showed a side of him that contradicted his disciplined pursuit of dreams. In short, what we have here—by the time the college years have ended—is two Scotts: one, the self-reliant dreamer and hard worker who will master anything he puts his mind to, and the other, the overconfident stimulation seeker who doesn't feel a need to keep working.

By the end of college, Scott had few career prospects and no social connections to open doors. Still, he had one hidden virtue, a second life theme that would eventually shape his career: *He was convinced that he could figure things out on his own.* He could learn sports, and he could figure out horse races. Scott's was an intellectual confidence, even though he was not leading the life of an intellectual. He believed that whatever others had figured out, he could as well. Interpersonal losses and the shattering of his baseball career did nothing to dampen that confidence.

PORTRAIT OF THE YOUNG TRADER

Scott's summer job experience, selling meat door-to-door, was hardly glamorous. The sales experience, however, helped land him a highly coveted internship at Smith Barney. Shortly afterward, Dan Lesinski, the best man at Scott's wedding, helped him land a job at the Chicago Board of Trade as a runner in the five-year options pit. His salary at the time was $200 a week. He worked in the pit for approximately two years before applying for a clerking position in the bond pit that he was hardly prepared for. Once again, he simply assumed he would figure it out. "I've never been so stressed in my life," Scott described, as he struggled to keep up with the rapid hand signals while traders yelled at him and millions of dollars of trades were on the line. "It got me battle tested," Scott insists. Gesturing at his current trading office, he jokes, "This is a massage parlor compared to working in the pits as an arb clerk."

> Our source of deepest confidence is the overcoming of worthy challenges and obstacles.

Despite day after day of being yelled at by brokers and customers and struggling to keep up with the order flow on the floor, Scott stuck with his new position. It was one more sign of the persistence he exhibited when he truly wanted something. What he ultimately desired, however, was to be a trader, not a clerk. His break came when friend Rob Ross brought him to Kingstree Trading, despite the initial concerns of owner Chuck McElveen. He got his shot as a proprietary trader; his earnings now were limited only by his talent.

Alas, Scott's timing could have been better. He joined Kingstree in August 2001, as the bear market gathered steam. He lost $2,600 his first day with the firm—trading one-lots! In fact, he lost money every single day for a month and a half. If anyone seemed destined for a brief trading career at that juncture, it was Scott Pulcini. Then, as if that weren't enough, the markets hit September 11 and closed following the attack on the World Trade Center. Not much was going right. He was broke and his job was far from secure.

Once again, let's freeze the frame on the life history. Take a moment to think about how Scott started his proprietary trading career. To lose $2,600 on one-lot positions means that you are down more than 50 S&P points in a single day. That's not just being wrong—it's being consistently wrong. Then imagine losing money every day after that for weeks on end. Scott felt desperate at the time—not because he didn't feel he could pick it up, but because he thought he would be fired from the firm before he actually picked it up. He was losing at trading, he was running out of cash, and profits weren't in sight. What possibly could have given Scott the fortitude to ride out this period?

Two things appeared to be working in his favor. First, he had already been in extremely stressful situations in the pit. If he could stay calm then, with everyone yelling at him simultaneously, he figured that he could surely handle this. Perhaps even more important, however, is that *the pit experience revealed that Scott had a unique talent: the ability to process orders rapidly under conditions of high risk*. He learned the hand signals and developed the ability to attend to many traders at one time to be successful as an arb clerk. Never once did he lose large money for any of his traders. How many people could jump into a busy pit and pull that off?

He didn't know it at the time, but Scott had found his niche—and the confidence to hang in during this new learning curve.

PORTRAIT OF THE SUCCESSFUL TRADER

After going on a fishing trip with Rob Ross, who recommended that he read *Reminiscences of a Stock Operator* to get a different outlook on trading, Scott returned to a closed market in September 2001. He came in at night and began trading the German market (DAX). It was lonely occupying the office by himself and struggling to master trading after so many losing trades. He kept himself entertained and uplifted by listening to the music of Grammy award winner Shawn Colvin, who would later figure in Scott's success. When he made his first profit in the DAX, he was especially proud. "How many people make $1,000 before 5 A.M.?" he asked himself.

He returned to the S&P market when it reopened and, in Scott's words, "One day it clicked." He began to make money, and his confidence grew. Indeed, his confidence had grown so much by January that he bet firm owner Chuck that he would finish the year as Kingstree's number one trader. He eventually won that bet.

"A lot of my motivation came from my competitive drive," Scott told me. "If these guys can make money, I can." While Scott certainly liked making money—he was up over $200,000 in January after making his bet and finished the year making more than $2 million—it was the competition against the other traders that Scott found most motivating. He wanted to be the best.

But let's step back for a moment. How can we explain a learning curve that has a trader losing money every single day for six weeks in August and September and then making consistent, serious money by January?

Much of the explanation, as I mentioned earlier in the book, can be found in Scott's distinctive trading style. (Note: In deference to Scott and Kingstree, I have attempted to be as detailed and accurate in my description of his trading as possible without revealing proprietary trading information. For that reason, I insisted that both Scott and Chuck, as well as the other traders named in this book, review and approve the material in the book.) In common trading parlance, a trader who places several trades a day is considered an active trader. Traders who close out their positions prior to the session close are called daytraders. Scott is an active daytrader, but that doesn't begin to capture his trading style. His degree of activity provides him with almost constant exposure to market information and patterns. In any day of market activity, he exposes himself to more trading information than a normal trader would obtain in weeks. I strongly believe that this, in conjunction with his talents and personality, accounted for his phenomenally accelerated learning curve.

> Through concentrated market experience, we can accelerate skill development.

You see, Scott functions as a market maker, providing liquidity to the marketplace. He will work bids below the market and offers above. The natural movement of the market ensures that many of his orders will be filled and that he will be in the market a good deal of the trading day. His goal is to buy bids and sell offers, profiting from the spread. Unlike the technical trader, who assesses chart patterns or trends over periods of minutes, hours, or days, Scott focuses on the very short-term shifts in supply and demand in the marketplace and rapidly responds to those to benefit from small, frequent movements. "I did the opposite of what the books tell you," Scott explained. "I wanted one tick fifty times rather than a fifty-tick move." Indeed, that is exactly how he succeeded. Over time, Scott grew his size as a trader, so that he was trading 40,000 to 50,000 round turns per day. A single tick may not seem like a great deal of money, but multiplied across such size and trading frequency, it accumulated into solid profits.

Scott attributes his success to his ability to read the patterns in the very short-term movements of the market. He is sensitive to the size and positions of orders above and below the market, and he tracks each trade, its size, and where it occurs. He has a keen awareness of when a market is slow and dominated by locals and when it is busier, with institutional (paper) involvement. This awareness allows him to rapidly adapt as conditions change over the course of the day. The same observational skills and quick reactions that helped him survive as an arb clerk in the pit provided him with his edge as a screen trader.

But think, for a moment, of what an edge he developed. Consider the commissions on tens of thousands of round turns in the S&P E-mini market, not to mention all the other fees and expenses associated with trading. *One would need to make thousands of dollars a day just to break even.* To make millions requires an edge of gigantic proportions—an edge that is replicated day after day after day for years on end. Only world-class talent and skill can account for such results.

If I had to single out Scott's greatest talent as a trader, I would say that it is his phenomenal concentration, accurate short-term memory, and speed of mental processing. He spends hours in front of the screen, actively tracking everything happening in the market. Most traders, including me, would find that completely exhausting. Scott is very different. Like that young boy who felt trapped when he had to sit still in class, Scott dislikes slow markets. His times of greatest frustration are when markets won't facilitate trade. He thrives off activity and finds such action to be stimulating and challenging. His rapid mental processing and superior short-term memory allow him to recall what has happened in the recent past both above and below the market, so that when business picks up in the ES contract, he is among the first to detect it and act accordingly. It is not at all unusual for Scott, when he is trading well in an active market, to be long, short, and long again in the span of a single minute, making money on both sides of the market.

These talents cannot be taught. Nor is his ferocious competitive drive something that can be acquired. The drive that had him waking up at 5 A.M. and taking batting practice as a child and shooting baskets in the rain is the same drive that enables him to make the outrageous bet that he will lead the firm in profitability. It was also the same drive that allowed him to sustain his learning efforts day after day, even in the face of continual failure. What is clear to me is that Scott's greatest asset has been his ability to persist at mastering markets under the most daunting conditions. He truly begins with the premise that if others can achieve, so can he.

These cognitive and personal talents combine with specific trading skills to create success. In Scott's case, the skills involve the reading of short-term patterns of supply and demand. Because he is in the market so much of the time, he has a firsthand sense of whether large traders are leaning to the buy or the sell side and can position himself accordingly. When a large order of his is only partially filled, he obtains information about the drying up of buying or selling and can exploit that valuable piece of data. Much of his processing and decision making is rapid and automatic, without a great deal of time spent in explicit analysis. It would not be far off to say that Scott trades the way a race car driver handles a vehicle: with well-honed instincts based upon experience gained in real-life performance. After the fact, he can tell you why he placed or canceled an order, but all of his reasoning is occurring on the fly, integrating large amounts of rapidly changing data.

> Talent + Personality + Performance Niche + Training = Success

In short, Scott succeeded quickly because he rapidly found his trading niche: a trading firm that encouraged trader growth, a market that allowed him to trade actively, and a trading style that exploited his action-oriented personality and distinctive cognitive talents. This propelled him from rookie trader to serious earner in less than a year's time.

But as markets change, so do niches.

PORTRAIT OF THE TRADER IN TRANSFORMATION

To date, Scott has not replicated his best year, 2003, in which he earned $10 million. Indeed, he actually lost money in 2005—about $300,000. It has been a challenging and even painful period of readjustment.

Several factors conspired to make very active, short-term trading difficult in the stock index markets—not just for Scott, but for many market makers. The wringing of volatility from the markets has changed the personalities of the popular ES and NQ indexes. My research shows that we have not experienced the present combination of low trending and low volatility in the past 70 years. One would think that a scalper such as Scott would not need trending and volatility, but that is not exactly the case. If markets become deep—they have large participation in the order book at all prices—and nonvolatile, they lock up. They trade back and forth, not fully moving through any price level. One's orders can sit in a book for minutes at a time and not be filled. This lack of movement turns the very short-term trader into a position trader.

In Scott's case, this loss of movement became psychological poison. It was as if he was back in school, forced to sit. Trading became more frustrating than fun. His office, like the classroom years before, began to feel like a jail. Worse, the markets no longer actively filled Scott's orders, so he had less information to work from. His core talents of observation, rapid information processing, and superior short-term memory were underutilized. Staying out of the market at times of market inactivity, he found himself feeling more and more like the kid defeated by the bully. He wanted to fight back, but this time there was no one to punch. Over time, the childhood feelings of being the wimp, not the man, crept back.

> The greatest market stresses are those that reactivate our early personal struggles: losses and powerlessness.

At first, Scott kept waiting for the market to return to its old ways. "It's human nature to stay in your comfort zone," he told me. "I didn't want to think about being in a different market." That's where confidence became overconfidence, leaving him unprepared as he had been when trying out for the college baseball team. As long as he was in his comfort zone, he wouldn't make the difficult changes: the adjustments of lifestyle, the extra work, and the modifications to his trading style. He knew about changing markets, but, in his words, "I didn't think it would happen to me."

Conditions in the marketplace only worsened, as automated trading became increasingly dominant. This made it difficult for short-term traders to be fast enough to get good prices. As I put it in one article, increasing volume in the ES market was chasing decreased market movement. Inevitably, at the end of the trading day, many traders found themselves without a seat in the market's musical chairs game.

Here we can see how traders become moderately traumatized, as Chapter 9 described. We are not talking about a trader who had a good year now having a bad year. Rather, this is a trader who had been ultrasuccessful year after year, who now found that what worked in the past no longer makes money. Imagine what it would be like for a center in basketball to suddenly face rims raised two feet higher and lanes doubled in width. It would no longer be possible to dominate the inside, either for scoring or for rebounding, as any incursion into the lane would likely bring a three-second violation. Basic moves that had always worked, such as posting a player up inside and making the turnaround jumper, would no longer be possible. This is what happens when markets shift: Their rules change. Scott was like that center, now forced to adapt to a new set of unforeseen market rules.

Relatively early in the market's change, Scott hit upon the idea of videotaping the day's trade and learning about his mistakes and the market's new patterns. He purchased a videorecording unit that contained a large hard drive so that he could save and replay multiple days of market action. This enabled him to see how and where he placed orders, how and where he was filled, and how he managed his positions. The expansion of his screen time allowed him to make crucial adjustments in his trading.

Unfortunately, those adjustments took Scott further and further from his niche. Position trading simply was not his strength; it did not capitalize upon his unique talents. As a longer-term trader, he was like Michael Jordan the baseball player: competent, but not world class. For Scott, that was not enough. Somehow he had to find a home for those talents. He was, after all, the kid in the rain, born to be a winner.

PORTRAIT OF THE TRADER AT HOME

Tiger Woods has gone through extended periods of not winning tournaments before regaining his dominance. After back-to-back 20-game winning seasons in 1973–1974, pitching great Nolan Ryan never again won 20 games in a year. Indeed, he experienced losing years throughout his career: 1976, 1978, 1985, and 1987. We don't recall the losing times, however. We judge him across an incredible career of 27 years and 323 career wins. Slumps are part of the business for most high-level performers, and Scott is no exception. He has read of trading greats, and he knows that many, if not most of them, have lost their first money. It's hard to adapt to markets until you learn the need to adapt.

Such perspective doesn't make the downtimes any less painful, however. Even those with the greatest resilience and most competitive spirits are apt to wonder if their day has passed. Scott's frustration was not only visible at times, but audible. More than once I would be in his office as he watched a locked-up market sit on a single tick minute after minute, loudly wondering how this could happen in a world marketplace. Such frustration takes its toll on trading discipline, as well as emotional outlook.

Much has been written about traders, but little about trader spouses. Many of these, I believe, should be on a fast track toward sainthood. The stresses of trading, the challenges of changing markets, and the day-to-day and year-to-year lack of certainty about income and performance make it impossible to not take problems home. It is a rare spouse who understands trading well enough to appreciate the stresses of their partners. It is also a rare trader who appreciates the difficulties of spouses who must tolerate ups and downs of mood and income, with little control over the situation.

Anne and Scott had known each other for $3\frac{1}{2}$ years before getting married in November 2004. It was a beautiful ceremony, with Shawn Colvin—the same singer whose music had kept the lonely young trader company in 2001—providing the music. Anne's work is in special education. This has provided her with extra doses of patience and understanding, as she works with students who struggle in school and are frequently frustrated.

"Anne has a calming effect," Scott explained to me. After bad days, "I have the ability to forget about it, but not right away. I think the world is coming to an end. Anne will say, 'It's going to be okay. Don't worry about it.' "

"Having been a teacher," Anne pointed out, "that's what I've done all my life: This isn't the end of the world. You're going to read at the end of the year."

> Expert spouses are ones who retain the perspective that their partners temporarily lose.

Then Anne said something revealing: "It sounds strange, but I went to school in order to marry him." Theirs is a team effort, with Anne providing a stabilizing influence.

With the recent birth of their daughter, Sofia, Anne and Scott have developed a workable division of labor. Anne knows that Scott needs his full concentration on his trading and his learning process. She pointed out that after his work, "he can play and take part in the fun stuff." Anne explained, "I want this to be a good addition to our lives, not a frustration." Indeed, that has proven to be the case. Scott says seeing Sofia when he gets home after a difficult day "makes me smile. I get in a better mood when I'm home."

My sense is that Anne is as talented and expert at what she does as Scott. So many other spouses would respond to their husband's frustrations with frustrations of their own, escalating an already difficult situation. Anne's core talents are patience and emotional stability. This makes her a successful facilitator of learning for students, but also an anchor for her competitive husband.

Success, even at an individual level, is so often a team sport. Without emotional support, few performers would survive slumps and fresh learning curves. It takes special partners to perceive and encourage the best in each other.

PORTRAIT OF THE DEVELOPING TRADER

As I write this, Scott has evolved tremendously. He is developing new ways to employ his talents and skills in niches that possess even more promise than his former one. He hasn't yet made any outrageous bets, but you can be sure that when he does, I won't be taking the other side. A sign on Scott's wall reflects his personal motto: "Those who endure, conquer." He is truly a self-made man; when he has endured, he has conquered.

Nolan Ryan realized in midcareer that he had to change to succeed. He learned to ease up on his fastball, develop other pitches, and cultivate his control. As a result, he was more of a threat to hitters at 90 mph than at 99 mph. He also protected his arm from the damage that would have resulted had he stuck with his original fastball edge. I'm sure Nolan had his share of frustrations during his rebuilding, contributing to those losing seasons. He is a Hall of Famer, however, because he stuck with the development process, committing himself to a long-term career.

Greatness is not an achievement, but a lifetime of achieving.

But Nolan Ryan did not find success by abandoning his strengths. He did not try to become a knuckleball pitcher, a hitter, or a football player. He adapted his strengths to changes in the game. Similarly, Scott will not find his long-term success by becoming a long-term investor or a system trader. His fastball is the speed of his mental processing, his quick perception of market patterns, and his ability to rapidly translate perceptions into actions. New facets of his game will supplement these strengths but not replace them. Nolan Ryan in 1976 was a losing pitcher. Little did he realize at the time that he had 17 years of success—and legendary performance—ahead of him. So it is with those who aspire to hall-of-fame-level trading.

Talent, skill, drive, and resilience: These are the building blocks of success we can learn from experts in all fields. In Scott, we see an embodiment of so many ideas from the previous chapters: the importance of finding a niche that exploits one's talents, the role of immersive experience in accelerating implicit learning, and the need to constantly evolve with markets. In Scott, we also observe the psychology of an elite performer: the young boy teaching himself baseball by hitting and fielding early in the morning, the pit clerk who adapts to unspeakable stress to establish his toehold in a career field, and the trader who concentrates years of market experience in months of self-directed training, building competence and confidence on the way to expertise.

Early in his trading career, when Scott lost every day for six weeks, he hit a financial low point and had to borrow $100 from his mother. "There's no bigger pressure than losing every day when you're broke," Scott explained. "If I can handle that, I can handle anything."

Four months later, when many would have given up—and many firms would have given up on him—Scott was earning a solid six figures. That's why I never give up on a skilled trader who is willing and able to make the effort to adapt to changing conditions. Having watched Scott, I realize, deep in my heart, that great things will always be possible when talent and preparation meet opportunity.

Conclusion

*Difficulties show men what they are. In case of
any difficulty remember that God has pitted you
against a rough antagonist that you may be a
conqueror, and this cannot be without toil.*

—Epictetus

We're nearing the book's end. It has been both a challenge and a plea-
sure to write. Writing is so much more than a mere transcription of
one's thoughts. In putting those thoughts into words, we inevitably
analyze them, play with them, and rework them. *Enhancing Trader Performance* has captured my ideas about what it means to become an expert
trader, but it has also honed those. If anything, it has made me even more
respectful of the talents and efforts of those who have sustained success in
the markets and developed themselves as elite performers. The writing has
also crystallized a few crucial ideas that, no doubt, will guide my work with
traders—and my own development as a trader—going forward. Let's see if
we can summarize those ideas and explore their relevance for your trading
career.

THE ESSENCE OF TRADING PERFORMANCE

In these pages, a few themes have emerged and reemerged, capturing the essence of trading success:

- *Trading is a performance field.* It is not a routine, mechanical task or the automatic expression of an innate talent. Trading, like athletics or the performing arts, is a field that demands an initial degree of talent and develops this talent over time to achieve increasingly refined performance. As a performance field, trading requires the high-level enactment of skill under competitive conditions and pressures.
- *Trading consists of a variety of performance niches.* Trading success hinges, in part, on finding an optimal fit between one's talents and interests, the markets one trades, and the ways one trades those markets.
- *Trading performance is a function of training.* This training may be formal and structured or self-initiated, but expertise in trading—like that in other performance fields—results from the learning initiated by deliberative practice.
- *Trading expertise is a developmental process.* Expertise in all fields progresses from beginning levels through competence and expertise. The tasks needed to move from phase to phase and the role of mentors at each phase vary considerably. Sustained success in trading, like that in other performance fields, requires years of development and exposure to a variety of market conditions.
- *The learning curve of trading expertise can be accelerated.* Learning is facilitated by breaking trading down into component skills; rehearsing these under realistic, simulated conditions; and gathering detailed performance feedback to guide future rehearsals.
- *Expertise development in trading is an ongoing process.* The changing nature of markets ensures that traders will experience learning curves throughout their career. Much of their long-term success will hinge on their risk management during these periods of relearning.
- *The majority of emotional disruptions of trading are preventable.* They stem from three sources: (1) inadequate training and resulting frustration, (2) mismatches between trader strengths and the demands of their trading niches, and (3) deficiencies in risk management leading to overtrading.
- *Emotional disruptions of trading tend to be episodic.* Triggered by distortions of cognitive and emotional processing under conditions of heightened perceived threat and danger, they result in altered coping and a diminished ability to act planfully.

- *Traditional talk counseling and self-help methods are of limited benefit to traders experiencing emotional disruptions.* These disruptions result from conditioning that has bypassed normal conscious processing and require interventions that similarly bypass explicit thought.
- *The most effective psychological help for traders is methods that have proven success in the treatment of trauma.* These include cognitive and behavioral methods that treat emotional disruptions as the results of partial traumatization. Such methods permit a reprocessing of conditioned patterns of thought, feeling, and action, extending traders' capacity for intentional behavior.

So what do these conclusions mean for you and your trading career? A few important implications stand out:

- *Build on your strengths.* You are most likely to find trading success by exploiting what you are already good at. Your trading niche will take advantage of distinct competencies that you already possess and already employ in other facets of your life.
- *There is much in the trading world you will need to filter out.* If trading is indeed a performance field, there is no reason to believe that elite performance will be found in better indicators, faster or more comprehensive software, newsletter tips, or coaching advice. Only a directed developmental process will allow you to internalize market patterns and act upon these with confidence. Better golf clubs will not turn a duffer into a pro; the finest wrenches will not make one a master mechanic. You will hear many promises of quick rewards in the trading world, but these cannot replace training.
- *Peaks and troughs in trading performance are likely to be the norm rather than the exception.* If markets indeed change their patterns of trending and volatility over time, traders never really reach the end of their learning curves. There are apt to be periods in which market cycles change and the new patterns have not yet been internalized. These are also likely to be periods of drought in traders' profits. What is important is to survive these performance troughs through proactive risk management, a prudent savings plan, and a determination to not traumatize oneself and thereby preclude fresh learning. An excellent predictor of long-term trader success is the ability to prepare for inevitable lean times when the earnings are good.
- *Your emotional experience in trading will reflect your success in structuring your training.* Properly structured training will generate sustained experiences of learning, mastery, and confidence. They will contribute to a sense of efficacy. These positive emotional experiences are precisely what you need to be able to handle the inevitable stresses

of risk and reward as you increase your size. Properly configured training will also serve as training to enter and sustain the flow state in which we activate our brain's executive functions and will make our best decisions. If your learning experience is understructured, you will be at greater risk of emotional frustrations and conditioning effects that disrupt coping.

In sum, my best advice is to truly treat trading as a profession if it is to be your career. A profession is a field that requires extended education and specialized training. It is a field that demands that you be responsible and that you execute that responsibility with professionalism. Trading can be a wonderfully challenging and rewarding activity, but it can also leave the unprepared emotionally wounded and financially bereft. Don't be too quick to put your account at risk in hopes of making money now. Take the time to learn and build a career that will sustain you for a lifetime.

CONCLUDING ADVICE FROM LARRY CONNORS

I recently posed this question to Trading Markets founder, money manager, and market author/researcher Larry Connors: "In your experience, what's the one thing traders most need to do to improve their performance?" Larry's response was so thoughtful that I present it in its entirety:

First, you need to find a systematic method which removes most (if not all) of the emotion and discretionary judgment from your trading. Be prepared . . . this could take years. Once you have identified a system that can be profitable over the course of time, then you have to develop a mindset in which you:

1. *Focus on executing your system perfectly for each individual trade;*
2. *Focus on weekly or monthly gains and not the results of individual trades;*
3. *Track and quantify your performance mercilessly;*
4. *At the end of each day, each week, and month evaluate your actions and then commit to doing better tomorrow;*
5. *Stay positive in your thoughts and spoken words;*
6. *Stay away from negative influences that cause you to have doubts and fears about your ability as a trader;*
7. *Teach others to maximize their performance and, in so doing, maximize your own.*

Please make note of what Larry is saying: *To succeed in the markets, first find your edge.* Then work on yourself. Your first task as an aspiring expert is to find your opportunity. Next to that, all else is secondary.

THE ULTIMATE GOAL OF TRADING

If a successful trading career requires such effort and training, why bother? Come to think of it, why trade at all? Why exercise every day, straining muscles and lungs? Why train to become a successful athlete, dancer, or chess master? Why try to master stress by exposing yourself to traumatic cues, not once but repeatedly? Why risk your life savings on an entrepreneurial vision? We could just as easily put our money in savings accounts, watch performance activities on television, avoid danger, and plant ourselves in secure jobs. We could avoid all risk and discomfort.

But we don't. Why?

There is only one reason that makes sense: *To become the best that we can be.* We'll never know our strength until it is tested; we can never increase that strength unless the tests become ever more stringent. Arrayed against all the potential pain, loss, and fatigue of the performance quest is but a single reward: the pride of accomplishment and the security of knowing that you have made something of yourself, that you have not squandered your time on earth.

I wrote this book about trading, but it is not a trading book. Rather, it is a book about freedom. Trading, like those other glorious performance fields we've touched upon, is simply one venue for the development of freedom.

WHAT IT MEANS TO BE FREE

Let us not forget what it means to be a trader. It means that I am free to own property: shares of a private company or contracts in a commodity. I can take delivery of my property and dispose of it as I wish, or I can trade it to others. My decisions are mine to make; I need not follow the dictates of those who would put other interests—those of gods, governments, or guns—above my own. If I lose, it is my loss. If I profit, the gain is mine.

Freedom means that I have a voice. If I like an investment, I can tout it in online bulletin boards and blogs. If I don't like the way the government is managing the economy, I can vote my conscience, not only at the ballot box, but in the marketplace by investing or withdrawing my funds.

But freedom is even more than that. Freedom is the ability to make one's living by one's judgment, and not being limited to subsistence through the toil of his or her hands. Freedom is the ability of a single individual sitting right here, right now, at a personal computer, to write words that can be read years later, in faraway lands. Freedom is downloading reams of market data and conducting research that, just years ago, would have taken weeks to complete. Freedom is the ability to see who is bidding, offering, buying, and selling in global marketplaces. It is the unfettered opportunity to participate in the economic vigor of developing nations.

Without freedom, there is no trading. Trading is a celebration of economic and political freedom. Slaves are traded; they do not trade.

All this freedom, however, is for naught if we, ourselves, are not free. It is the deepest of ironies that we experience greater freedom—far broader potentials—than those who came before us. And yet, in our lives, in our abilities to master ourselves, we are no freer. Amid opportunity, we remain partial: tethered to our conditioning.

What it means to be free is to be able to choose, to live with intention. The free life is one that we guide: a life lived with purpose, direction, and meaning.

Trading, like all the great performance activities, is an opportunity to cultivate the intentional life. Pursued properly, it is a path to freedom.

TRAINING FOR FREEDOM

What are we really developing when we train for expert performance in any domain? We develop skill and knowledge, to be sure, but we also develop more than that. *We cultivate will: the ability to formulate goals and direct our actions toward reaching those goals.* Every training session is a battle of will: a struggle to overcome our limitations and reach a particular performance goal. Was it really so important, when I was at Duke University, for basketball team members to make 10 consecutive free throws before they ended practice for the day? As a foul-shooting exercise it perhaps had benefit, but as training of the will it was exquisite. When every fiber of your being wants to get home after a hard practice, you learn to focus your foul shooting under pressure. Filtering those pressures out helps you tune out pressures on game day—and those help you overcome pressures in the tournament. We train for freedom—freedom from external and internal constraints.

To formulate and follow a trading plan in the absence of pressure is relatively easy. It is in the heat of trading, when profit beckons and loss threatens, that our abilities to plan and execute plans are tested. Military officers refer to the "fog of war": the uncertainties surrounding all decisions and actions. A great deal of military training is designed to help soldiers perform high-level tasks automatically even amid the fog. Trading, too, is conducted in fog. It offers substantial risk and reward, opportunity and danger. There is no certainty—ever. The trader who trains for expertise is no different from the soldier in training: expanding his or her capacity to act intelligently and intentionally in the midst of fog. To create and follow a plan in the face of every conceivable disruption—that is freedom.

Ultimately, however, training brings freedom from our limitations. The artist finds new and better means of expression; the scientist develops better ways to study, identify, and predict facets of nature; athletes better their scores or times. When the pit crew performs at the NASCAR race and sends its car off in record time, it has overcome one more limitation. To that degree, it is less controlled by outside forces; it is more self-determining. Look at the self-control developed by ballet dancers, race car drivers, Major League pitchers, and world-class marksmen. Theirs is the victory of intention over randomness and chance.

When you enhance your performance as a trader, you replace a small piece of randomness with intention. To that degree, your outcomes are self-determined. If you train yourself properly, you will become not only a successful trader, but a more self-determining human being. What places you in the state of flow will also be what enhances your skill and enables you to perform in any facet of life. *Flow is the path to freedom.* It will immerse you in the activities you require to be self-determining. Gradually, inexorably, training will lead you to your freedom.

WHAT IS IMPORTANT: A PARTING WORD

It is not important that you make money on your next trade. It is not important that you trade at all.

What is important is that you discover a focus for your life that develops you as a free, self-determining human being. It is not critical that you become a world-class trader or an elite performer in any particular field. What is crucial is that you have *some* field of performance, some domain that expresses your talents and allows you to become what you can be.

Maybe it will be as a parent, as a businessperson, as a teacher, or as a healer. Perhaps it won't be as a trader.

It doesn't matter.

All that matters is that you have a limited time on this earth, a finite set of talents, and the freedom to make the most of these. If that involves trading, my deepest hope is that you find some of the ideas in this text eye-opening, helpful, and inspiring. If trading is not your path, my equally fervent wish is that you find your performance niche and the deep satisfaction of a life well lived.

Live free, and you will live well.

Resources for Performance

The bibliography includes many of the written resources that went into the writing of this book. Following are specific resources that I have found useful in my own trading and in my work with traders. Please note that I am not commercially affiliated with any of these products or services.

TRADING PLATFORMS

- NeoTicker (www.tickquest.com). This is a very impressive platform with considerable depth of features. It includes flexible charting, customized market scans, and a variety of unique indicators such as Neo-Breadth (customized breadth measure for any basket of stocks) and customized TICK measures. It links to many brokerage services for order execution and is particularly powerful for system development. The simulation capability is powerful and flexible, with excellent replay features.
- Ninja Trader (www.ninjatrader.com). This platform has many strategy management features that automate the order execution process, taking advantage of specific tactics (such as automatically adjusting stop losses to breakeven when a profit target is hit). The simulation version of the program is free, and it includes a module for the collection of trading metrics as well as market replay capability. It connects to many

brokerages and data feeds; flexible charts depict traders' orders and positions.

- CQG (www.cqg.com). This platform has evolved tremendously, with a chart trader feature that allows order entry directly from a chart, side-by-side depth of market information and charting, a trade flow measure to track demand and supply, and highly customizable charts. The platform supports simulation and market replay, and the charts can depict almost any indicator formula or stock basket you define. Charts also display traders' orders and positions, with room for annotation. A deep database supports the platform, including up to 999 days of tick charts, and a backtesting feature facilitates system development.
- Trading Technologies (www.tradingtechnologies.com). TT, as it's known, has recently added a number of charting and data features to its well-known depth-of-market and order execution capabilities. The charting includes volume analysis and spread charts. The platform also comes with a simulation module and a module called Trade Analyzer for collecting metrics. Order entry and execution are right off the depth-of-market display, with support for multiple order types.
- TradeStation (www.tradestation.com). TradeStation is best known for its trading system development program, but this program is now embedded in a larger discount brokerage service. There is a large forum of users who support each other in system development and a large number of third-party vendors who offer trading tools that integrate with TradeStation.

MARKET DATA AND CHARTING

- Decision Point (www.decisionpoint.com). Best single resource for sector charting and technical indicators.
- Pinnacle Data (www.pinnacledata.com). Excellent source for daily indicator data and end-of-day prices for indices and commodities.
- Tick Data (www.tickdata.com). Best source I've found for historical intraday data on futures and individual stocks; includes very useful software for breaking data into time frames.
- RealTick (www.realtick.com) Actually a charting and order execution platform, but its historical data and links to Excel particularly stand out.
- Barchart (www.barchart.com). Flexible charting of futures and stocks, but the real draw for me is the wealth of data on sector and individual issue performance.

STOCK SCREENING AND MARKET ANALYTICS

- Market Delta (www.marketdelta.com). Intraday real-time charting that segments volume based upon whether it occurs at the bid versus ask price. Best measure of short-term sentiment that I know of.
- WINdoTRADEr (www.windotrader.com). Very flexible implementation of Market Profile that includes many features for volume analysis. Excellent graphics and highly customizable.
- Trader DNA (www.traderdna.com). The best implementation of trading metrics I've yet found, with charting of trader performance statistics and numerous breakdowns over a variety of measures and time frames. My favorite feature is a breakdown of markets into their type (trending, nontrending, etc.), so that traders can separate out their P/L as a function of market condition.
- *Mind Over Markets*. This Jim Dalton classic text is the best source of insight into the market auction process that I know of.
- Trade Ideas (www.trade-ideas.com). Comprehensive and creative screening tool that really shines in intraday analyses. Allows for layering of screens on multiple time frames. This is my favorite program for scanning the market for historical patterns that possess a directional edge.
- Jon Markman (www.jonmarkman.com). Jon's columns for MSN Money offer some of the best stock-picking insights I've encountered. Jon also edits two publications, *Strategic Advantage* and *Trader's Advantage*, which provide longer- and shorter-term stock selection, respectively.
- MSN Stock Scouter (www.moneycentral.com). Longer-term screen that includes technical, fundamental, and institutional ownership criteria. Quite likely the best free trading/investment tool on the Web.
- PowerRatings (www.tradingmarkets.com). This relatively new service rates stocks from 1 to 10 based upon projected short-term performance utilizing historical pattern research. There is much information on the site for using the ratings to construct strategies and portfolios.
- Adaptrade Software (www.adaptrade.com). Mike Bryant's work on system development (www.breakoutfutures.com) is excellent, and he publishes an informative newsletter. His System Analyzer software aids position sizing and risk management, with detailed performance reports.

HISTORICAL PATTERN RESEARCH

- TraderFeed (www.traderfeed.blogspot.com). This is my free research blog that tracks short-term historical patterns, primarily in the stock indices. Daily postings identify where there might be an edge in short-term trading.

- *Stock Trader's Almanac* (www.hirschorg.com). Very interesting and useful research on seasonal and daily patterns in market history. The companion book and newsletter called *The Almanac Investor* also include historical patterns among sectors, supplemented by an online research feature.
- SentimenTrader (www.sentimentrader.com). First-rate research on a variety of sentiment measures, as they influence the stock market. Jason Goepfert tracks short-term and intermediate-term market models for trading guidance.
- Market History (www.markethistory.com). Excellent statistical analyses of market patterns. The real draw here is the coverage of multiple trading markets, including stocks, fixed income, and currencies.
- *Trade Like a Hedge Fund.* James Altucher's book describes a number of specific trading patterns and also provides insights for developing new ones.

INFORMATIVE WEB SITES, BLOGS, AND BOOKS

- Trading Psychology (www.brettsteenbarger.com). This is my personal site, and it includes the largest archive of articles on trading psychology on the Web. Also part of the site are performance resources for traders, a weekly blog devoted to trader performance, and a daily summary of the stock index market that incorporates a number of unique measures of strength and weakness.
- Daily Speculations (www.dailyspeculations.com). This site, led by Victor Niederhoffer and Laurel Kenner, offers a treasure trove of insights into markets, often drawing upon ideas from other disciplines.
- Trading Markets (www.tradingmarkets.com). One of the most comprehensive sources of market perspective. It includes columns from well-known analysts, blogs, educational programs, mentorship resources, market data, and stock ratings based on Larry Connors's research.
- MSN Money (www.moneycentral.com). Excellent comprehensive resource for market data, news, and perspective from columnists. Stock selection is a particular strength, with experts sharing their portfolios.
- Minyanville (www.minyanville.com). Todd Harrison's site is distinguished by expert commentary on markets in real time. The commentary is archived, and Matt Ford reworks the content to provide teachable moments.

- Trade2Win (www.trade2win.com). Online community of traders, with articles from guest writers and many discussion boards. Lively and active.
- Teach Me Futures (www.teachmefutures.com). John Conolly has done a fine job of coordinating and archiving a variety of online educational programs for traders, including many sponsored by the futures exchanges.
- PIT Instruction and Training (www.pit-now.com). This is the site for the training school that trains NASCAR pit crews. The articles in the press archive on performance are most enlightening.
- The Kirk Report (www.kirkreport.com). Charles Kirk is an excellent source of market insights scoured from all over the Web. He offers market and stock selection ideas in a down-to-earth manner and conducts monthly Q&A sessions with readers.
- Trader Mike (www.tradermike.net). One of my favorite stock selection blogs that also includes a comprehensive set of links to other blogs and resources.
- CXO Advisory Group (www.cxoadvisory.com). This is my favorite blog for original market research, including regularly updated trading models and summaries of academic research.
- Abnormal Returns (http://abnormalreturns.wordpress.com). An excellent compendium of market-related material from around the Web and well-organized by category. Many fresh perspectives.
- The Big Picture (http://bigpicture.typepad.com). Barry Ritholtz brings his experience and vantage point as a money manager to this blog. His "apprenticed investor" articles model ways of thinking about markets.
- Daily Orphan Report (http://adamsoptions.blogspot.com). This blog covers the world of options and volatility, with astute and engaging commentary from Adam Warner.
- ETF Trends (www.etftrends.com). This is an excellent, comprehensive resource for tracking developments in the rapidly expanding world of exchange-traded funds.
- Stock Tickr (www.stocktickr.com). Very interesting social investing resource that allows you to view and monitor the watch lists created by users. An excellent set of interviews provides windows on different trading approaches.
- Declan Fallond (www.fallondpicks.com). Very impressive stock selection resources and an enormous database of market blogs and sites. His trading blog provides nice insight into the stock selection process.
- Fickle Trader (www.fickletrader.blogspot.com). Jon Tait offers regular watchlists for stock selection, a large number of links to other resources, and valuable trading perspectives.

- Ticker Sense (www.tickersense.typepad.com). Excellent market research blog with a unique sentiment survey of other bloggers.
- John Mauldin (www.frontlinethoughts.com). Well-known blog with unique perspectives on markets and the economy. Consistently thought provoking.
- *The Psychology of Trading.* This is my synopsis of trading psychology, the emotional factors that influence traders, and strategies for changing patterns that disrupt trading.
- *The Education of a Speculator.* Victor Niederhoffer's autobiography is a fascinating look at the life and mind-set of a performance-oriented trader, with plenty of insights into markets as well.
- *Practical Speculation.* Victor Niederhoffer and Laurel Kenner debunk a great deal of received wisdom in the markets and illustrate the relevance of the scientific method in market analysis.
- *The Essentials of Trading.* John Forman has assembled a much-needed market primer, with excellent guidance on developing trading plans.
- *How Markets Really Work.* Larry Connors's research into short-term market patterns, including many interesting countertrend strategies.
- *Mastering the Trade.* John Carter's book covers a range of trading topics, from hardware and software to trading psychology, specific trading patterns, and business planning.
- *Trading Risk.* Kenneth Grant's book is the best nontechnical presentation of risk and risk management that I've seen, with guidelines for portfolio managers and traders of individual positions.
- *Encyclopedia of Chart Patterns.* Thomas Bulkowski's thorough exposition of chart patterns and statistical evidence of their value is a landmark work.

MENTORING RESOURCES

- Woodie's CCI Club (www.woodiescciclub.com). Ken Wood has pioneered the use of hotComm conferencing to create a variety of trading rooms in which traders can watch experienced traders follow the markets in real time. There is a great deal of teaching, much of it focusing on patterns in the Commodity Channel Index (CCI). Very supportive and dedicated group.
- Linda Raschke (www.lbrgroup.com). Linda offers online trading rooms for the futures markets and individual stocks, with an emphasis on short-term trading. She illustrates setups and trade management, and an online room allows members to learn from each other. Guest lectures and classroom sessions supplement the real-time trading

rooms, and trading room transcripts are available on an end-of-day basis.

- Trade The Markets (www.tradethemarkets.com). John Carter's service offers a live trading room featuring short-term setups across a variety of markets, including the mini Dow and fixed income. The service teaches specific strategies and makes these available for TradeStation users. Seminars supplement the online teaching in the trading room.
- Trading Markets (www.tradingmarkets.com). The Trading Markets site offers a variety of books, video courses, and mentoring services for daytraders and swing traders. Many of these also include daily alerts for trade ideas. Many of the courses and systems emphasize original research on trading patterns.
- Journey to Wild Divine (www.wilddivine.com). This is an excellent introduction to biofeedback, consisting of software and hardware that allow you to play games on the computer and control your heart rate and skin conductance levels.

Bibliography

Abernethy, B. "Attention." In R.N. Singer, H.A. Hausenblas, and C.M. Janelle, eds. *Handbook of Sport Psychology*, 2nd ed. New York: John Wiley & Sons, 2001. 53–85.

Albert, R.S., ed. *Genius and eminence*. 2nd ed. Oxford: Pergamon Press, 1992.

Allard, F., and J.L. Starkes. "Motor-skill experts in sports, dance, and other domains." In K.A. Ericsson and J. Smith, eds. *Toward a General Theory of Expertise: Prospects and Limits*. Cambridge, MA: Cambridge University Press, 1991. 126–152.

Altucher, J. *Trade Like a Hedge Fund*. New York: John Wiley & Sons, 2004.

Armstrong, L. *It's Not About the Bike: My Journey Back to Life*. New York: Berkley Books, 2001.

Armstrong, L., and C. Carmichael. *The Lance Armstrong Performance Program*. New York: Rodale, 2000.

Beck, J.S. *Cognitive Therapy: Basics and Beyond*. New York: Guilford, 1995.

Beck, J.S., and P.J. Bieling. "Cognitive therapy: Introduction to theory and practice." In M.J. Dewan, B.N. Steenbarger, and R.P. Greenberg, eds. *The Art and Science of Brief Psychotherapies: A Practitioner's Guide*. Washington, DC: American Psychiatric Press, Inc., 2004. 15–50.

Bloom, B.S., ed. *Developing Talent in Young People*. New York: Ballantine, 1985.

Bohrer, D. *America's Special Forces*. St. Paul, MN: MBI Publishing, 2002.

Bollettieri, N. *Bollettieri's Tennis Handbook*. Champaign, IL: Human Kinetics. 2001.

Brown, C. "In the balance." *The New York Times Magazine*, January 22, 2006. 43–49.

Buckingham, M., and D.O. Clifton. *Now, Discover Your Strengths*. New York: Free Press, 2001.

Bulkowski, T.N. *Encyclopedia of Chart Patterns*, 2nd ed. New York: John Wiley & Sons, 2005.

Burton, D., S. Naylor, and B. Holliday. "Goal setting in sport: Investigating the goal effectiveness paradox." In R.N. Singer, H.A. Hausenblas, and C.M. Janelle, eds. *Handbook of Sport Psychology*, 2nd ed. New York: John Wiley & Sons, 2001. 497–528.

Carter, J. *Mastering the Trade*. New York: McGraw-Hill, 2005.

Ceci, S.J., S.M. Barnett, and T. Kanaya. "Developing childhood proclivities into adult competencies: The overlooked multiplier effect." In R.J. Sternberg and E.L. Grigorenko, eds. *The Psychology of Abilities, Competencies, and Expertise*. Cambridge: Cambridge University Press, 2003. 70–92.

Charness, N. "Expertise in chess: The balance between knowledge and search." In K.A. Ericsson and J. Smith, eds. *Toward a General Theory of Expertise: Prospects and Limits*. Cambridge: Cambridge University Press, 1991. 39–63.

Charness, N., R. Krampe, and U. Mayr. "The role of practice and coaching in entrepreneurial skill domains: An international comparison of life-span chess skill acquisition." In K.A. Ericsson, ed. *The Road to Excellence: The Acquisition of Expert Performance in the Arts and Sciences, Sports and Games*. Mahwah, NJ: Erlbaum, 1996. 51–80.

Chase, W.G., and H.A. Simon. "The mind's eye in chess." In W.G. Chase, ed. *Visual Information Processing*. New York: Academic Press, 1973. 215–281.

Cleeremans, A., and L. Jiménez. "Implicit sequence learning: The truth is in the details." In M.A. Stadler and P.A. Frensch, eds. *Handbook of Implicit Learning*. Thousand Oaks, CA: Sage, 1998. 323–364.

Collins, J. *Good to Great*. New York: HarperBusiness, 2001.

Connell, M.W., K. Sheridan, and H. Gardner. "On abilities and domains." In R.J. Sternberg and E.L. Grigorenko, eds. *Abilities, Competencies, and Expertise*. New York: Cambridge University Press, 2003. 126–155.

Connors, L., and L.B. Raschke. *Street Smarts*. Los Angeles: M. Gordon Publishing, 1996.

Connors, L., and C. Sen. *How Markets Really Work: A Quantitative Guide to Stock Market Behavior*. Los Angeles: TradingMarkets Publishing Group, 2004.

Costa, P.T., Jr., and R.R. McCrae. *NEO PI-R*. Odessa, FL: PAR, Inc., 1992.

Couch, D. *The Warrior Elite: The Forging on SEAL Class 228*. New York: Crown Publishers, 2001.

Csikszentmihalyi, M. *Creativity: Flow and the Psychology of Discovery and Invention*. New York: HarperPerennial, 1997.

Csikszentmihalyi, M., and I.S. Csikszentmihalyi, eds. *Optimal Experience: Psychological Studies of Flow in Consciousness*. Cambridge, MA: Cambridge University Press, 1994.

Curran, T. "Implicit sequence learning from a cognitive neuroscience perspective: What, how, and where?" In M.A. Stadler and P.A. Frensch, eds. *Handbook of Implicit Learning*. Thousand Oaks, CA: Sage, 1998. 365–400.

Dalton, J.F. *Markets in Profile: Profiting from the Auction Process*. New York: John Wiley & Sons, in preparation.

Dalton, J.F., E.T. Jones, and R.B. Dalton. *Mind over Markets: Power Trading with Market Generated Information*. Chicago: Probus, 1990.

Deakin, J.M., and S. Cobley. "A search for deliberate practice: An examination of the practice environments in figure skating and volleyball." In J.L. Starkes and K.A. Ericsson, eds. *Expert Performance in Sports*. Champaign, IL: Human Kinetics, 2003. 115–132.

Dewan, M.J., B.N. Steenbarger, and R.P. Greenberg, eds. *The Art and Science of Brief Psychotherapies: A Practitioner's Guide*. Washington, DC: American Psychiatric Press, Inc., 2004.

Duval, S., and R.A. Wicklund. *A Theory of Objective Self-awareness*. New York: Academic Press, 1972.

Ericsson, K.A. "The acquisition of expert performance: An introduction to some of the issues." In K.A. Ericsson, ed. *The Road to Excellence: The Acquisition of Expert Performance in the Arts and Sciences, Sports and Games*. Mahwah, NJ: Lawrence Erlbaum, 1996. 1–50.

Ericsson, K.A. "Development of elite performance and deliberate practice: An update from the perspective of the expert performance approach." In J.L. Starkes and K.A. Ericsson, eds. *Expert Performance in Sports*. Champaign, IL: Human Kinetics, 2003. 49–84.

Ericsson, K.A. "The search for general abilities and basic capacities: Theoretical implications from the modifiability and complexity of mechanisms mediating expert performance." In R.J. Sternberg and E.L. Grigorenko, eds. *The Psychology of Abilities, Competencies, and Expertise*. Cambridge: Cambridge University Press, 2003. 93–25.

Ericsson, K.A., and N. Charness. "Cognitive and developmental factors in expert performance.: In P.J. Feltovich, K.M. Ford, and R.R. Hoffman, eds. *Expertise in Context*. Cambridge, MA: MIT Press, 1997. 3–41.

Feltovich, P.J., R.J. Spiro, and R.L. Coulson. "Issues of expert flexibility in contexts characterized by complexity and change." In P.J. Feltovich,

K.M. Ford, and R.R. Hoffman, eds. *Expertise in Context.* Cambridge, MA: MIT Press, 1997. 125–146.

Folkman, S., and R.S. Lazarus. 1988. "The relationship between coping and emotion: Implications for theory and research." *Social Science Medicine,* 26: 309–317.

Forman, J. *The Essentials of Trading: From the Basics to Building a Winning Strategy.* Hoboken, NJ: John Wiley & Sons, 2006.

Gable, D. *Coaching Wrestling Successfully.* Champaign, IL: Human Kinetics, 1999.

Goldberg, E. *The Executive Brain: Frontal Lobes and the Civilized Mind.* New York: Oxford University Press, 2001.

Grant, K.L. *Trading Risk: Enhanced Profitability through Risk Control.* Hoboken, NJ: John Wiley & Sons, 2004.

Greenblatt, J. *The Little Book That Beats the Market.* Hoboken, NJ: John Wiley & Sons, 2005.

Gutman, B. *Tiger Woods: A Biography.* New York: Archway, 1997.

Hall, C.R. "Imagery in sport and exercise." In R.N. Singer, H.A. Hausenblas, and C.M. Janelle, eds. *Handbook of Sport Psychology,* 2nd ed. Hoboken, NJ: John Wiley & Sons, 2001. 529–550.

Hatmaker, M. *Boxing Mastery.* Chula Vista, CA: Tracks Publishing, 2004.

Heller, A. (2005, December 26). *Israeli is world's top blind golfer.* www.ocusource.com/main.cfm?page=info&topic=pressroom&article=362.

Hembree, E.A., D. Roth, D.A. Bux, and E.B. Foa. "Brief behavior therapy." In M.J. Dewan, B.N. Steenbarger, and R.P. Greenberg, eds. *The Art and Science of Brief Psychotherapies: A Practitioner's Guide.* Washington DC: American Psychiatric Press, Inc., 2004. 51–84.

Hirsch, J.A., and J.T. Brown. *The Almanac Investor: Profit from Market History and Seasonal Trends.* Hoboken, NJ: John Wiley & Sons, 2006.

Hirsch, Y., and J.A. Hirsch. *Stock Trader's Almanac 2006.* Hoboken, NJ: John Wiley & Sons, 2006.

Janelle, C.M., and C.H. Hillman. "Expert performance in sport: Current perspectives and critical issues." In J.L. Starkes and K.A. Ericsson, eds. *Expert Performance in Sports.* Champaign, IL: Human Kinetics, 2003. 19–48.

Lavallee, D., J. Kremer, A.P. Moran, and M. Williams. *Sport Psychology: Contemporary Themes.* New York: Palgrave Macmillan, 2004.

Lazarus, R. S. *Stress and Emotion: A New Synthesis.* New York: Springer, 1999.

LeDoux, J. *The Emotional Brain: The Mysterious Underpinnings of Emotional Life*. New York: Touchstone, 1996.

Lee, T.D., C.J. Chamberlin, and N.J. Hodges. "Practice." In R.N. Singer, H.A. Hausenblas, and C.M. Janelle, eds. *Handbook of Sport Psychology*, 2nd ed. Hoboken, NJ: Wiley, 2001. 115–143.

Liker, J.K. *The Toyota Way*. New York: McGraw-Hill, 2004.

Locke, E.A., and G.P. Latham. *A Theory of Goal Setting and Task Performance*. Englewood Cliffs, NJ: Prentice-Hall, 1990.

Lonsdale, M.V. *Raids: A Tactical Guide to High Risk Warrant Service*. Los Angeles: STTU, 2000.

Machowicz, R.J. *Unleash the Warrior Within*. New York: Marlowe & Co., 2002.

McNab, C. *The SAS Mental Endurance Handbook*. Guilford, CT: Lyons Press, 2002.

———. *The SAS Training Manual*. St. Paul, MN: MBI Publishing, 2002.

Niederhoffer, V. *The Education of a Speculator*. New York: John Wiley & Sons, 1997.

Niederhoffer, V., and L. Kenner. *Practical Speculation*. Hoboken, NJ: John Wiley & Sons, 2005.

O'Donohue, W., J.E. Fisher, and S.C. Hayes, eds. *Cognitive Behavior Therapy: Applying Empirically Supported Techniques in Your Practice*. Hoboken, NJ: John Wiley & Sons, 2003.

Ouspensky, P.D. *The Fourth Way*. New York: Vintage, 1971.

Patel, V.L. and G.J. Groen. "The general and specific nature of medical expertise: A critical look." In K.A. Ericsson and J. Smith, eds. *Toward a General Theory of Expertise: Prospects and Limits*. Cambridge: Cambridge University Press, 1991. 93–125.

Patel, V.L., D.R. Kaufman, and S.A. Magder. "The acquisition of medical expertise in complex dynamic environments." In K.A. Ericsson, ed. *The Road to Excellence: The Acquisition of Expert Performance in the Arts and Sciences, Sports and Games*. Mahwah, NJ: Lawrence Erlbaum, 1996. 127–167.

Patel, V.L., and M.F. Ramoni. "Cognitive models of directional inference in expert medical reasoning." In P.J. Feltovich, K.M. Ford, and R.R. Hoffman, eds. *Expertise in Context*. Cambridge, MA: MIT Press, 1997. 67–99.

Pirsig, R.M. *Zen and the Art of Motorcycle Maintenance: An Inquiry into Values*. New York: William Morrow, 1974.

Ranger Training Brigade. *Ranger Handbook*. Washington, DC: Pentagon Publishing, 2004.

Root-Bernstein, R., and M. Root-Bernstein. *Sparks of Genius*. New York: Mariner, 1999.

Rose-Smith, I. "Angry young man." *Trader Monthly*, Dec./Jan. 2006. 76–81.

Ryan, N., and T. House. *Nolan Ryan's Pitcher's Bible*. New York: Simon & Schuster, 1991.

Salthouse, T.A. "Expertise as the circumvention of human processing limitations." In K.A. Ericsson and J. Smith, eds. *Toward a General Theory of Expertise: Prospects and Limits*. Cambridge: Cambridge University Press, 1991. 286–300.

Scardamalia, M., and C. Bereiter. "Literate expertise." In K.A. Ericsson and J. Smith, eds. *Toward a General Theory of Expertise: Prospects and Limits*. Cambridge: Cambridge University Press, 1991. 172–194.

Schwager, J.D. *Market Wizards: Interviews with Top Traders*. New York: Perennial, 1990.

Schwarzer, R., and R.A. Wicklund. *Anxiety and Self-focused Attention*. London: Routledge, 1990.

Shekerjian, D. *Uncommon Genius*. New York: Viking, 1990.

Simonton, D.K. *Greatness: Who Makes History and Why*. New York: Guilford, 1994.

Sloboda, J. "Musical expertise." In K.A. Ericsson and J. Smith, eds. *Toward a General Theory of Expertise: Prospects and Limits*. Cambridge: Cambridge University Press, 1991. 153–171.

Sloboda, J.A. "The acquisition of musical performance expertise: Deconstructing the 'talent' account of individual differences in musical expressivity." In K.A. Ericsson, ed. *The Road to Excellence: The Acquisition of Expert Performance in the Arts and Sciences, Sports and Games*. Mahwah, NJ: Lawrence Erlbaum, 1996. 107–126.

Smith, S. *The Jordan Rules*. New York: Pocket Star Books, 1993.

Starkes, J.L., J.M. Deakin, F. Allard, N.J. Hodges, and A. Hayes. "Deliberate practice in sports: What is it anyway?" In K.A. Ericsson, ed. *The Road to Excellence: The Acquisition of Expert Performance in the Arts and Sciences, Sports and Games*. Mahwah, NJ: Lawrence Erlbaum, 1996. 81–107.

Starkes, J.L., and K.A. Ericsson, eds. *Expert Performance in Sports: Advances in Research on Sport Expertise*. Champaign, IL: Human Kinetics, 2003.

Starkes, J.L., W. Helsen, and R. Jack. "Expert performance in sport and dance." In R.N. Singer, H.A. Hausenblas, and C.M. Janelle, eds. *Handbook of Sport Psychology*, 2nd ed. New York: Wiley, 2001. 174–204.

Steenbarger, B.N. "The importance of novelty in psychotherapy." In W. O'Donohue, N.A. Cummings, and J.L. Cummings, eds. *Strategies for Becoming a Master Psychotherapist*. New York: Academic Press, 2006. 277–290.

Steenbarger, B.N. *The Psychology of Trading: Tools and Techniques for Minding the Markets*. Hoboken, NJ: John Wiley & Sons, 2003.

——. "Solution-focused brief therapy: Doing what works." In M.J. Dewan, B.N. Steenbarger, and R.P. Greenberg, eds. *The Art and Science of Brief Psychotherapies: A Practitioner's Guide*. Washington, DC: American Psychiatric Press, Inc., 2004. 119–156.

Steenbarger, B.N., and D. Aderman. "Objective self-awareness as a nonaversive state: Effect of anticipating discrepancy reduction." *Journal of Personality*, 47: 330–339.

Stoneberger, B.A. *Combat Leader's Field Guide*, 12th ed. Mechanicsburg, PA: Stackpole Books, 2000.

Tinius, T. *New Developments in Blood Flow Hemoencephalography*. Binghamton, NY: Haworth Medical Press, 2005.

Walters, J., and H. Gardner, H. "The crystallizing experience: Discovering an intellectual gift." In R.S. Albert, ed. *Genius and Eminence*, 2nd ed. Oxford: Pergamon, 1992. 135–156.

Williams, A.M., and J. Starkes. "Cognitive expertise and performance in interceptive actions." In K. Davids, et al., eds. *Interceptive Actions in Sport: Information and Movement*. London: Routledge, 2002.

Williams, A.M., and P. Ward. "Perceptual expertise: Development in sport." In J.L. Starkes and K.A. Ericsson, eds. *Expert Performance in Sports*. Champaign, IL: Human Kinetics, 2003. 219–250.

Williams, T., and J. Underwood. *The Science of Hitting*. New York: Simon & Schuster, 1986.

Wilson, C. *New Pathways in Psychology: Maslow and the Freudian Revolution*. New York: Taplinger, 1972.

Winner, E. "The rage to master: The decisive role of talent in the visual arts." In K.A. Ericsson, ed. *The Road to Excellence: The Acquisition of Expert Performance in the Arts and Sciences, Sports and Games*. Mahwah, NJ: Lawrence Erlbaum, 1996. 271–302.

Womack, J.P., and D.T. Jones. *Lean Solutions: How Companies and Customers Can Create Value and Wealth Together*. New York: Simon & Schuster, 2005.

Zavorel, N. *A Season on the Mat: Dan Gable and the Pursuit of Perfection.* New York: Simon & Schuster, 1998.

Zeitz, C.M. "Some concrete advantages of abstraction: How experts' representations facilitate reasoning." In P.J. Feltovich, K.M. Ford, and R.R. Hoffman, eds. *Expertise in Context.* Cambridge, MA: MIT Press, 1997. 43–65.

About the Author

Brett N. Steenbarger, Ph.D., is associate clinical professor of Psychiatry and Behavioral Sciences at SUNY Upstate Medical University in Syracuse, New York, and author of *The Psychology of Trading* (Wiley, 2003). As director of trader development for Kingstree Trading, LLC, in Chicago, he has mentored numerous professional traders and coordinated a training program for traders. An active trader of the stock indices, Brett utilizes statistically based pattern recognition for intraday trading. Brett does not offer commercial services to traders, but maintains an archive of articles and a trading blog at www.brettsteenbarger.com and a blog of market analytics at www.traderfeed.blogspot.com. His work on brief therapy has been featured in several reference volumes in psychology and psychiatry, and he has published over 50 peer-reviewed articles and book chapters in the field.

Index